The Best of
Best
Jewish
Sermons

The Best of
Best
Jewish
Sermons

Edited by
Rabbi Saul I. Teplitz

JONATHAN DAVID PUBLISHERS, INC.
MIDDLE VILLAGE, NEW YORK 11379

Library of Congress Cataloging-in-Publication Data

The best of Best Jewish sermons / [compiled] by Saul I. Teplitz.
    p. cm.
  ISBN 0-8246-0387-7
    1. Jewish sermons, American.   I. Teplitz, Saul I.   II. Best
Jewish sermons of . . .
BM735.B483 1996
296.4'2—dc20   96-12375
                                                     CIP

Printed in the United States of America

Table of Contents

Introduction

Preaching is a creative and dramatic art. It is not enough for a sermon to read well. It must sound so compelling as to convince the listener that everything depends upon its realization.

Henry Ward Beecher, the eminent Protestant preacher of the last century, once wrote, "A preacher is a teacher; but he is more. A teacher brings before man a view. The preacher looks beyond mere knowledge to the character which that knowledge is to form. It is not enough that men shall know. They must *be*. Preaching is the art of moving men from a lower to a higher self." The rabbi is essentially a teacher of Torah, and the sermon is his prime instrument to instruct the congregation of the truths of Judaism, and to uplift them spiritually by quickening their conscience.

Through the sermon the rabbi is able to relate the relevancy of the weekly scriptural portion to Jewish wisdom and tradition. A well structured sermon accompanied by a passionate delivery will, it is hoped, inspire the listener to greater involvement in Jewish life and move him from "ought to be" to "want to be." In essence, the sermon is a marching order that asks the congregation to change a course of conduct or alter an idea or attitude. It is said that when Pericles spoke, the people said, "How well he speaks." But when Demosthenes spoke, the people said, "Let us march."

The Jewish sermon must in the main address itself to the manifold problems which beset Jewry today. Guidance on how to face them, and the strength required in order to solve them, should be drawn from the Torah and Jewish classic literature. Answering questions that nobody is asking makes the sermon an exercise in futility.

George Bernard Shaw wrote the following about preaching: "Some preaching is like wine—it has color and sparkles, but does no permanent good; some is like drinking coffee—it stimulates, but does not nourish; some is like carbonated water—a fuss over nothing; some is like spring water—good, but hard to get."

Because it is often difficult for the preacher to come up with new ideas each and every week, some forty years ago Rabbi Alfred J. Kolatch, of Jonathan David Publishers, Inc., suggested that I invite rabbis to submit recent sermons that they would like to share with their colleagues. I undertook that assignment, and over the course of the years 5713 to 5732 produced twelve volumes of *Best Jewish Sermons* to which hundreds of rabbis from all parts of the United States and Canada contributed. These volumes, which have served as an invaluable tool for rabbis of all denominations, are now all out-of-print, unavailable to a whole new generation of rabbis.

My publisher suggested that since twenty-five years have passed since the publication of the last volume of *Best Jewish Sermons*, it might be a good idea to select the best of the sermons in the entire series, those that still have relevance, and present them in one volume. Thus, I have reviewed all of the material in the twelve volumes and now offer this volume of *The Best of Best Jewish Sermons*. My hope is that the material selected for inclusion will inspire the preacher and elevate the listener to greater Jewish commitment.

RABBI SAUL ISRAEL TEPLITZ
Woodmere, New York

The Best of
Best
Jewish
Sermons

1

Making People Out of Children

Rabbi Kassel Abelson

TRADITIONALLY, Rosh Hashannah is the *yom haras olam*, the day on which the world was created. It marks also the anniversary of the creation of man. One would, therefore, expect that the day would be dedicated to cosmological themes—to discussions of meta-physical problems of universal significance. But quite the contrary is true. Surprisingly, the wonders of the physical world are scarcely mentioned at all, nor are the vast problems of the destiny of man the main concern of the liturgy. Judging from the Torah readings chosen by the rabbis for this holiday, they were far more concerned with the prosaic problems of everyday life. The Torah readings for this holiday, for example, are an account of events in the household of Abraham.

Abraham and his wife, much like you and I, had to face and solve problems that arise in bringing up children. The sacrifices parents must be called on to make to maintain their ideals and pass them on to their children, is another theme. The relation between parents and children is characterized for us in the Haftorahs we read on both days.

Selected from *Best Jewish Sermons 5719-5720*

Now these readings for Rosh Hashannah are not the result of mere accident. It was no whim which guided our sages to these selections. Our spiritual architects were very practical in their world outlook. They realized that on the day set aside to commemorate the creation of the physical universe, special attention must be given to the problem of maintaining and developing the spiritual universe. They felt that it was in the home that the foundations of the future were being laid. Children were not only sons of the past but the builders of tomorrow—humanity's second chance to make good its mistakes and to realize its fondest aspirations, its hopes, and its dreams for the future. And so it is, that on this day of universal aspirations, the rabbis directed our attention to our homes, our families, and asked us to reexamine our relations with our children.

Though Americans are very sentimental about the family—glorifying it in song and story, something very serious is happening to the American home. The rapidly increasing divorce rate, the frightening growth of juvenile delinquency and the great increase in emotionally disturbed people are all symptoms of the disintegration of the family.

It wasn't so long ago that the house was a home for a friendly family doing things together and living with each other, with common interests and activities. Now many homes have become houses of strangers thrown together by the ties of blood—and no more. Time was when the family would gather after dinner, in the family parlor, read aloud and talk with one another. Today, a family rarely sits together for a meal—and if it does, each member, as he finishes, hurries off—each to his own interest, oblivious of the fact that he is a member of a family.

It is said that once a real estate agent was trying to

sell a home to a young woman. After hearing his sales talk, she replied:

"A home? Why do I need a home? I was born in a hospital, educated in a college, courted in an automobile and married in a church. I get my food at restaurants and delicatessens; I spend my mornings at golf, my afternoons at bridge, and my evenings dancing or at the movies. And when I die, I will be buried from the undertakers. All I need is a garage."

Though this is undoubtedly an exaggerated picture, it portrays faithfully the culmination of the trends now dominant in our society where houses are bought, not for a lifetime, but with an eye towards their resale value.

And our Jewish homes are not exempt from these trends. Though we Jews are the heirs of a pattern of family life about which Mark Twain wrote: "The Jewish home is a home in the truest sense," we don't need social scientists to tell us: "the Jewish home is today subjected to all the strains which affect family life in a sick society, plus those which come from identification with victims of extermination or arise from increasing discrimination."

It is common knowledge that the warm closeness, the sense of belonging, the feeling of being wanted, and the concern of each member for the happiness of all, which characterized the Jewish home is rapidly disappearing. Our homes, which once were the germinal cells from whence came the spiritual and ethical values which shaped the Jewish character, are rapidly becoming the graveyards of our highest aspirations. It is almost as though what the High Priest of old feared would happen to the inhabitants of the valley of Sharon is happening today. On Yom Kippur, the High Priest prayed on behalf of those who lived in Sharon: "May it be Thy will, that they may not make their homes their graves."

The home had the responsibility, not only of conveying Jewish values, but also of *machen fun kinder mentschen*—of making people, fine human beings, out of children. Today, in too many cases, our homes fail to give our children the proper opportunities for mental, spiritual and character growth which are so essential to the development of a happy and effective human being.

It would be unfair for me to oversimplify the situation and to pretend to be able to diagnose the causes and prescribe the remedy. Instead, I would like to point out several factors that contribute to the problem—factors which are in our power to remedy. We do hope that even if we are unable to solve the broad problem we can make our own homes what they should be.

First and foremost, I believe, the disintegration is due to a change in the role of the Jewish father. In the past, he was the head of the family, the court of last appeal, both revered and loved. He was never too busy or too tired to spend time with his children, to inquire about what was happening at *Heder* and, on occasion, to communicate a beautiful thought or memory from his father or grandfather.

Today, however, the Jewish father is almost a stranger to his family. His children plan and have their most important experiences without even a sign that there is a father around the house, for he is absent from early morning until the dinner hour. Moreover, when he comes home from work, he is in no mood to deal with the whims of his children. He is irritable, tired, hungry and worried about some business deal. After supper he is rarely ready to help his children with their lessons or to discuss their problems with them. Instead, he hides behind his paper or stretches out before the TV set—for an evening of oblivion.

I have the impression that many men are eager to

shift all family responsibilities to their wives, alibiing: "I run the business end of things; it's up to her to run the family." They seem ready to abdicate all responsibility for family life, and leave the raising of their children to their wives—but they little realize what they are doing to their children.

Students of family life may differ on many points, but on one fact they are all united. They agree that the major cause of mal-adjustment in the lives of the children is due to what they call "child rejection." I know that most fathers would be quite shocked if they were accused of rejecting their children. They would point to the beautiful homes, the fine clothing, the good schooling and the luxuries they have provided their children as signs of their love and devotion. But child rejection takes on many aspects. Very often fathers unconsciously do things that warp the healthy spiritual growth of their children. An unwillingness to listen to the excited chatter of children as they talk about things important to them; an impatient, "are you finished?" or "don't bother me!" or "go away, I'm tired," coupled with being just too busy to share experiences—implants in children seeds of doubt about whether their father really *loves* them or only feels *responsible* for them. Out of this grow feelings of rejection, accompanied by all sorts of mal-adjustments. Recently, a father wistfully remarked to me that he hoped that as his teen-aged children approached maturity that they would begin to understand him and forgive him for neglecting them while they were growing up. His business made too many demands on him to permit him to be the father he knew he ought to have been.

Most fathers that I meet are truly troubled because they feel they do not have enough time to develop the proper relationship with their children. Hence, it is important that they use wisely whatever time they do have. It is a good thing for husband and wife to go away together, for a brief period, but it is more important that vacations be planned where the family does things together as a family unit. Unfortunately, such opportunities come very seldom. But there is an opportunity to act as a family unit which comes regularly, which every father should take advantage of—that is to celebrate *Shabbos* with the family as a whole. At the *Shabbos* dinner, the father can take his proper place as head of the family—leading the *Kiddush*, turning the conversation at the table to subjects that involve the entire family, sharing his experiences with them, interjecting a thought about some ethical or spiritual principal. Though the time spent together may be briefer than is desired, when it is spent in the emotionally charged atmosphere of the Sabbath, it is most effective in strengthening family ties.

But the abdicating father is only one facet of a complicated problem. Very often parents are deeply concerned about developing a close relationship with their children—but don't quite know how to go about doing it. The method advocated today is that parents should become "pals" to their children. "Go to ball games," "take them to the movies," "be interested in their social life," that is the advice. "Be a pal," is the refrain, and you will be able to reach your child. You must establish a rapport with him. And what better way is there to establish that relationship than getting on his own level?

It sounds very good, doesn't it, and truthfully, there is a great deal of merit in this advice! But there is a fatal weakness, and that is, that children have many pals at their own level already. What they really need are *parents* to guide them.

In Judaism the parent-child relationship is a very clear and important one. The parents' responsibility is to teach, to educate. The Hebrew word for parents is *horim*, and it comes from the same root as *moreh*, *teacher*. The parent is, and remains, the first and most important teacher that the child will ever have.

Being a pal is good and has an important role in a parent-child relationship. But the parent must ever be aware that it is his responsibility to teach, to lead, to set an example.

But unlike classroom teaching, where the aim *is* primarily conveying facts, the parent is charged with setting standards, transmitting ideals and giving the child a sense of values which will guide him when he is confronted with a moral problem. This type of teaching is done when we "are sitting in our house, when we are walking on the road, when we lie down and when we rise up."

Rev. A. Fox tells us in his thoughtful book, *The Child's Approach to Religion*: "The child will get a conception of goodness because you are good to him and to other people; of love, because you and your husband increasingly love each other as well as him; of truth, because you are unfailingly truthful; of kindliness of speech, because your words and tones of speech are never harsh; of constancy, because you have kept your promise; of consideration for others, because he sees these things in you."

The burden this places upon us is captured for us by the poet in a *Boy's Message to His Dad*:

> His little arms crept 'round my neck
> And then I heard him say
> Four simple words I shan't forget,
> Four words that made me pray. . . .
>
> They turned a mirror on my soul,
> On secrets no one knew,
> They startled me, I hear them yet;
> He said "I'll be like you!"

It is a sobering thought to realize that we are making our children into people like ourselves. Rosh Hashannah puts on us the responsibility of determining whether we are the sort of people we want our children to become!

There are other implications also in the attempt of parents to become pals to their children.

The parent too often becomes more concerned that the child likes him rather than respects him, that the child has a good time rather than seeing that he does what is good. As a "pal" the parent is supposed to have full faith in his child, and though he may discuss the advisability of certain activities, he does not forbid them, particularly when the child explains, "all the other kids are doing it!"

This weapon of "all the other kids are doing it," is used to force the parents into condoning activities they feel are wrong, into hesitating to set time limits when the children must be home from dates—lest they be different from the others—into forbidding steady dating even when they instinctively recognize the dangers of this practice.

"Going steady" has become a wide-spread practice in our day and it begins at an earlier age each year. Little girls of eleven and twelve are permitted and, in some cases, encouraged to go out on dates or to formal parties. It seems so cute to see these children all dressed up in fashionable gowns and doing the intricate steps of the latest dance, but it seldom occurs to parents that they may be permitting their children to have experiences for which they are mentally and emotionally unprepared, and laying the groundwork for future tragedy.

It is not unusual for girls of twelve and thirteen to be worried about being old maids when they are not invited to parties, and boys of the same age questioning their masculinity when they are ignored by girls. And, unfortunately, parents also add to their children's insecurity by their own concern that their children "be popular" and go out regularly.

Is it surprising then to find even very young children pairing off at an early age and going steady with one person for long periods of time to insure themselves against being left out. We see, know, and condone all this and yet we are shocked when sociologists and family counselors trace the alarming increase in the number of unwed schoolgirl mothers to the practice of going steady.

These experts warn us that "going steady" leads to increasing intimacy often with tragic results. This is not a question of trusting your children but one of placing upon their shoulders more responsibility than they can legitimately be expected to bear.

During the past few months recognition of the gravity of this situation has forced itself upon the Minnesota Rabbinical Association. The situation was discussed at length at many meetings. Experts were invited to present the facts to us. And this week a Yom Kippur message will be issued by the Rabbinical Association urging parents to direct their children into properly chaperoned activities and to discourage "going steady" until it can serve the realistic purpose of being a preliminary to an engagement. We do so in the hope and prayer that our Jewish Community, aware of its priceless heritage of family living and high standards of personal morality, will act to preserve the family and ensure the happiness of their children.

This Rosh Hashannah, our eyes have been directed to that which is closest and dearest to our hearts, our homes and our families. Fathers have been asked to answer the question whether they are "parents" also! Parents have been challenged to examine themselves and learn whether they are worthy teachers of their children or only "pals"; whether they have the courage to say "no" to them, to insist on what is good, rather than simply permitting them to have a good time. Rosh Hashannah challenges us all to face the question—*What sort of people are we making out of our children?*

On the answer that we give to this challenge hinges the future of our people and of humanity!

2

Creative Discontent

Rabbi Morris Adler

"AND JACOB DWELT in the land of the sojournings of his father."

The Rabbis comment that wherever Scriptures speaks of "dwelt" and the desire for ease which it suggests there is an undertone of sorrow and distress. (Sanhedrin 106a)

If the books that are read, the lectures that are announced and the private conversations of people that one hears are any criterion, then our age wants one thing above all else. It craves for peace. I refer not to peace among countries, but rather to peace of mind, to serenity, to ease. This is the kind of peace the patriarch wanted, when he took up dwelling in Canaan. "Jacob sought to live in tranquillity." "*Bikesh Yaakov leshev b'shalva.*"

This age has not incorrectly been designated "the age of anxiety." We are haunted by multiple insecurities and ridden by diverse fears. Our world in particular is shaken by uncertainty and concern and we are shaken with it. In addition of course there are always "the thousand natural shocks that flesh is heir to." In our troubled state we crave calm. Agitated and restless, we

Selected from *Best Jewish Sermons of 5714.*

yearn to be quiet and at ease; full of tensions, we hunger for rest.

Hence, it is that the popular literature of our time addresses itself to the malady which overwhelms so many.

Those who profess to be experts in this area, frequently advise "don't let anything bother you." Or, we ask in our agitation, to be left alone. "Leave us alone," we are prone to demand of our relatives, our associates, society, life, thinking to find in isolation, the relaxation that has heretofore eluded us. No wonder that "peace of mind" has become the object of intense pursuit of restless millions. Indeed it bids fair to become one of the idols of the age, to be added to the list of idols which Francis Bacon described as shackling the mind and holding men's spirits captive.

This then is what we devoutly wish—comfort, unruffled living, an existence unpained, undisturbed, uninconvenienced. Inertness has become the Utopia of multitudes. Lolling on a beach, carefree and irresponsible in what may be described as a vegetable state appeals to us as the greatest and most desirable goal. It is a kind of Miami Beach philosophy of life.

Our tradition seeks to remind us that such insensibility and calm do not constitute life's prime aim or its most worthy purpose. Such a fretless and unworried existence charts the path to stagnation, to atrophy, to the staticism that is death in life. Adulthood and stature can never be achieved this way. Two peoples in antiquity began their group life in the wilderness. Both moved against the same background, both were faced by identical circumstances and possibly shared the same ancestry. One remained poor, unfruitful and insignificant and was soon lost in the trackless sand of the desert from which it had emerged. The other went forward to a career unequaled in history and made a lasting contribution to human life and thought. Moab and Israel both lived in the same environment, one became great—the other remained stagnant. The prophet Jeremiah suggests the reason in a chapter devoted to Moab. The prophet says, "Moab hath been at ease from his youth and he hath settled on his lees. And hath not been emptied from vessel to vessel, neither hath he gone into captivity. Therefore, his taste remaineth in him and his scent is not changed." (Jeremiah 48:11) Untroubled Moab was uncreative Moab. Living on the flat level of complacency, Moab remained unstimulated and unchallenged. It lived for a while and in passing from the scene of history left nothing behind as an enduring consequence of its labors. It is known today solely because of its contacts with Israel.

Our text suggests the inadequacy of ease as a goal of life. Jacob wanted serenity. A great destiny lay before him. A great people was to spring from his loins and a great Law was to be given to his descendants for all mankind. One with such a future to achieve must not be permitted to sink into placidity. His must be the restlessness that is a prelude to creativity.

The chief problem in our day, it seems to me, is not that we do not enjoy a stolid equanimity, an unbroken peace of mind. We miss the heart of our crisis when we place the emphasis here. Our major weakness resides in the fact that we surrender "peace of mind" for things that are unimportant and unworthy. One has not been taken into the membership of an allegedly exclusive club and he becomes upset and distressed. Another has less wealth than his neighbor and hence bears the stigma of despair and failure. A third has not been invited to a dinner party and he (and not infrequently she) is straightway cast into the throes of dejection and lamentation. Pinpricks become Mt. Everests. Trifles are turned into tragedies. We become smaller as we allow paltry setbacks to affect us as if they were major catastrophes. A man is measured by the things which disturb him and by the tensions which upset him.

· Man's life is insipid unless it is excited and disquieted by significant wants and high needs. Out of such intranquillity comes great living. Life is a process of growth and in the nature of things, growth is associated with travail and effort. Not peace of mind should be our goal, but creative tensions.

We should seek to grow in knowledge. Painfully aware of the immense gap between what we know and what there is to be known, we should eagerly and restlessly seek out new frontiers of study and understanding. Seeing ourselves as explorers of new seas, we should set sail and courageously face the hardships of such an adventurous voyage. The rabbis say: "*Talmidei chachomim eiyn lohem menucha.*"

"The true student and sage never knows satiety of peace." And then they add this interesting supplementary comment, "neither in this world, nor the next." For the glory of the student is his turbulent questing of knowledge; his determination to learn more and more. If heaven meant ease and relaxation, it can't be heaven for the scholar. Here is a tension we ought to incorporate into our lives, the tension that will give us no rest and will stimulate us to pursue knowledge and more knowledge.

Character is never a finished product. It is capable of a lifetime of growth. To be content with ourselves as we are is to perpetuate a comatose existence. Too many live a life of hibernation. One of the saddest experiences is to meet a college classmate twenty years after graduation and find him unchanged. He is the same sophomore or junior you knew so long ago. He is older, bald and portly but in every other respect he is frighteningly the same. Twenty years have passed him by. The new experiences and new responsibilities have left him untouched and have released no hidden potentialities. Each of us in moments of illumination, becomes aware of his ethical weaknesses, moral shortcomings and spiritual inadequacies. What a challenge confronts us in our own life! Through creative discontent that challenge can become opportunity.

Growth in social understanding and participation is another area that should appeal to us. We live in a complex and intricate society. All about us there are social ideals to be comprehended and absorbed; procedures to be refined and improved; social agencies to be strengthened. Despite our massively organized life there are still social needs unmet and social purposes unharnessed to an adequate instrument for their implementation. To become a participant rather than a passive spectator, in the social process of our community or nation is a goal unworthy of none. But we cannot content ourselves merely with sending a monetary contribution. We must enter the fray, take on the burden of responsibility, become deeply dissatisfied with many things as they are and through the struggle and discontent raise ourselves to greater heights.

Jewish history is perhaps the greatest chronicle of human experience. Israel's history is a masterwork worthy to be placed alongside of the religion and the book which it created. It is no record of calm and uninterrupted ease. It is a story marked by storm and thunder without and a divine restlessness within. Sorrow there is in abundance but with sorrow came great wisdom and growth. Always there was a reaching out, an inner wrestling, a great and constant quest. In the commentary of

Rabbi Samuel ben Meir, known as Rashbam, the grandson of Rashi, there is an interesting aside included in the interpretations of this Sabbath's Scriptural portion: "I often discussed the matter of the proper method of interpretation with my grandfather and he admitted that if he had the leisure he would revise his commentary in accordance with the new insights and exegesis that are constantly developing."

And these words came from Rashi, known as "Parshandasa," the Prince of Commentators. The life of the Jew was marked by spiritual and intellectual ferment.

Abraham, tossing and wrestling and searching the very heavens, refusing to acquiesce to the heathen faith of his time, found a new religion for his descendants and for mankind; the prophets, stormy petrels of discontent and fury, erupting with anger against injustice and evil, set up social goals we must centuries later still struggle to attain; the Maccabees rebelling against a Hellenism which having blanketed the whole Eastern world sought to cover them too; Jews unwilling to make peace with dispersion and rightlessness keeping alive a fire whose flame is now visible in the reestablished state of Israel—all these implanted within Judaism something of their eternally restless, questing, tossing spirit. Discontent begot achievement. Struggle and not resignation; rebellion and not complacency led to fulfillment.

Always there was a reaching out for greater knowledge, for more learning and understanding even on the part of those esteemed by their contemporaries for their scholarship. Always there was the striving for greater holiness, greater piety, greater accomplishment. No matter how far man has traveled on the road to progress he is still an infinite distance from perfection. The existence of that gap should never give him ease. It is in such uneasiness that man's chief glory resides.

These reflections suggest a major weakness in American Jewish life. We are satisfied with what we have established. We are complacent about our record. "We have done well thus far," say our leaders. "We have built strong and adequate organizations," say our executive directors. "We are proud of our attainments," our parties, and agencies proclaim at every annual meeting. Ferment is lacking. It is all quiet on the Jewish front except when the pride and vainglory of one national organization meets in collision with the presumption and vanity of another. We live from day to day. We are the prisoners of urgency and the blind worshippers of the immediate. There is no looking beyond, there is no reaching upward. No large vision beckons to us. We do not dream of a community, self-determining, informed and conscious of Judaism's part, its ethical values and sensitivities, its spiritual outlook upon life. We do not plan to release the powers frozen by indifference, unawareness, self-minimization. During the last war I heard of a large tank going full speed that came to a sudden stop. When it was examined it was found that it had enough gas to continue. There was nothing mechanically wrong with it. When the officer in charge was asked why the tank had come to a halt, he answered, "we have come to the edge of our map." Our maps are small and local. We need larger maps.

Individual Jews too are smug with their Jewishness. "I contribute, don't I," says one. "I am a member of a shul," affirms another. "I send my children to a Sunday School," boasts a third. We know enough. We do enough. We are good enough. We are hemmed in by narrow boundaries. The wide horizons that once ringed the Jewish community are no longer here. We pay for our self-satisfaction with stagnation. Our ease bears a distressing resemblance to boredom. We must not forget that where there is *vayeshev*, quiescence and calm, there is *tsar*, the distress of spiritual pauperism and intellectual insolvency. Let us awaken. Let us bestir ourselves. Not peace of mind is our aim—but rather that blessed dissatisfaction, that divine discontent which bring advancement, growth and achievement in their wake.

3

Idolization of Nature

Rabbi Max Arzt

IN RECENT YEARS Bible study has been considerably advanced by research into the languages, laws and folkways of the peoples of the ancient Near East. Among the linguistic discoveries is an entire language, *Ugaritic*, which was spoken by the Canaanite and even pre-Canaanite inhabitants of Northern Syria. These studies help us understand the cultural *sitz im leben* out of which Biblical religion developed. They acquaint us with the lifestyle of our ancestors, and reveal the startling similarities as well as the astonishing differences between their respective insights and cosmic outlooks. The differences between the religion of Israel and the religions of its more "civilized" neighbors testify to the revolutionary nature and the inspired origin of the faith of our fathers.

Deeply rooted and widespread among Israel's neighbors were certain "gut" beliefs and practices. The gods were believed to reside in nature and nature itself was so sacralized that it could be bent to man's will only through magical rites. All natural impulses, urges, and instincts were of the gods in that the unbridled expression of these compelling and often competing desires

Selected from *Best Jewish Sermons of 5733-5734*.

became a means of winning their favor. They demanded man's ritual obedience and would withhold the fruits of the womb in man and beast as well as the fruits of the soil, until they were cajoled and propitiated through incantations and rituals. There arose among the pagans fertility cults in which lust was sacralized, nature deified and sensuality hallowed. Because pagan temples were peopled by hierarchies of male and female cult prostitutes, we can understand the intent and import of the verse, "No Israelite woman shall be a cult prostitute nor shall any Israelite man be a cult prostitute (Deuteronomy 23:18). One of the ancient gods was Molech whose belly was an oven into which grateful parents threw their firstborn sons in anticipation of blessings to be bestowed upon them for their piety. We can now understand the story of the *Akeda* which encapsulates the idea that the God of Abraham was only *testing* Abraham's loyalty but was not expecting human sacrifices. We can applaud the genius of the Torah which ordained the rite of *pidion ha-ben* as a transmutation of the hideous practice of child sacrifice—a transmutation which made the occasion a joyful family celebration rather than a tragic performance of infanticide. Southeast of Jerusalem there was a valley known as *Ge-hi-nom* where, in Jeremiah's days, Israelites addicted to heathen practices offered up their children in honor of Molech.* The word, "Gehena," is derived from the name of that ancient crematorium. Into such a primitive milieu came the Israelites with their covenantal relation to the God of all nature and of all men, the God who is the Author of nature but who is wholly other than nature and above it. He is the Creator of all that is and He speaks to man with overpowering ethical demands, with "You

---

*Jeremiah 7:30-32.

shall" and "You shall not" commands and imperatives. He accepts ritual worship only when it is accompanied by righteous conduct and His Temple Mountain may be ascended only by one "who has clean hands and a pure heart" (Psalms 24:4). The God of Israel denounces lust and the worship of nature and demands not the suppression of one's natural impulses but that they be regulated through self-discipline in order that man's humanity may transcend his animality.

The Torah reading for Yom Kippur afternoon details and denounces the practices of the highly civilized and culturally advanced Egyptians and Canaanites. Israel is warned not to imitate their practices of incest, sodomy and other perversions for, "These abhorrent things were done by the people who were in the land before you, and the land became polluted" (Leviticus 18:27). The moral pollution of a people was deemed to threaten its very survival and Israelites were admonished to refuse to "adjust" themselves to the vile, nauseating degradations of human nature practiced by the heathen peoples around them.

You have a right to ask me: Why talk of the barbaric, primitive practices of peoples that have long gone to the dust-heap of history. Why not talk about contemporary problems? The answer is that in Rabbinic tradition Yom Kippur is the day on which the Israelites were forgiven for the worship of the golden calf. The Rabbis explained that Yom Kippur was the one day of the year when the high priest did not put on (for the sacrificial service), the golden vestments which he wore on other days, because the gold would be a reminder of the golden calf worship. The golden calf symbolizes that which was central in nature worship: the belief that man must seek instant gratification for every lust, that he must "do his own thing" now and never deny himself a satisfaction which his animality demands. We live in an age of permissiveness, in which man is believed to be a "noble savage" whose instincts need to be obeyed, not educated and regulated, and in an age in which self-discipline, self-control and even self-respect give way to self-fulfillment, self-indulgence and self-realization. Judaism rejects the notion that we must obey our nature. Only a rock obeys its nature and registers the geologic imprints of the ages. We need not say to a rock, "Be a rock," and we need not say to a dog, "Be a dog." But we do say to a man, "Be a man." A man can make things happen and he can thus be more than a product of blind fate. Man must arbitrate between the conflicting demands made on him by instinct, time, place and circumstances. Yom Kippur's theme is, "And you shall practice self-denial."* We cannot live in a society if we obey every natural impulse. We are all driven by acquisitiveness, aggressiveness and lust. We must govern these drives to make ourselves fit to live with. Professor Hocking of Harvard University summarized man's uniqueness in these words:

> Human nature is the most plastic part of the living world. In man, heredity counts less than in any other animal; and conscious building force counts most. Man's infancy is the longest, his instincts the least fixed at birth, his brain almost unfinished. What sets man apart from and above other living beings is his great capacity to shape and mold himself. To anyone who asserts as a dogma, "Human nature never changes," we reply, "It is human nature to change itself."

Yom Kippur calls on us to grasp the handle of our being and to make ourselves the willing instruments of God, His partners in perfecting ourselves and in making the world a better place for human beings to live in.

---

*Leviticus 23:27.

4

People Without Souls

Rabbi Ephraim I. Bennett

IN THE PORTION of the Torah describing the consecration of the High Priest Aaron and his sons to the service of God (Leviticus Chapter 10), we are told of a peculiar incident which occurred. As the ceremony was about
to conclude, the two eldest sons of Aaron, for some
unknown reason, brought impure and unholy fire to the
altar and, according to the story, a flame burst forth
from heaven and destroyed them. Thus what was to
have been one of the joyous days in Aaron's life was
converted into a grim tragedy.

Our rabbis, in commenting upon this event, use a
very striking and suggestive phrase to describe the death
of these two sons, Nadab and Abihu: "Their souls were
destroyed, but their bodies remained untouched." The
flames seared and shriveled their souls, yet their bodies
remained unmarked.

This is a very suggestive phrase for it hints at what is
wrong with much of our present day world. Everywhere
about us we find men and women who are in this same
state—individuals who are perfectly sound of mind and

Selected from *Best Jewish Sermons of 5713*.

limb, but who suffer from one grave defect—they have no souls. Either their souls have never been allowed to develop fully, or they have atrophied from lack of use. Nor should this surprise us, for if we survey the contemporary scene we find that endless attention is focused upon the development of healthy bodies and the cultivation of sound minds, but the growth of the soul is almost completely ignored.

What is meant by the word "soul?" I do not use the word in its ordinarily accepted sense, as though it were a separate organ in the human body, but rather as the sum total of those qualities which human beings possess which cause them to aspire to live on a higher level. It is those elements in us which make us truly human. As such, the soul is a very complex entity and has innumerable facets. For example, it is that power within us which makes us capable of loving our fellow men, of sharing in their sorrows, of desiring to assist them to the best of our ability and even of sacrificing our own interests so that others might benefit thereby. It is that which motivates the Jews in America to undertake to raise each year vast sums of money in order to bring a measure of relief to their forlorn and destitute fellow-Jews. It is that which causes Americans to be concerned about the welfare of human beings in Greece, in India, in China, in Africa, or wherever there are people in need. It is the love of a mother for a child and a child for its parent, a relationship which reveals the human soul in its noblest and clearest expression.

From another point of view, the soul is the faculty in us which enables us to appreciate the good and the beautiful; whether it be the beauty of a glorious sunset which spreads its golden hues across the sky, the sight of a lovely tree or garden which stirs something deep within us and evokes a tender response, or the appeal of a magnificently constructed musical composition, or a profoundly moving poetic work. It is the common bond which unites Beethoven, struggling to create and articulate that which is within him; Toscanini, striving to interpret that which Beethoven had written; and the audience, desiring to comprehend the combined efforts of both these artists. More simply, our soul may be our ability to understand and thrill to the reflection of the divine which is revealed in every ordinary act of kindness.

Or again, the soul may be that quality which some men have within them which compels them to fight against tyranny, to sacrifice their lives to achieve a greater measure of freedom for others, to consider bondage an affront to the human personality, and to resist any limitations and restrictions imposed upon the human spirit. It is Moses standing up to Pharaoh and demanding of him, "Let my people go!" It is the Prophet Nathan denouncing King David for his crime against an ordinary citizen, Uriah the Hittite. It is Elijah turning to Ahab the King with the bitter words, "Now that thou hast murdered, wilt thou also take possession?" It is Patrick Henry articulating the feelings of his people when he exclaims, "Give me liberty or give me death!" It is Abraham Lincoln standing on the battlefield at Gettysburg, reaffirming the proposition that all men are created equal. It is the innumerable people in Germany, France, Denmark, Sweden, Norway, and Yugoslavia who defied the might of the Nazis and were thrown into concentration camps to meet a bitter yet glorious end.

Then again, the soul may be that element in human beings which leads some of them to devote their lives to the pursuit of truth. It is that quality which drives men to be untiring and relentless in their efforts to arrive at a more correct understanding of the nature of man and the universe; that which forces men to be fearless in their quest, which gives them the courage to stand up against the accepted, conventional opinions of their day. It is that which moves men to blaze new trails, to chart the unknown, to explore the darkness; that which causes men to expose themselves as guinea pigs to the germ of yellow fever or to the rays of an atomic pile, in order to increase the collective fund of human knowledge. It is that sense of curiosity which gnaws at us and goads us to want to know what is the truth. All this and much more is inherent in the word "soul." For the soul of man is his highest aspirations, his noblest visions, his loftiest ideals and his finest actions.

It should be obvious to us that no person possesses a perfect soul. No one individual begins to contain within himself all the above mentioned virtues in their fullest expression. For to be so would be to be like God, and, as our Sages long ago pointed out, "There is no righteous man on Earth who does not sin." We all fall short of the mark, for that, too, is human. Similarly, it should be obvious that rare indeed are those individuals whose souls are completely extinct within them. For to be so would be to have lost all human qualities and to have sunk to the animal level.

The important question which must be faced by us, individually and collectively, is: "How much of a soul do we have?" How much effort do we expend to cultivate within ourselves and to plant within our children this thing which we call a soul—to teach ourselves as well as them to have a sense of sympathy for those in need and an eager, ever willing, and helping hand for those in want; to train ourselves to appreciate and to respond to the beauty which in all forms so abundantly surrounds us; to develop within ourselves an ineradicable desire and love for human freedom, and a readiness to fight to preserve a maximum of human dignity everywhere. How anxious and determined are we to seek the truth or even to face the truth? It is when we attempt to answer these questions that the words of our rabbis acquire a striking relevancy, for there are many warning signs which indicate that many of us are rapidly approaching the point of seeing our souls shriveling and withering away to nothingness.

Let us examine briefly our modern world and see what some of these danger signs are. Was not Nazism in Germany a conscious attempt on the part of a group of individuals to destroy the German and, if possible, the human soul? How close it came to succeeding! Were not the Nazi leaders able to persuade millions of individuals, not only in Germany, but in many other countries, to sell their souls, like Faust, for baser and more material values—to exchange freedom for security, mercy and kindness for cruelty and brutality, beauty and tenderness for naked, ugly power and human dignity for human degradation. The warning of Nazism is contained not in the fact that a small group of individuals were misguided by their lust for power, but that they were able so easily to convince so many millions that this change in values was desirable. Indeed the Nazis brought a strange fire to the altar of God and they came perilously close to destroying man's soul.

Is not Communism, as it has developed in recent years, akin to Nazism in this respect? As a matter of fact it is far more dangerous than Nazism. For whereas the latter was an open and bold denial of the human soul, Communism disguises itself by posing as the savior of the human being and justifies all its actions by proclaiming that they are the means to the salvation of the soul. Communism presents itself as a religion with claims that it will achieve the Utopia for mankind and that it possesses the secret for the attainment of the King-

dom of God here on earth. But stripped of all this cam-
ouflage, it represents the sacrifice of the individual on
the altar of the state and the destruction of human freedom in the name of national interests. It has generated
an atmosphere of fear, suspicion, hatred and oppression—an atmosphere in which it is extremely difficult for
the individual soul to develop freely and grow in stature.

Getting closer to home, here too, we have our danger signals. On the one hand, America possesses a wonderful climate for the flowering of the human soul. Our
country was conceived in liberty and born in freedom
and has always been amongst the staunchest defenders
of these ideals. It has a tradition of kindness and hospitality. In days gone by it reached out to the homeless
and the oppressed and welcomed them to her shores.
The Statue of Liberty with its warm words of understanding and mercy was a beacon light which attracted
the attention and the hopes of all who were in despair
or who were deprived of their fundamental rights as
members of the human race. Our country has a deep
and abiding thirst for knowledge and truth. Witness
how it has moved to the forefront in the fields of science, medicine and other areas.

And yet despite this rich and noble heritage so full of
promise, America's soul faces the prospect of being sti-
fled by an over-abundance of wealth. We have formulated a philosophy which says that material things—security, money, luxuries, comfort—are the most important
values in human life and represent the goals toward
which one ought to strive. We have made these the scale
of success and are pushing into the background those
traditional ideals and values which for so many countless centuries have been cherished as the finest expression of the human soul. Thus, for example, America,
which fifty years ago accepted so gracefully and eagerly

the teeming millions of persecuted and hounded individuals who came to her shores, now finds it impossible to open her doors to more than a handful of the distressed human beings who are knocking desperately on her gates. She finds it difficult because of her fears that this immigration may cause economic difficulty, may increase unemployment, or may in some way interfere with her comfort and her standards of success.

We who live in this country cannot help but be influenced by the general atmosphere and the surroundings in which we dwell. As a result, many of us have adopted this philosophy as our guide. We have set up wealth, fame, power and security as the most desirable goals which we can attain. If in the process of reaching these ends we become selfish, cruel, thoughtless, unsympathetic, insensitive and blind to all the higher regions of the human spirit, we justify our spiritual failure on the grounds that we are too occupied with our daily affairs and with the pursuit of success to concern ourselves with other matters. We rationalize our soullessness with the soothing thought that after we have achieved security and slaked our thirst for material things we shall be free to turn our attention to the intangible, more remote values of the spirit. To those of us who think this way our Rabbinic comment on the story of Nadab and Abihu offers a very significant message. It contains a warning which may be applied directly to our own lives. Beware of setting up false values and standards. Take heed not to bring false fires to the altar of God for if you do so, what happened to Aaron's sons may very easily happen to you. You may lose your soul in the process and destroy the humanity which is in you.

5

Empty Spaces

Rabbi Bernard Berzon

As I face you, dear friends, year after year at Yizkor, I am always pained to observe the new faces that have joined the congregation of mourners—those who are reciting the memorial service for a departed loved one for the first time. From private conversations with bereaved children I know that a number of them experience pangs of regret and anguish in these moments of soul-searching and reminiscence. As they recall with nostalgia the faces of their dear ones, they ask themselves the disquieting questions, "Have we done our duty by them? Have we fulfilled the precept of honoring our fathers and mothers in the traditional Jewish manner?" The poet may well have expressed these thoughts when he said:

> What silences we keep year after year
> With those who are most near to us, and dear;
> When out of sight and out of reach they go,
> Those close familiar ones who loved us so.
>
> When death had claimed them, and in their place
> We find instead an empty space;

Selected from *Best Jewish Sermons of 5721-5722*.

We think with vain regret of some harsh word
That once we might have said and they have heard.

"Ah!" we say to ourselves. "If we could but recall the years and have them back again; if we could but see their faces, feel the pressure of their hands, and hear the sound of their voices, what contentment and peace it would bring to our troubled souls! We would be good to them and fill their hearts with *nachas* and joy."

But let us face the truth. The fact is that not so long ago they were with us, willing and eager to guide and advise us, but on numerous occasions we flaunted their guidance, ignored their teachings, and sometimes even raised our voices to them. And now, when they are no longer with us, now that they have been lowered into the bosom of mother earth, we would like to turn the clock back and make amends. But, alas, it is too late!

There is an old Jewish legend concerning two students of the *Kabalah*, of Jewish mysticism. They lived at a time when the plight of Israel was so pitiful that there seemed to be no hope in sight. The two men resolved to intervene on behalf of their unfortunate brethren. They began to fast and pray for the advent of the Messiah. One evening both had an identical dream in which they were told to go to the Holy Land and there, near the city of Jerusalem, they would find a cave in which King David was asleep. On a certain day, precisely at the break of dawn, the old king would stretch forth his hands. If at that exact moment they would pour water on his hands and help him rise, David would leave the cave, redeem his people, and usher in the messianic era of brotherhood and peace.

The next day the two scholars set out on the long trek to the Holy Land. They met countless obstacles on their way. They suffered hunger and privation, but they were not deterred. Finally, on the appointed day, they reached the cave of David at midnight and found the old king asleep. They prepared a pitcher of pure water and placed it at his bedside. But inasmuch as there were still a few hours left before the crack of dawn, the men decided to explore the other chambers of the cave.

As they walked about they beheld many treasures which reminded them of the glories of Israel's past. They saw the sword with which David slew Goliath, and the famous harp upon which he played his prayerful tunes to God.

The two men were dazzled by the precious jewels and the ancient relics—they were so absorbed by the magnificence of the cave and its contents that they forgot about their important mission and the great task at hand. When they reminded themselves, and rushed to David's bedside, it was much too late. Dawn had already broken; David had stretched forth his hands and had waited anxiously for someone to pour water on them and help him rise, but no one had appeared. So, frustrated and utterly discouraged, the old king had dropped his hands and went back to sleep. The two scholars, heartbroken and remorseful, cried out, "Woe unto us! We arrived at his bedside too late!" How typical of life this legend is!

A surgeon is summoned to the bedside of a dying man, and after a thorough examination he turns to the worried members of the family and says, "See! A year ago a simple operation might have saved his life. Five years ago a change in his diet and habits might have prevented this disease altogether. But at this point there is very little that medical science can do for him. I am very sorry, but it is just too late."

A crowd stands gazing at a tenement building on fire. A woman is trapped inside the blaze. She could have left her apartment in time, but she tarried in order to save a few of her trinkets until it is impossible for her to get out alive.

"We reached him too late!" I heard these agonizing words last summer on the beach as lifeguards and policemen were desperately trying to pump water out of the lungs of a drowned man who ventured out too far from shore.

During the last war reports reached us from the far-flung battlefields that many of our boys died because the heavy weapons—the tanks or the air support—arrived too late to do any good. Winston Churchill immortalized this failure in the phrase, "too little and too late."

From bitter experience we know that the time to prepare for battle is not when the enemy is within the gates, and that the time to insure your furniture is not when your house is on fire. Yet, we are victimized by this failing all the time. We keep putting off tasks that should be done *now* until it is too late.

But why talk in generalities! Let us come closer to home. A friend is ill and there is a visit to be made. We know that we should do it, yet we keep postponing it until it is too late. A poem by Charles Hanson Towne entitled, "Around the Corner," drives this point home with great force:

> Around the corner I have a friend,
> In this great city that has no end.
> Yet days go by, and weeks rush on,
> And before I know it a year is gone,
> And I never see my old friend's face,
> For life is a swift and terrible race.
>
> He knows I like him just as well
> As in the days when I rang his bell
> And he rang mine. We were younger then,

> And now we are busy, tired men.
> Tired with playing a foolish game,
> Tired with trying to make a name.
>
> "Tomorrow," I say, "I will call on Jim
> Just to show that I'm thinking of him."
> But tomorrow comes—and tomorrow goes,
> And the distance between us grows and grows.
>
> Around the corner!—yet miles away ...
> "Here's a telegram, sir" ... *Jim died today.*
>
> And that's what we get, and deserve in the end ...
> Around the corner, a vanished friend."

We realize that it is time to provide a worthwhile Jewish education for our children, but we procrastinate and delay. First we say, "What's the rush!," and then we say, "It's too late."

We are aware of our responsibilities as Jews. We know that we should be loyal to the faith of our fathers, but we defer observance to a more convenient time. We put it off from adolescence to adulthood and from adulthood to old age—until it is too late.

If you wish I can give you some familiar quotations. Says one man, "I shall be generous when I will make my bundle." Says another, "When I will retire from business I will study the history and culture of my people, and attend religious services regularly."

But the poet warns us:

> Thou knowest not tomorrow's sun,
> Tomorrow's light is not thine own.
> And what today is left undone
> May forever become undone.

Whatever it is thou has to do,
Beneath whatever load to bow,
Be to thy sphere of duty true—
Be up and doing—do it now.

Alas, that we disregard the pertinent fact that time waits for no man, and ignore the wisdom of the old adages, "Never put off until tomorrow what you can do today." And that "one today is worth two tomorrows!" Ah, if we would but heed the words of Hillel, *ve'im lo akhshav emotai* "and if not now, when!" (Abot 1:14).

Repeatedly the Torah's emphasis is on *hayom*—today. *Hayom im be'kolo tishmau*, "Today if you will hearken to His voice" (Psalm 95:7). And one of the concluding prayers of the High Holiday service has a refrain of that word. *Hayom te'amtzenu; hayom te'vorkhenu; hayom te'gadlenu* ... "*Today* let us be strong! *Today* let us be blessed! *Today* let us be exhalted!"

There was a great rabbi in the city of Safed by the name of Isaac Luria, otherwise known as the Ari. Legend has it that the Ari died suddenly, at the prime of life. Long after his death, a story circulated that the rabbi had an infant grandson who was gravely ill. The Ari went to the synagogue and prayed before the open Ark. "Master of the universe!" he cried. "I plead with you to take the remainder of my allotted days on earth and give them to my grandchild that he may live and continue my work." His plea was answered. The infant recovered and the Ari died.

Years rolled by and the grandson grew up to be a strong and fine looking boy, but of a mean disposition. When he was of age, the father sent him to a Yeshiva in another city, in the hope that new contacts and a different environment would make a *mentsh* of him. But the reports that he received from the head of the school were discouraging, for the young man spent his time in bad company and was wasting his life.

One day his father sent him a letter requesting that he come home immediately, as some urgent matter had arisen. The young man, fearing the worst, took the first coach back home. His father met him, but instead of explaining to him the reason for asking him to come home, he took him to the cemetery and stopped at the grave of the Ari. There he told his son of the story how the Ari had prayed to God to take him, instead of his grandson, so that his grandson might continue his noble work. After finishing the narrative, he said to the young man, "Now my son that you know the circumstances of the passing of your grandfather, face his tombstone and tell him that it was worth it."

Tears streamed down the cheeks of the young man. He broke down, buried his face on the shoulders of his father and shook with sobs. "Father," he moaned. "I know that thus far I have failed you and your sainted father. But it is not too late. I promise at this sacred place that I will make it up to you and to him."

On this Yizkor day let us admit that in many ways we have failed our fathers and grandfathers, but let us also realize that it is not too late to make amends.

6

Alone in the Storm

Rabbi Eli A. Bohnen

On Yom Kippur we read the story of Jonah, the man who was bidden to go to Nineveh, to prophesy there that the city would be destroyed unless the people repented of their sins. As you remember, Jonah did not want to go. In fact, in order to escape this assignment he boarded a ship which was going in another direction. The story tells us that while Jonah was aboard, a great storm came up and threatened the ship with destruction. Jonah convinced the sailors that he was responsible for their plight, whereupon they threw him overboard, and a great fish came along and swallowed him.

It is unfortunate that the story of that fish has tended to obscure the fact that the Book of Jonah has a great deal to teach us. The Book of Jonah, as we find it in the Bible, and as it is discussed in later literature, has shed light on many human problems, and it is to one of these that I wish to address myself this morning as we prepare ourselves for our *Yizkor* service.

The Midrash, in discussing the story of Jonah, describes the storm that threatened to destroy the ship.

Selected from *Best Jewish Sermons of 5721-5722.*

The rabbis write: *"v'chal aniyot shebayam ovrot v'sha-vot b'shalom, v'ha-aniya sheyarad ba Yona haita b'tzara gedola ...* All the other ships which were plying back and forth sailed peacefully along; only Jonah's ship was in terrible distress."* (Midrash Yona)

What did the rabbis mean by that? How is it possible for a ship to struggle in a terrible storm, while all the other ships in sight sail along quietly and peacefully? On the surface it seems as if the rabbis are describing an impossible situation.

Actually, when we look into it more deeply, we become aware of the great insight the rabbis were showing into the nature of trouble and sorrow. What were they saying? Jonah finds himself in the midst of a situation which is fraught with tragedy for him. The storm is raging around him. But as he looks elsewhere the sun is shining. Others are sailing blithely along. For others, life seems to be filled with happiness and laughter. But not for him. How lonely he feels! How absolutely alone in an unfriendly world!

As we come together this morning for our *Yizkor* service we know that the hearts of many who are here are torn with grief. In many instances there are wounds which have not yet begun to heal. Even those of us who lost some dear one many years ago can still recall the utter loneliness into which we were cast at the time. Here is a woman who has lost her husband. To be sure she still has her children, but the feeling of being all alone is nevertheless an overpowering one. Here is a husband who has lost his wife and recalls the loneliness of spirit which assailed him. Parents who have lost a child, even though they have each other, cannot help feeling that there is an area of their life in which they walk alone now. We who have suffered bereavement in the loss of parents or a brother or sister can well remember how our grief was made so much more difficult to bear by the feeling of loneliness which came over us, particularly because we knew that the world was proceeding on its merry way as if nothing had happened.

So we can well understand what the rabbis were trying to tell us when they described Jonah in the midst of the storm. It wasn't merely the storm which was tormenting him: there was the crushing thought that he was being singled out by fate.

Is it not a fact that this is what happens whenever troubles come upon us in the course of our lifetime? Is it not the feeling of isolation that makes our troubles so much more difficult to bear?

I think of some of those whom I visit in the hospital. The doctor has informed them that they will never be completely well again, that they must accustom themselves to the idea that they will not be able to do all the things they did before, nor indeed all the things which their friends and neighbors will be able to continue to do. Their lives will be circumscribed by rules and restrictions. I sense the feeling of loneliness which comes upon these people until they are able to adjust themselves to the idea that their way of life will have to be changed. How shall I approach such a person? Obviously, we don't like to enter a hospital room with a long face, looking like the personification of gloom. We want to have a cheerful countenance. And yet we are afraid to walk in with too sprightly a step. We do not want to appear as if we have no cares in our world. How can we avoid making this person feel that those who visit him are in a world apart, a world in which there is no sickness, no restrictions and no rules? We don't want to add to the burden of loneliness which the patient must bear as part of his troubles.

Again we are conscious of the wisdom of our religion

which has made the *loeg larash* a terrible sinner. Literally the words *loeg larash* mean "one who mocks a poor man." Originally it referred to one who was wealthy and flaunted his luxuries in the face of a poor man. But it came to mean more. It came to mean one who spoke enthusiastically of a sunset in the presence of a blind man, it meant one who gloried in his good health in the presence of an ailing person. It meant, in brief, anyone who added to the feeling of loneliness which someone who was sick or underprivileged might be experiencing.

I think of the story of the rabbi who was late for the *Kol Nidre* service. The congregation could not understand how the rabbi could be tardy on this most important day. The time came to recite *Kol Nidre* and still he was not there and they began without him. What had happened to the rabbi? He had started for the synagogue and on the way he had overtaken another Jew who was also going to hear *Kol Nidre*. But the other Jew was lame. He could not walk fast. The rabbi knew he should hurry. The congregation was waiting for him. But the rabbi did not hurry. He walked beside the lame man, refusing to walk faster than he. The rabbi knew what it would have meant for him to hurry forward in great strides. He would have left the lame man behind, overwhelmed by a feeling of inferiority, weighed down by a sense of overpowering loneliness. So the lame man and the rabbi arrived together, too late for *Kol Nidre*.

Granted that, like Jonah, we find our troubles and our sorrows more difficult to bear because of the accompanying feeling of being all alone, is there anything we can do about it? I believe that we can find some relief in facing the facts of life. For it is a fact that actually we are not alone. We are *all* beset with trouble and sorrow, and rare indeed is the human being who goes through life without his full measure of them. *The thing which con-*

fuses us is the timing. We do not all have our setbacks at the same time, but it is a fact that we all have our sorrows. It seems difficult for us to believe this at times. We see so many with smiling faces and cheerful countenances. Like Jonah, we think that the storm has engulfed only us while the sun is shining on everyone else. It simply isn't true. We know it could not have been true that there should be a storm which endangered only Jonah's ship. Storms are not selective nor discriminatory in that way. So it is with the storms which come into our lives. We are not alone. The wave merely strikes one ship before it reaches another. If we could only understand this, the sense of being alone would not be so strong within us.

Many of you are familiar with the old folk-legend about the little village in which one person after another came to the rabbi with his troubles. Each one felt it was only his ship which was in the storm. You recall how, when each of the complaining persons was given an opportunity to exchange his bundle of troubles with those of others in the community he sheepishly decided to keep his own. How much wisdom there is in that little story!

So it is with all of us, my friends. From time to time we find ourselves in the midst of a storm which threatens to engulf us. In our unhappiness it seems to us that only our ship is beset by the storm and that others have clear skies and smooth sailing. But as we look more carefully we realize it isn't so. It is merely a mirage, an optical illusion. We need not feel all alone.

The point is not that we should derive comfort from the feeling that others suffer too. This would be unworthy of us. But we should remember that we have not been singled out and separated from the rest of mankind by our troubles, but that on the contrary, it is this which makes us part of the human race. It is this which joins us to our fellows.

In a moment we shall rise for *Yizkor*. The hundreds who will rise with us will help us to understand that we are not alone, indeed, that come what may, we are never alone.

7

Call of the Open Road

Rabbi Ben Zion Bokser

ONCE MORE WE ARE assembled at a Rosh Hashanah service. What does the dawn of a new year mean to us? What message does our tradition have for us during this season when we must search our hearts and mend our ways?

Judaism has characterized the good life by a variety of metaphors, but none is more striking than the conception of the good life as an open road. The Bible regularly employs the term "derekh," a road or a way as a synonym for life. The Psalmist in offering praises upon God-fearing people employs this very term: "Praised are those who are upright in the way, who walk in the law of the Lord." Our own phrase commonly used in the English language, "the way of life," is undoubtedly derived from the Biblical conception. The famous Rabbi Dov Beer of Mezeridge, one of the pioneers of Hasidism, gave this conception its most explicit formulation when he declared: *derekh nikra zaddik*, "the life of a righteous man is an open road."

What is the significance of seeing life as an open road?

Selected from *Best Jewish Sermons of 5713*.

43

A road, in its most essential nature, is a means of moving forward. This is the first quality which a good life must have. It dare not be static; it is the opposite of the smug acceptance of the time, the place, and the circumstance in which we find ourselves. It is always a restless surge forward toward new movement and growth.

The Torah frequently emphasizes the importance of tradition, of respecting what is hallowed by the past. But this only directs us to preserving the worthwhile elements which the past has handed down to us. It does not invite us to halt in our forward movement, to stop the march of progress. God Himself is described to us as making new again every day the work of creation. In our own world too, there must be newness, growth, a continued striving for what will make us better than we are.

It is not an easy goal. Most of us are afraid of change and resist the call to grow. Every step forward in civilization had to be taken against the resistance of those who were too timid to follow the call of the open road. Even among people of culture the suspicion of what is new is often pronounced. Recently there was a show of art forgeries in Amsterdam, Holland. They assembled a museum-full of canvases which were so brilliantly executed that they all seemed like the works of the great masters. It took the greatest art connoisseurs to detect the forgery, and some of them were fooled too. If these artists were so gifted that they could paint like Rembrandt and Raphael and Durer, why didn't they present these works to the world as their own creations? The answer is that even lovers of art do not readily appreciate the master when he is a contemporary. In his own lifetime Rembrandt himself was also spurned and he was left to starve in a garret by an unappreciative world.

The art lovers of his time were no different than their descendants today. Their minds are too often fixed on what is hallowed by the past, and they are not ready to accept the fruits of new creations which life, in its forward movement, is constantly bringing us. This fear of change has afflicted all life. They burnt the books of Maimonides because they abounded in unfamiliar ideas which were therefore, presumably, dangerous. Galileo was tortured because he taught that the earth moved around the sun. Those who projected the steamboat and the airplane were laughed at as impossible visionaries. Dr. Herzl was ridiculed as mad when he projected the idea of a Jewish State. A sound idea will eventually win out, but the initial reaction of the world to it is expressed in ridicule, if not outright hostility.

Many of us are often like that. There are people who have remained at a standstill in business. Great opportunities passed them by because they could never learn to try something new. There are people who know just what it would take to mend the breach in their family life, but they suffer from inertia and cannot change. There are people who have not added a single new fact or a single new idea since they left school, despite all the revolutionary changes in all phases of life which have gone on all about them. Indeed when a new idea is brought to them they often resist it stubbornly. Watch, for example, the programs offered by Jewish organizations in every community. Invariably you will find year after year, the same dish served to the public with no variation from past performances. And if anyone ever proposes a change, the stalwarts will shout that down as an innovation which cannot be countenanced.

One of the reasons that some people are bored with existence is that their lives lack the movement and change which is embodied in the call of the open road. Anyone who remains forever on one spot grows tired of it. And this is the cause of much distress. We are tired of the same old self that we have continued to remain despite the passage of the years. Nervously, we sometimes try to change the externals of life. We re-do our homes and change the furniture; we move into a new neighborhood; we switch hotels for our vacations; some even change their names. There is many a woman who goes shopping each time she feels blue. But no matter where we go or what we do in externalities, the "we" remains the same, and in our new surroundings we take our boredom with us.

Let us not take too seriously the advertising slogan of a certain paint manufacturer: save the surface and you save all. A new coat of paint on the surface is not the change we need. The prophet asked his people: "And make unto yourselves a new heart and a new spirit." It is inner growth we need. It is new emotions, new visions, which is all-important. It is this deeper change to which the open road summons us.

A road is not only a forward movement. It is a movement with a purpose. Roads are not built toward dead ends. They are built to link us with the world beyond ourselves. The life of a good man is like that too. It is not an isolated, segregated existence. It is linked to all kinds of people in space and in time. It is part of the very life-beat of the universe.

The tragedy is that many people build fences around their lives, instead of open roads. They are set in the tiny corner which they occupy in the world and look with disdain at those who are outside their own charmed circle.

We are outraged when a resort puts a restricted sign on its door. But the truth is that we do not really rebel against the principle of restriction. We object for selfish reasons, because we are its victims. But given the chance, we would not hesitate to practice the same principle ourselves. We don't want our children to mix with the children who live on the other side of the tracks. We have a distinct consciousness of our social worth or of our financial position, and we instinctively reject those whom we judge to be our inferiors. The wife and children of a representative of Pakistan were once arrested in Westchester as vagrants only because their dress seemed so different to their middle-class American neighbors among whom they had ventured out on a shopping tour. In our own community I have heard sneering references to new arrivals, to apartment house dwellers, to refugees, to Galicians, to Hungarians—these, if taken seriously, are symbols of provincialism, the sin of people who have not mastered the wisdom of the open road.

The open road of the spiritual life extends also to the past and to the future. Our tradition has created all kinds of pathways to our people's past. This is one of the purposes of the ceremonies and rituals of our faith. He who observes them has built a mighty road that will offer him precious links to a wonderful world beyond himself. With Abraham he will smash the idols of a pagan world and proclaim the oneness in God. He will be with the Israelites in Egypt, suffering their bondage and exulting in their freedom. With Moses he will stand at Sinai and share in the announcement of the law to mankind. He will experience vicariously the two thousand years of Jewish history, dreaming great dreams, fighting great battles, performing a mighty service to the cause of civilization through the centuries. And the open road of his life will go winding down into the future as well. He will participate in movements and causes that are helping to shape the world of tomorrow, to build it toward justice and freedom and peace for his own people and for all mankind.

The open road is a forward movement, aiming at a

destination. But it is important to remember that it is not always a perfectly paved, smoothly running highway. It often extends over rough terrain, across rock and gravel and mud, up mountains and down valleys, with sharp turns and narrow lanes. But a good traveler is not intimidated by the rough terrain, proceeding undaunted to his destination. The life of a good man is like that, too. It must pursue its goals regardless of the resistant surface through which we must reach them.

Many people prefer to travel on an easy surface without resistance and struggle. They want comfort above everything else. I am thinking of a young man who aspired for a career in medicine. He was fortunate in being admitted to one of the leading medical schools in the East. But the first few months at school convinced him that he would have to work hard, and that some five years of stern self-discipline would intervene between him and his goal. So he chose the path of least resistance and gave up school. He is now selling rayons for his father's firm. There is nothing wrong with selling rayons, if that is what one wants. But it is a tragedy to become a rayon salesman when one has the ambition and also the opportunity to become a doctor.

Anyone who has ever endeavored to define greatness of character must surely have recognized that one of its major attributes is the pursuit of a destination even though it is necessary to cross a rugged terrain to get to it. I was once privileged to spend a weekend with Ludwig Lewissohn. We both attended services on Saturday morning, and Mr. Lewissohn was honored with an *aliyah*. I later complimented him on the beautiful Sephardic Hebrew with which he pronounced the prayers. And then he told me the story of his own self-education as a Jew. His parents never gave him a Jewish education. In fact, he had never been *Bar Mitzvah*. He learnt his

Hebrew as a grown man through his own efforts. He built the road of his life over a rugged surface, but once he sighted his destination, hardships did not deter him.

This is the mark of every great character. Weaklings follow the road which leads across a smooth area, with little concern to where it will take them. Men and women of character pursue primarily a goal, and then they will blaze a trail to their goal across any land by which it may be necessary to reach it. The pioneers who built America moved toward their goal across a wilderness beset by all kinds of hardships. Those who built the State of Israel traveled on a road which proceeded over rock and swamp, across a land that resisted them at every turn. Those who have built our own Jewish community have journeyed across the same kind of road, a rough and rugged surface, resisting and impeding at every turn.

The defiance of the hardships of travel on life's open road is not only a means of reaching great destinations. It is also a vital condition of our happiness. Life is aglow with interest when we have challenges to face, hardships to overcome. Without challenge life becomes languid and dull. Roads like the New Jersey Turnpike have been characterized in a recent article in the *New York Times* as "Speedways to Death." They are so perfectly paved, so straight and smooth, that they become monotonous and induce boredom and drowsiness in the driver. The life of the open road is like that too. To sustain our interest it must have elements that challenge us. Continued smoothness makes for monotony and boredom.

There are great lands in the far horizon which beckon us. There is the call of service to our community. There is the call to improve our knowledge of Jewish tradition, to learn the thrilling story of our heritage and the role it has played in civilization. There is the call to make the synagogue part of our lives by claiming its power to lift and inspire us. There is the call to bring the Sabbath and festivals and other Jewish ceremonials into our homes, to endow them with beauty and Jewish distinctiveness. It is not easy to reach these ends. Yet if we keep our minds toward our destination, we shall conquer the rugged terrain and build a highway toward our idea. As the prophet put it: "Clear a road for our people. Make straight in the wilderness a way for our God." Yes, the life of a good man is an open road and it proceeds across all kinds of barriers, even across the wilderness. It is an unswerving pursuit of our God.

The Ethics of the Fathers teaches us that the art of happiness is to rejoice in one's lot. This is true. The art of making the most of what we have or what we are, of rejoicing in whatever is worthwhile in our portion is indispensable to happiness. But no man dare remain as he is. That which he is must serve as a base from which to proceed in an unending quest for what is better.

On this day of Rosh Hashanah we are summoned to the unending quest for the ennoblement of life. On this day of Rosh Hashanah we continue to sound the call for growth, for linking our lives with the larger world which the Lord hath made, for the courage to face undaunted whatever life may offer in an unswerving pursuit of the visions that beckon us. All this is conveyed in the simple maxim of the Rabbi Mezeridge: "To live the life of a good man is to follow the call of the open road."

8

Divinity and Dividends

Rabbi Eugene Borowitz

It was a lovely June morning. We men sat in a room with windows on three sides, and around us, so it seemed, there flowed the expanse of Long Island Sound. An occasional cloud blotted out the sun from time to time, but never enough to darken the room or dampen our spirits. Surrounded by this beauty, we sat and talked of death.

Not openly, of course. It was too nice a morning for that. Openly, we spoke of life, our life, of the tensions which crowd our days, and the pressures which drive us through the weeks. We spoke of why we push ourselves so hard and why we punish ourselves so much—and we confessed we did not know why we did, only that we did.

We spoke of life, but thought of death, for the un-mentioned subject of our discussion that morning was the coronary thrombosis, now clearly more than the ulcer, the symbol of our American way of life.

If Damocles could not enjoy a banquet with a sword suspended by a hair over his head, at least he was the

Selected from *Best Jewish Sermons of 5719-5720*.

victim of another's displeasure. This killer it is reasonably clear, we make for ourselves by the way we live.

Why then do we live this way? Are our wives the true demons of the piece, making us provide for them at a pace we cannot support? No, say the men, it is we who wish to work for them. No, say the women. We prefer them to their purchasing power—and if the truth be known, they prefer paying our bills to paying us attention, they would rather give us gifts than give us love. It is no one's fault, we say. It is just the way we live.

Then, can we not stop it and save ourselves the anxiety of anticipation and the pain of the reality? But you can't work halfway, say the men. But you can't nag and hope to be helpful, say the women. The epitome of 20th-century American chivalry is the sincere declaration of one of our more realistic regulars who said: "All I'm trying to do is to provide for my family before my coronary comes." Love speaks here. Devotion speaks here. Honesty speaks here in a way that betrays fears, hidden in us all.

We do not wish to face the realities of our way of life or else having done so, we quickly exile the inevitable from consciousness. We live by a sort of spiritual resignation, with a touch of the gambler's despair. We know we're in a crooked game, but it's the only game in town.

Judaism does not believe in fatalism, openly preached or quietly lived by. Judaism says man is free to choose his way of life—his sins of the past year need not be his sins in the New Year. This day with its call to confession, repentance and resolution is founded on that freedom. What does it say to us who yearn to be inscribed in the Book of Life? What is its message to this congregation which has been wondrously free of death, and yearns for another year and more of such blessing?

There are no precedents for what we seek to learn

this evening. Never has there been a Jewry so blessed with comfort, with convenience and with the opportunity for yet even more, as is this American Jewry. For this we are grateful. Would that our great-grandparents could see how we live! To recall now their childlike folk song, of the banquet they would eat when the Messiah arrived, is to realize how limited even their imagination had become in the straitened life of the ghetto. Their prayer was that their children, or their children's children, that even *we* might someday live another kind of life—and this country, with its unparalleled opportunity, with its appreciation of ability despite the source, this country has more than fulfilled their highest aspiration. We are grateful in a way that is reinforced not only by our present pleasures but by the memories of 2,000 years of tribulation. America has been unique to us among the nations.

But these riches have had their price, and this luxury has brought its pain. The term Jewish drunk was once a wry commentary on the incapacity of the ghetto Jew who took an occasional schnapps, to hold much more than that. America has made the Jewish drunk a reality, and Jewish alcoholism is for the first time in the history of our people a serious problem. The ghetto Jew had no time for extensive beauty treatments and no money for expensive wardrobes. He did not marry for love or raise children by psychology. But his home was filled with respect and understanding between parents and children, and with faithfulness and devotion between husband and wife. The ghetto had its delinquent parents and its problem children. It even had its divorces. But these were nothing as compared to the American scene where the Jewish divorce rate continues to climb and where the stability of the Jewish family has had a sickening decline.

The truth is that America has not been an unmixed blessing to us. It has taught us evil with the good but we have been so happy with its benefits that we have been eager to accept them whatever the cost.

Are we still so insecure in our new-found freedom that we cannot reject or criticize any part of America? Or do we trust our democracy? Are our free institutions so weak that Jews must never differ too much from the majority? Or does the American way of life appreciate and even benefit from differing opinions and vigorous dissent?

We Jews have integrated well into American life—in fact too well. What we need now is to learn to stand off a little from it. We need now to withdraw from it enough for honest criticism. We need now to find that clear perspective which will not make us blind to its faults because we are in love with its virtues.

All higher religion seeks to remove man from the seeming reality of his society to the *lasting* reality behind it. The Buddha like to speak of the wheel of life on which we are impaled. Ceaselessly it revolves and we are carried up by hope and desire only to be ever plunged anew into the depths of despair and disappointment. The Buddha sought to free man from the wheel by breaking its cycle, by killing desire in a complete withdrawal from the world, into mystic contemplation. The adequacy of the Buddha's diagnoses and therapy is proved by the increasing numbers of westerners who have found them and their off-shoots of value, including such redoubtable figures of modern literature as Aldous Huxley and Christopher Isherwood.

Judaism, too, has dealt in social criticism since its earliest days. Indeed, one of the great Protestant theologians of our time, Reinhold Niebuhr, has called this one of Judaism's greatest contributions to Christianity, the doctrine that religion's loyalty is to God, not to society, and that on the basis of its faith in God religion must constantly bring society into judgment.

But we Jews do not criticize so that we may withdraw from the world, but only so that we may participate in society in a way which leads to sanctity. We Jews can see too much good in the world to want to hide from it in silent meditation. And, at the same time, we have found too much value in our American freedom and opportunity to want to rebuild the ghetto walls.

Precisely because we love our country and cherish what it offers us, we need our religion to lift us out of our hectic way of life, and show us where we are running. We need our religion to release us from our gilded execution and release us to a life of freedom.

If anything, our Judaism is uniquely suited to perform this function.

The informed Jew always looks at the world around him not only as something of a clear-eyed stranger, but as one who has lived through so much before that he can tell the transient from the lasting. To be a Jew means to have lived through Egypt and Palestine, Babylonia and Spain, Poland and Germany. It means to think in terms of centuries and millennia rather than, at the most, of five or ten year plans of business expansion. It means the ability to think of our problems in the context of Jewish suffering, and of our goals in the framework of human destiny.

The beauty of Judaism is that these are not merely ideas with which the mind can toy. They are a way of living one's life. America rewards the successful business man by allowing him an occasional afternoon off for golf, a world series game, or even more, time for a winter vacation. But these are apt to be characterized by the same compulsion and straining for achievement that mar the rest of his life. Judaism says rather, take time off to celebrate the festivals of your people—not just the High Holy Days, which are generally considered excused absences from business—but the first and last days of Sukkos and Pesach, and Shovuos as well. Observe them in a way that has nothing to do with business, but with the prayer and relaxation that will refresh your soul. Let them break up the rhythm of your year with their teaching about the Source of blessing and of woe, and let them restore you to the sane kind of life you should be leading.

But the Sabbath does this best of all—not just the Friday night Sabbath, but the all day Saturday Sabbath in particular. Here the week is punctuated by a non-working, a non-tiring, a non-exhausting day. Here the work of the week is given its proper direction and limit as we deliberately take time out to think, to study and to rest.

And just precisely because most Americans do not observe these days, just precisely because they and all the other meaningful practices of our religion are the minority, the non-conforming thing to do, they break us out of this desperate American race with life, they make it possible for us to choose our own goals and live our own lives. Religion *is* a valuable therapy for the ills of our society. There can be no question that it is the sickness of our culture today which is driving many to the church and synagogue to seek remedy. In the process of helping men overcome the tension of these times, religion has found a new and useful role for itself. Did not Dr. Paul Dudley White comment that religion was one of the great aids in preventing the kind of life that invites a coronary. How many a Temple bulletin carries this kind of item quickly to its readers, reminding them that this or that authority recently said that regular attendance at services tends to reduce high blood pressure and other nervous ailments. How often do they include a prescription from *Peace of Mind* or *The Power of Positive Thinking.* The phone numbers where you may call for a prayer any time of night or day are increasing so that, like the doctor, religion is never far away.

It is true that religion offers a cure for our ailment, but like all advanced therapies, it has a high price. That inescapable price is sincere repentance.

How weak-kneed, how simpering, how maudlin even, the word repentance sounds in English, as if it described a beaten child come blubbering to its parent. How different from the strength, the affirmation of the Hebrew word *T'shuvo. T'shuvo* means literally "turning" and it is this "turning" that we need. We need to turn from our old way of life and find a new one. We need to turn out of our American culture and into our Judaism, and we need to do it in the only way it works, with a full and sincere heart.

It would be so much simpler if religion could be taken like aspirin, one or two prayers every four hours, not to exceed eight a day. Three Friday evening services, or two study groups a month for men and women of average ambition. Add daily prayer and a ten minute Bible reading, before meals, for more advanced cases.

But religion works in the heart, and what we need is to turn our hearts, our desires, our longings, our very selves, away from the cars, and the cruises, the expansion, and the expensive, the deals, and the delights, the progress, the profits, and the professional standing, that set the awful tempo of our lives.

The soul cannot serve two masters, the profit system and God, and as much as we would like to merge these interests, He is One, Alone and Unique. We cannot turn Divinity into dividends.

What has distorted our lives is that we have made a religion of business and a business of religion. The passion, the dedication, that once went into prayer, into study, or good deeds, now is given to the god of business or social success. We read the financial section of the paper in the morning with the devotion and intensity proper to the prayerbook, and we size up our professional journals, our economic reports, or the latest community gossip with the personal involvement that exercised the Jew of another day over his Mishnah or Talmud. With all our heart, with all our soul, with all our might, sitting in our house, walking by the way, lying down and rising up, we try to be more successful. And the tremendous effort we made to be casual about it all, to keep it from being obvious, is only another example of modern man's peculiar notion that he must not display to others what is most dear to him.

Business is not necessarily evil, nor is economics the devil's domain. Work has an enormously valuable part to play in the relations between men. It can be a means of glorifying humanity and enriching the individual life, as long as we recognize it for what it is—a road to be driven, but not the city to be reached; a shelter to be lived in, but not the home that love must build. We should not live to work, but work in order to live. We have turned our work from a means into an end, and if we would save our lives from the savage pressures and silent fears of our day, we must turn again, again to make our goals the goals of our God, again to have our lives find their meaning in the love, the helpfulness, the wisdom which are beyond the categories of success or failure.

Can we turn? Can the heart of a man be taken out of him and then be put back in again? This was the question which Rabbi Bebai Ben Zabdai asked one fast day and he said: "If a man holds an unclean thing in his hand, he may dip in all the seas of creation and he will never become clean. But let him throw away the unclean thing and a very small amount of water will suffice to wash him clean."

We can be made clean, but we must give up the goals that defile. We can turn, if we will be honest with what we are and find the courage to be what we ought to be.

Ezekiel set the message of this day in a form that will be classic as long as self-interest and self-delusion rule the life of man. Ezekiel said:

Yet saith the house of Israel: The way of the Lord is not equal. O house of Israel, is it My ways that are not equal? Is it not your ways that are unequal? Therefore I will judge you, O house of Israel, everyone according to his ways, saith the Lord God. Return ye, and turn yourselves from all your transgressions; so shall they not be a stumbling block of iniquity unto you. Cast away from you all your transgressions, wherein ye have transgressed; and make you a new heart and a new spirit; for why will ye die, O house of Israel? For I have no pleasure in the death of him that dieth, saith the Lord God; wherefore turn yourselves, and live."

That is the message of this day—turn yourselves, turn yourselves and live.

9

Giving of Yourself

Rabbi Samuel Chiel

IT IS A RARE THING nowadays to hear anybody say a good word about the Biblical concept of sacrifice. Sacrifices, we are told, are primitive and archaic and have no meaning nor message for modern man. And yet, in the second verse of today's *Sidrah* which deals in the main with the details of the sacrificial system, we are taught something in regard to sacrifices which is perhaps one of the most basic and important ideas ever promulgated in an ethical document. *Adam ki yakriv Mikem Korban Lashem*, the verse says, "When any man from among you brings an offering unto the Lord." The rabbis were quick to note that the word *Mikem* is superfluous, and they ask why the Torah could not have said: *Adam ki yakriv Korban Lashem*, without the additional *Mikem*. With penetrating insight, they answer that the word *Mikem* is placed in the verse for a very special reason—to teach us the unique and distinctive feature of true sacrifices. The Talmud interprets *Mikem* as meaning *Mishelochem*—the true meaning of sacrifice, the true concept of giving—is that it must be from—*yourself*.

Selected from *Best Jewish Sermons of 5714*.

It took many generations of human life for man to discover this profound truth about the nature of giving. Indeed, in our own religion, we see this development in the change of emphasis in the notion of sacrifices as expressed in the detailed instructions of Leviticus and as enunciated by the prophets. Hosea unquestionably reached a high point in religious thinking when he exclaimed in the name of God: *Ki chesed chofatzti v'lo zovach*—"For I desire mercy and not sacrifice." And similarly, the verse from Proverbs: *Alo tzedokoh umishpot, nivchor lashem nizovach.* "To do righteousness and justice is more acceptable to the Lord than sacrifice."

What causes this change of emphasis on the part of Hosea and the other prophets? It is not that they are opposed to sacrifices per se; what they are opposed to is the fact that the people of their day failed to comprehend the *true* meaning of sacrifice—the people of their day were prepared to offer up lambs and bullocks at the altar, but were not willing to truly give of themselves to their God.

What then, you may ask, is the meaning of "giving of one's self?" Is that not precisely what we all do, for example, whenever we give a contribution to charity? The answer is decidedly—no! We do not have in mind only the giving of material possessions; "giving of one's self" implies more than that. Its meaning is alluded to in this same verse: *Adam ki yakriv mikem korban.* The words *korban* and *mikem* are integrally related; the verse implies that if our giving is really to be *mikem*, of ourselves, it must represent a *korban*—a sacrifice.

Would you say there is a difference between the Texas oil-millionaire who gives a million dollars to the United Nations and the Pennsylvania coal miner, who gives a dollar to his Community Chest fund? Of course, there is. For the millionaire, the philanthropic act represents a fine gesture; he could have invested his money in making more money or he could have used it for some less worthy cause. But it goes without saying that this gift represents no real deprivation for him. But for the miner, this dollar signifies an hour of sweat under the most perilous kind of working conditions—for him the dollar represents a deprivation, a denial, a true sacrifice—he has given of *himself.*

Let us consider for a moment what it is in our lives that represents this kind of sacrifice. To most of us, money is neither as unimportant as it is to the millionaire or as meaningful as it would be to a poor miner. For us, living in our kind of society, where we are forever punching either real or imaginary timeclocks in the mad scramble for existence—for us, the real sacrifice, the real giving of ourselves is the giving of our time and energy, whether it be to the synagogue, to our homes and families, or in any other realm of human activity.

Unfortunately, most people in our society, as in the days of Hosea, have never learned the true meaning of giving of themselves. Let us look at our synagogues, for instance. Very few members of a congregation will refuse to respond to a Yom Kippur appeal or even to place an ad in the annual congregational journal. But only a handful of people are willing to give of their time and energy to participate in the synagogue committees and boards, to join in the hard work which gives true life and spirit to a synagogue.

And, so too, in the political interests of the average individual. Most intelligent people go to the trouble of casting a vote, but very few "give of themselves" by spending the time necessary to inform themselves of the relative merits of the various local state and national candidates. The sad truth is that very few people enter into the fight for democracy by joining and working actively in organizations which attempt to give them better representation in their government.

And what about our own personal lives? The lives of most parents, for example, are motivated and given meaning by their desire to give their children a good education, an opportunity to make good in the world of the future, and to provide them with some of the comforts which they themselves never enjoyed. But very few parents bother to give their children the best kind of education—the education which comes with a home where parents spend many hours with their children, learning to understand them better, by listening to their worries, their problems, their plans, their hopes and their ideals.

But why, someone may ask, should we give of ourselves? Can this kind of giving help us in any way, enrich our lives or broaden our perspective? The answer, it seems to me, is that giving freely of ourselves, is not an option which we can decide to take or leave—it is the essential quality of being human. In this respect, the human being is marvelously different from the animal in that he can think of the needs of others as well as of his own. In the final analysis, whom do men think of as being the real human being—the Lot or the Abraham, the Korah or the Moses, the grasping and aggressively acquisitive individual or the person who can sincerely extend his hand to his fellow man and say: "Is there anything I can do for *you*?"

Jewish history, and perhaps all of world history, might be written in terms of its great men and women who reached the highest point of human fulfillment by their willingness and desire to give of themselves. The Bible is replete with stories of self-sacrifice and with examples of such wholehearted unequivocal giving of oneself. Is it not this very quality which gives the beauty and grandeur to the story of Ruth, who is willing to sacrifice and give of herself in her loyalty to Naomi, a woman who has lost life's most treasured possessions, her husband and her sons. We may fail to recall Naomi's words as she pleads with her daughters-in-law to return to their own homes, but as long as man continues to live on this planet, he will thrill to the sublime words of love and self-sacrifice, uttered by Ruth: "Entreat me not to leave thee, and to return from following after thee; for whither thou goest, I will go; and where thou lodgest, I will lodge; thy people shall be my people, and thy God, my God; where thou diest, will I die, and there will I be buried."

In prophetic times, we have manifold examples of prophets who are ever prepared to sacrifice their lives, if necessary, to preach the word of God, in the perennial struggle for justice and truth. It is difficult to imagine anybody in our own day with the courage and spiritual stamina of a man like the prophet Nathan, who is not afraid to rise and tell the mighty King David that he has sinned and that he is guilty of murder in the eyes of the Lord and that he will receive his due punishment. *Atah haish*—"You are the man," cries the prophet, knowing well that his words jeopardize his very life. And yet he persists in giving of himself, completely and unflinchingly, knowing that his cause is a just one; it is the cause of the Lord.

As we proceed through the pages of Jewish history, we are confronted with the tragic portrayal of the martyrdom of the saintly Rabbi Akiba. Never can we forget his last words, which were uttered as he was being tortured by the Romans, words which were meant to comfort his weeping disciples: "All my days," he cries, "I have longed for this hour. I have loved God with all my heart, and I have loved Him with all my might; now that I can love Him with my whole life, I have found complete happiness." He rejoices in the fact that he can give *Kol Nafsho*—his very soul, in making the supreme sacrifice.

And in modern times, a man like Theodore Herzl, imbued with an ideal of reestablishing the ancient homeland of Israel, gave of his life to help make this idea into a reality, thereby making of himself a great human being. And finally, in our own day, we have but to look to the people of the tiny State of Israel who gave of themselves completely, first as Halutzim in the struggle to make a fertile land out of a parched desert, and then as soldiers and fighters, giving their lives to retain their precious land and even now, continuing to give and sacrifice in order that any Jew who wishes to do so may find a refuge in the Promised Land.

How can we know if we are really "giving of ourselves?" There is a very good test. For there is an amazing and wonderful quality about giving of oneself. We usually think that when we part with something, we are of necessity left with less for ourselves; but actually the true sign of "giving of oneself" is that the person loses nothing; on the contrary, he adds a great deal of meaning and significance to his life. When we participate actively in the life of the synagogue; when we give freely and ungrudgingly of our time and energy to the Sisterhood, the Men's Club, and the various other activities—we are not only helping the synagogue—we are thereby adding spiritual wealth and beauty to our own lives.

If we join and give of ourselves to a political organization which has as its goal the elimination of corruption from government and the strengthening of democracy, we become through this work better citizens and more complete human beings.

Every parent knows that the sacrifices he makes for

his children in turn makes him richer in spirit and understanding—never poorer. When we really give of ourselves to our children, we are not only helping them to grow up to be better men and women—we are helping to make ourselves more tolerant, more sympathetic, finer human beings.

The Hebrew writer, Judah Steinberg, has written a very beautiful story which I would like to share with you. In this story he explains why of all the sections of the Temple of old, the only part which has remained standing is the *Kotel maaravi*—the western wall. It seems that when King Solomon was about to erect the Temple, he decided that in order to make it a Temple of the entire Jewish people, he would have everybody who wished to do so, take part in its construction. And when the wise king made this proclamation throughout the land, people from the farthest corners of Israel gathered together in Jerusalem, all of them eager to share in this holy venture.

Now the people, it seems, were divided into a number of groups—the wise men, the priests, the mighty men and the poor people. The wise men chose to work on the southern wall for they recalled that even when the *Mishkan* stood, the place of the Menorah was always in the southern portion, and so they ordered their slaves to build the southern wall.

The *Kohanim* asked permission to build the northern wall, for they remembered that in the *Mishkan*, the table and the showbread stood in the northern portion, and when they received permission to construct the northern wall, their servants promptly went to work and put it up.

The rich and mighty men of the land rushed toward the eastern wall and commenced its erection. For some reason the rich men have always liked the *Mizrach* wall, and their slaves constructed it with expert skill.

And finally the poor people, with fear and trembling, knowing full well that they were neither wise nor strong nor mighty, begged to be permitted to assemble the bricks and stones for the one wall that was left—the western wall. This permission was granted and with great joy and fervor, the needy and the indigent, struggled and labored to put up the western wall.

And the legend continues, when the Temple was completed, God chose for the habitation of the *Shechinah*—the western wall, for it was the handiwork of men and women who had constructed it in a labor of love with their own hands.

Then, when Israel sinned, God forsook His House, and the *Shechinah* returned to Heaven. And when the enemies of Israel set fire to the Sanctuary, it destroyed every corner of the Temple, except the western wall which till today stands firmly on its original foundations—foundations made strong and everlasting by people who gave of themselves.

Adam ki yakriv mikem korban—perhaps the deepest meaning of the verse is this: to really reach the status of *Adam*, of a real person, one must be prepared to give sincerely and completely of oneself.

10

The Hidden Light

Rabbi Seymour Cohen

THERE IS A VAST difference between the fast of Yom Kippur and the fast of the ninth day of Av. The fast in the summer is known as the black fast, and this day of abstinence is called the white fast. On the ninth of Av, the synagogue is darkened. One can hardly see his prayer book before him. On Yom Kippur Eve, the synagogue is aglow with light. In the old house of worship, before the invention of the incandescent lamp, there were many, many candles that were brightly burning. A light, a candle was lit for the living. It was called the light of living and a candle was lit for the dead known as the candle of the soul.

Why was the synagogue so full of light on Yom Kippur Eve? Why was this day solemn, but not sad?

I think that the explanation to our question lies in the attitude which the rabbis had towards light. What a wonderful thing light is! Light permits us to look into the recesses of darkness, to probe the mysteries of the night and to fathom new depths. Close your eyes for a moment and feel how life is in the absence; and then you open your eyes again and the illumination of many

Selected from *Best Jewish Sermons of 5715-5716*.

sources of light brings a new glow into your heart. The radiance of spiritual light permits us to look into our soul, to examine the inner workings of our spirit, to find new truths and to partake of new adventures in the mystery of life.

There is an ancient legend of our people which relates that when God created the world, primeval light blazed forth and covered the entire world. God, looking ahead into the history of mankind, saw evil generations ahead. He took his great creation and hid it away from the wicked. Job, speaking of this, wrote, "But from the wicked their light is withholden." God hid light, bits of light here and there. This light is hidden for the righteous who are to come, to rediscover it. This is the meaning of the verse which says, "Light is sown for the righteous and gladness for the upright in heart." Each righteous person, each individual must go out and rediscover the hidden sources of light. He must find once more these sources of spiritual pleasure which will help him to find his way through the dark cavernous passages of the world.

Light is planted for the righteous. Like a seed, the righteous must go out, discover the sources of light, cultivate it and in its growth, make richer his own life. Had light been hidden away altogether, the world could not have existed for a single moment. But it was only hidden like the seed which generates other seeds and fruits, and the whole world is sustained by it. There is not a day that something does not emanate from the light to sustain all things, for it is with this that the Holy One, blessed be He, nourishes the world.

"Light is planted for the righteous and gladness for the upright in heart."

With these words, the service of the synagogue begins on Kol Nidre night. We are persuaded to become, for the few fleeting hours of Yom Kippur day, seekers after this spiritual light. On this night, I would like to tell you of the account of two men who found their way back to God and rediscovered, as do the righteous, the light of their lives.

One was a German philosopher, a man who was so typical of his generation in Germany at the end of the 19th century and at the beginning of the 20th. His personality and the story of his life, the gripping account of his groping in the darkness, the story of his stumbling and his near fall are the tale that I would like to relate to you.

Franz Rosenzweig was a brilliant student of philosophy. His young mind was bestirred with the intellectual difficulties which are felt by so many of the sensitive minds of our young people. The meager Judaism which he had been taught gave him little spiritual sustenance. There was little to sustain the lusty, intellectual appetite of this young man. The Judaism which he knew could not satisfy the needs and the hunger of his soul. In the year 1913, Rosenzweig had committed himself to take the path that so many other German Jews had taken before him. He was not motivated by any desire for social advance. He did not seek to find acceptance in a Christian society. Rosenzweig felt that rather than live his days out as a pagan, he would prefer to convert to Christianity. He did not want to live as a man without any faith.

And then the Day of Atonement came, the day on which Rosenzweig was to make his final break with Jewish life. Being a typical German, systematic and conscious of the historical significance of his intended deed, he had only one proviso. He would become a Christian and enter the fold of Christian life, but not as a pagan, rather as a Jew who had broken with Judaism.

He decided to attend the service of the synagogue in the little German city of Cassel on Rosh Hashonah and on Yom Kippur. He was a Jew who did not wish to break off, but wished to go deliberately through Judaism to Christianity.

On Yom Kippur day when the synagogue is bathed in light a great experience of his life occurred. The event came about with swiftness and in the spirit of absolute finality that is reported in other accounts of great conversion and other moments of great discovery. On the Day of Atonement, he stood together with his brothers in the synagogue. The deep meaning of the day when a Jew is nothing other than a man and when God is nothing other than the great Judge of the world had the most profound psychological impact upon him. The moving character of the Day of Atonement has been understood by many a writer. Many a Jew and non-Jew has grasped the meaning of this day. Meyerbeer, the great composer, could never erase from his mind the lilting strains of the Kol Nidre melody. In all his compositions, the Kol Nidre theme runs through and through.

On Yom Kippur day, the Jew strips himself of all pretenses and stands before his Maker, asking for a year of life. Rosenzweig came into the synagogue that day determined that it would be the last in which he would be numbered among the Jewish people. He left the House of God that day resolved to find a new path in life. Here he had been determined to break with the heritage of his people; to cast aside centuries of tradition; to break family ties; to sever the link with his own loved ones; to find haven in another faith. Then Rosenzweig discovered some of the light which God had hidden away centuries before. Rosenzweig found some of that light which God has set aside for the righteous. In the great mood of discovery, as others have found before

him and others will find surely after him, Franz Rosenzweig found the road to return. His family had been
greatly troubled that holy season. They were fearful,
having some inkling of what he intended to do, that he
would convert after Yom Kippur day. Yes, Franz
Rosenzweig converted. But he converted back to the
faith of his people, led by the great light of the Lord that
he himself had uncovered.

What transpired after Rosenzweig's great return
should be of interest to us. He served as a soldier during
the First World War. He met with Jews of Eastern Europe
and saw the full meaning of their type of devotional
worship. Every night he would send a short postcard or
a letter back to his mother marking down some of his
philosophical ideas. His mother treasured these cards,
and after the war, they formed the notes upon which
Rosenzweig's great book "Star of Redemption," was written. Franz Rosenzweig remained until the last years of
his life a great interpreter of Judaism in Germany. He
was a Jew who was greatly devoted to tradition. Though
in the last decade of his life he was incapacitated by
crippling paralysis, he still continued his work in trans-
lating the Bible, in writing commentaries upon the
prayers and upon the poetry and ritual of our people.
He set up schools and institutions of learning. Some of
his students and co-workers are still active in Israel and
in America. Rosenzweig discovered the light that is hidden for the righteous and the gladness which is the
share of the upright of heart.

The second man who found his way to Judaism due
to the emotional impact of Yom Kippur was not a member of our faith. His name was Amie Palliere. Amie
Palliere was a typical young Frenchman. He lived in the
city of Lyons, a city which has been described as a city
with a soul.

A great experience happened to Palliere on Yom Kippur day. As he was walking along one of the streets with a companion, he noticed some of the shops were closed. He had had little dealings with Jews before. Typical of Christians who live in small communities, where there is limited social contact with Jews, the only Jews that he had known were three boys—three Cohen boys—who would sit in their class during the Sabbath day. In France, classes met six days a week. As the teacher would dictate, they would sit with their hands either in their pockets or on their desk. Palliere knew little about Jews or Judaism. The only Jews he had known were those whose illustrations were found in a Dore Bible, an illustrated Bible. One Yom Kippur afternoon, as he walked along noticing these stores closed, he asked his friend what sort of a holiday it was, and his friend told him that this was a great festival of the Jews and suggested that perhaps both of them might go into the Temple and see the service. Palliere debated in his mind whether or not he should enter. A pious Catholic does not permit himself to attend the religious service of another faith. Something in Palliere's heart attracted him closer and closer to the synagogue that day, as if he were drawn on by a magnetic lodestone. There was no reasoning or reflection of why he did what he did. For a long time, nothing was to happen in his life to reflect the fact that he had gone into the synagogue that day. Palliere was like a traveler who makes up his mind at the crossroads to take one route in preference to another, and then after a long journey finds that he has arrived at a point many, many miles away from where he was trying to reach. Palliere went into the synagogue that day and something struck him. All of his life, he had been taught the doctrine that the Jews were a rejected people, that the only purpose of the Jewish people in the world was to be part of the preparatory stage before Christianity. The Jews were a dejected people, a people who were spiritually impotent. Then for the first time in his life, he saw a large number of Jews assembled together. Their shoulders were covered with prayer shawls. Suddenly to his mind was revealed the fact that these Hebrews were the very same Hebrews that he had seen in the Dore Bible. They were on their very feet standing before him. He was struck by the fact that many in the Congregation wore a Tallit. He thought for a moment that they were all officiating. Some of them scattered here and there in the Congregation were dressed in the white robes of Yom Kippur day, just like the priests who remained in the center of the pulpit of the synagogue. Here was an entire people officiating. Here, for the first time in his life, he had the lightening experience of learning that in Jewish life all of us are part of the kingdom of priests, all are holy people—and then he was struck by another fact. The silent assembly was in expectancy of something about to happen. "What are they waiting for," he asked his companion. This double aspect which Judaism disclosed to him held nothing that could trouble his faith at that time, but here was revealed to him the two great characteristics of Jewish life—that each one of us is a priest and is holy, and that each one of us is waiting for the great event of our life. Israel appeared suddenly in its full meaning in the life of Amie Palliere. He suddenly found that light which is planted for the righteous. The light of revelation came to Palliere that day. Though for awhile he continued within the Christian faith, though for awhile he even trained for the Catholic priesthood, he did not find the spiritual moorings which would help to give firmness to his soul. The impact of this moment—the revelation of Neilah, as he preferred to call it, gave his soul little rest. Palliere became a wanderer. He searched about to find his spiritual home. He attempted for a while to find satisfaction by becoming a member of the Salvation Army and then he went to the Evangelists, wandering, seeking, searching, groping, looking for his spiritual moorings. At long last, he came to a pious Italian Rabbi, a Rabbi by the name of Elijah Benamozegh in this old city of Leghorn in Italy. Rabbi Elijah advised him to accept the Seven Commandments of Noah which the righteous of the world are to take on. Palliere was not completely satisfied and continued his studies of Judaism. He became an ordained Rabbi, and for awhile spoke in one of the synagogues. In the synagogue in Paris, he introduced the old customs once more and insisted upon more Hebrew in the service. He wrote his book, *The Unknown Sanctuary*. He lectured even in America. He worked with the Zionists and with youth groups. Light is planted for the righteous and gladness for the upright of heart. Palliere found his way on Yom Kippur day. The revelation of Neilah brought him to his spiritual home. Thus good friends, you have heard of two who found their way on Yom Kippur day.

As I look out upon you, a veritable sea of humanity, let me tell you that your very presence in this synagogue on this Yom Kippur night places you in the class of those of the righteous who are seeking the light of the Lord. You know full well in your hearts that the lamp of religion, that the light which God has planted can be found only in the House of God. You know that this is the source of light. "This is none other than the House of God and this is the very gate of heaven." Each of you knows that you can find a bit of that light which God himself has hidden for the righteous. Each one of you can find that source of spiritual satisfaction as did Franz Rosenzweig and as did Amie Palliere.

Franz Rosenzweig and Amie Palliere could not have found their spiritual home, their light, were it not for the fact that there was a synagogue existing in Cassel, a temple existing in Lyons where they would undergo their great experience. The spiritual message of the synagogue can only be brought to us when there is a physical surrounding in which the spiritual message can be told, related and unfolded. This House of God serves as the spiritual home for each one of you. Each one of you can, on this Yom Kippur day and throughout the year, with the assistance of the synagogue, with the majestic beauty of our service, with the inspiring manner of our religious teaching, help to find that bit of light which is planted for the righteous and the gladness which will be the share of the upright in heart.

The Poet Laureate of our people, Bialik, in one of his poems called, "Im Shemesh," urges us to rise early and go to the hills. There with the rising of the sun, there is to be found the pure golden light. Let each man draw sufficient sustenance to satisfy his soul. Let the light purge that which is within us. Let us always safeguard this light as a precious possession to satisfy our souls.

"Live, work hard, be hopeful—and be sustained by that light which you will discover."

11

Teshuvah Is the Answer

Rabbi Myron M. Fenster

I STOOD A FEW WEEKS ago before a painting by Vincent Van Gogh in the municipal Museum of Amsterdam, Holland. The painting is called, "Bedroom at Arles," a picture of the artist's room in a period of intense productivity.

Its simplicity is poignant; it had a moving effect upon me. All of the artist's possessions are there—two chairs and a bed, a table and a basin, a jacket, a glass. Of it the artist had written, "Just simply my bedroom by its simplification giving a grander style to things." This painting I believe has much to do with why we come to synagogue on this Rosh Hashanah.

All year the world of things and events occupy us. All year long the world is too much with us, late and soon we get and spend. All year long we run and hide, run and hide, but on these days we hold a mirror up to our lives and ask ourselves what life is all about. For these days come to remind us that life is not all work, rest and entertainment; that our purpose on earth is not only to make a living and enjoy ourselves. The Days of Awe come to teach us that life is a responsibility and a trust.

Selected from *Best Jewish Sermons of 5717-5718.*

For the next two days, indeed for the next Ten Days of Repentance, we will try to make sense of our running and going, of our getting and spending. We will try to fit the pieces together, to see if we, "by simplification, may give a grander style to the things" in our lives. We come to forget the momentary, the banal and the commonplace, to concentrate as all great artists have done, on the permanent behind the fleeting. We will try to strip away the frivolous and the unnecessary and search for the real and the significant. For in this, Van Gogh in his field, and many others in their own, come close to that which rabbis sought to discover for us. They sought to answer the question of how to seek the Eternal.

Across the stretches of time we shall try to unite during these days with those who prayed and who sought to make of their lives a prayer; with men who searched and tried to make of life a searching and finding in God. Men who understood the art of living and tried to etch it boldly into our tradition.

Out of the breath of their wisdom they ordained ten days of *Teshuvah*; ten days of return as, at least, a partial answer to the complex problems that we all face. *Teshuvah* means to look into the mirror of our lives, to discover what is ungainly, unseemly and inappropriate in it and to "return O Israel unto the Lord, our God." *Teshuvah* in Hebrew also means an "answer." What sort of an answer is *Teshuvah*?

Teshuvah is an answer to those who believe that life is a problem. This idea is one of the prevailing moods of our time. Man is pictured by many of our poets and writers, thinkers and even theologians as being a prisoner of circumstances, trapped by forces beyond his control. They speak of us as though we were inevitably and inextricably caught and weighed down by the nature of our being. They speak of yawning despair, the certainty of doom, the persistence of sin. This is their unvarying variation on their most prevalent theme.

Nowhere is this more evident than in Eugene O'Neil's brilliant, but desolate, *Long Days Journey Into Night*. It is a graphic picture of the breakdown of a modern family. The father is a miser and a drunkard, the mother is a dope addict. Each son has been afflicted with his own sickness. The play wallows in mutual contempt and self-pity. And at one point the mother blurts out: "None of us can help the things life has done to us. They are done before you realize it and before you know it, you have lost your real self forever."

Into this gloomy atmosphere steps *Teshuvah* to say that it is simply not so. Life is not a long journey into nothing. Spiritual night is not inevitable. No moving finger points toward defeat and having pointed, ensnares us. Your real self must not necessarily be lost. Very often we can help the things life has done to us. Montaigne's gloomy prediction to the contrary, man is not a moral creature forever committed to a moral enterprise. There is before us this day a new year; each day there is a new page. If he wishes, man can turn over a new leaf.

Along comes our tradition to declare: "There is nothing that stands in the way of one who returns, of one who has The Answer." Those who say with our liturgy, "Our Father, our King return us with full repentance before Thee," can and do return. And this is true on every level of our personal as well as our national life. Have we failed in this last year in our duty toward ourselves, our family and our faith? It must not necessarily be so. Man can change his ways and if he persists, can prevail.

That man can return and be reinstated is the underlying theme of the day and the season. With this in mind we gathered in the silence of midnight for Selihot and this is why we are here today. This is the hope of the Sabbath of Repentance and this will be our expectant hope on the Great White Fast of Atonement. It is written boldly into our tradition. It is held out luminously before us—there is nothing that stands in the way of the *Baal Teshuvah*.

Are there then among us those who are burdened by a sense of guilt, a feeling of wrongdoing in the past? Are there those among us being eaten up by envy of someone else's good fortune or possessions? Are there among us those who are soured by jealousy, driven by passions or haunted by the past? Our tradition teaches us that our God is merciful and compassionate, that He abounds in loving kindness and in truth. *Teshuvah* then beckons us to confess our sin and to be reinstated in His sight. Our liturgy teaches us that God desires not the death of the sinner, but that he return to Him and live.

The Talmud reports that Rabbi Meir was once so provoked by some highway robbers that in a moment of desperation, he prayed that they should die. His wife Beruria censured him: "Rather pray for them that they should repent." Rabbi Meir like many wise husbands heeded the admonition of his wife. He prayed for them, the story concludes, and they did repent.

One moment or one hour of *Teshuvah* will not erase all of our problems permanently. But *Teshuvah* that brings with it a renunciation of past wrong doing, a strengthening of the inner will, a resolution toward the future could help us start a journey on the road toward complete repentance. Thus, our rabbis extolled even one hour of repentance and good works. For out of simple beginnings and firm resolutions we stand to be remade for the entire year.

Let the weak be strong only once and a beginning has been made. Let the fearful show courage only once and he is on the road toward overcoming his difficulty. Let the intemperate control his anger on one occasion and he is on the way toward whipping his failure. We have been promised: "Open the door of repentance only the width of the eye of a needle and God will open it wide enough for carriages and wagons to pass through." We are not today required to finish the entire task of returning. We are required to make a beginning.

Are there among us those who have been postponing a beginning toward closer observance of our faith? Have we been putting off bringing the light of the Sabbath into our lives? How long have you been promising yourself the "luxury" of enrolling in a course of Hebrew study? How often have you remarked how wise it would be to set a daily period aside for prayer, devotion and thanksgiving? Now is the moment for firm resolution. Now is the time to make a beginning.

This idea that we are caught in a web of encircling circumstance has not only affected us individually. The idea that evil, corruption and bribery are here to stay seems to have become a part of our collective thinking. "Go Fight City Hall," we say. The fact of the matter is that once a few irate mothers in Central Park not only fought City Hall, but prevailed. The fact remains that there is a court of appeal for vice and corruption, as national scandals in the fields of labor and management have demonstrated. This notion that corruption is here and there is nothing to do about it is defeatist in addition to being untrue. It suffers from the lack of *Teshuvah* spirit. It fails to reckon with the fact that people inevitably will become aroused, that they will resist the inequities in their society and ultimately will expose them. This is the implicit faith of *Teshuvah*.

The life of the Jewish people shows that nothing stands in the way of a resolute will. Theodore Herzl, himself one of the Master Repenters of the modern age said, "If you will it, it is no dream." The Jewish people have since been *willing* their return to their ancient homeland. It is no longer a dream.

The Psalmist held out for us the great promise of *Teshuvah*. "Have faith that you will see the goodness of the Lord in the land of the living." Have faith and you will see it. Return and you will experience it. *Teshuvah* is the way to see the goodness of the Lord in the land of the living.

When you see a great painting or hear the blast of the *Shofar*, when we say our prayers in these Days of Awe, let us be aroused out of our complacency. Let us remember the responsibilities of our life. Let us recall the expectant hope of being reinstated in the sight of God. Let us remember what *Teshuvah* means. It means a new lease on life, the beckoning possibility that we are not today committed, either individually or collectively, to yesterday's mistakes.

Again it was in the lovely city of Amsterdam that a young girl, hounded by unbelievable torment, looked into her life. The world was then beset by its greatest folly. It was just at this moment that Anne Frank wrote, "I still believe that people are really good at heart. I simply can't build my hopes on confusion, misery and death. I feel the sufferings of millions and yet when I look up into the heavens I think that it will all come out all right. This cruelty will end and peace and tranquillity will return. I believe in the goodness of man...."

On this Rosh Hashanah, let us look into the heavens. We too cannot build on misery and confusion. But we can build on our own possibilities, on the potential for good resident in each of us. Let us look into the heavens and believe in our own power to return. Let each of us look into the heavens and into our lives and discover the answer which is *Teshuvah*. Let us say today with Anne Frank, "I believe in the goodness of man." Let us resolve to look into our lives and remake them into the image of our living God.

12

Power of Negative Thinking

Rabbi Alfred Friedman

THE POWER OF POSITIVE THINKING has been pop-
ularized by the Rev. Norman Vincent Peale through his
books and newspaper columns. There is certainly value
in approaching life and its problems in a hopeful, constructive and positive frame of reference. But there is
also much to be said for "the power of *negative* thinking."

While most people associate "negative" thinking
with pessimism and obstructionism, the fact is that
such an approach can not only be constructive, but also
much more practical and hence more attainable.

Judaism has an optimistic and constructive approach
to life, despite the fact that many of its directives are
couched in *negative* terms. According to traditional
teaching, there are six hundred and thirteen commandments which the observant Jew must fulfill. It is of interest to note that more than half (365 to be exact) are
expressed by *negative* prohibitions!

Furthermore, of the Ten Commandments, *eight* are
in the negative form! Thou shalt have *no* other Gods
before Me . . .

Selected from *Best Jewish Sermons of 5721-5722*.

Thou shalt *not* make unto thee a graven image ... Thou shalt *not* take the name of the Lord Thy God in vain ... Thou shalt *not* murder ... etc.

In the same vein, we find many other biblical injunctions in a *negative* form. To cite but a few: "A stranger shalt thou *not* wrong, nether shalt thou oppress him, for ye were strangers in the land of Egypt." (Exodus 22:20). "Thou shalt *not* follow a multitude to do evil or to pervert justice. ..." (Exodus 23:2). "Thou shalt take *no* gift—for a gift blindeth them that have sight and perverteth the words of the righteous." (Advice to judges—Exodus 23:8).

It is surely no accident that we find the Golden Rule mentioned in the Talmud in Hillel's name, in the *negative* form! He said: "Do *not* do unto others as ye would have them do unto you." The positive enunciation, "Do unto others" is beautifully idealistic but impractical and unattainable—for there is no end to the good things we want done unto ourselves, while the evil acts of man toward his neighbor are more definable and avoidable. Looking further into the Ethics of the Fathers in the Mishna, we find other supporting examples:

"Do *not* associate with the wicked." (Avot, Chap. 1)

"Separate *not* thyself from the community." (Avot, Chap. 2)

"Pass *not* judgment upon thy neighbor until thou art come into his place." (Avot, Chap. 2)

"Do *not* say when I have leisure I will study. . . ."

When we look at the historic experience of the Jewish people, a minority everywhere, we find that they often had to say "nay" to the majority. Otherwise, they and the values they held dear would have been wiped out.

Thus, when the heroic Mattathias initiated the Maccabean revolt against Antiochus, he called upon his fellows to support him, saying: "We will *not* hearken to the king's words. ..." (I Maccabees).

In American, as well as in Jewish history, we recall the negative rallying cry of the colonists, "*No* taxation without representation!"

Does the power of negative thinking have anything to do with the lives of young people in twentieth century America? I think it has a great deal to say to them.

Teen-agers, generally, think that going along with the gang, conformity, is the right thing to do. They're afraid to stand up and say "No," lest they be labeled "squares" or be thought "queer." I am not claiming that it is evil to conform, but when saying "Yes" means compromising ethical or moral principles, then we must have the courage and the will to say "No, I won't." It's not correct to justify our behavior by saying, everybody's doing it—everyone drinks or smokes or cheats on examinations. Nor should we keep out of our fraternities, sororities, and schools those who differ from us in race or religion or disagree with our political ideas. If you feel that in relationship with your parents, you have a right to independence and individuality, then by all means be consistent enough to accord your fellow teenagers the same rights.

In the South, there has been a fairly successful effort spearheaded by Negro college students calling the country's attention to discrimination against Negroes in lunch counters and bus stations. These young people are saying a loud "nay" to inequality. Guided by the organization CORE, the Committee for Racial Equality, the students are oriented by such warnings as:

"*Don't* strike back or curse if abused."

"*Don't* laugh out."

"Remember, *no* violence."

It takes real strength of character to fulfill these negative prohibitions in the face of attackers and jeerers. They deserve not only our admiration, but also our unstinted support.

From all that has been said here, it should be quite clear that there is a tremendous power which inheres in him who uses negative thinking for constructive ends. Let us, therefore, learn to respond to life's challenges negatively as well as positively. Let us learn to say:

"I will *not* surrender my heritage for material gain."

"I will *not* compromise with truth and decency."

"I will *not* bend the knee before the idols of popularity or conformity."

"I will *not* sacrifice my ideals for social acceptance."

Then we shall build a worthy life based on the ancient rabbinic prescription: "In a place where there are no men, strive thou to be a man."

13

Solving Man's Permanent Paradox

Rabbi Theodore Friedman

FOR SOME YEARS now I have been searching the literature of our people in quest of answers to the persistent problems of life. No problem of man's existence is more universal and more permanent than that posed by the fact that "the days of our years are three score and ten and it is speedily gone and we fly away." To all the inevitable, unchangeable facts of life, the wise man soon learns to say, "Yes, I accept them. I readily accept all my limitations. I am reconciled to the limitations of my physical strength. I make peace with the fact that my intellectual power has its bounds, that my economic resources are not inexhaustible, that my capacity for goodness has its breaking point. With all my limitations, intellectual, physical, moral and material, I can somehow reconcile myself. But try as I will, I cannot look with unruffled spirit at the fact that some day time will run out, the sun will darken and I shall be gone." The foot soldier going into battle with death hovering around him puts it very bluntly. "Any man who says he

Selected from *Best Jewish Sermons of 5713.*

is not afraid is either a fool or a liar."

The soldier's observation is true as far as it goes, but it does not go far enough. Some men can overcome fear, any kind of fear. But no man yet has overcome the thirst for life, a thirst so insatiable that no matter how deeply we have drunk from the cup, at the end we cry, "More, more."

Consider Moses, the father of the prophets. Who had ever drunk more deeply of the cup of life? Who had ever experienced so much, achieved so much, known God so intimately? Yet, at the age of a hundred and twenty when God tells him, "Behold thy days approach to die," Moses will not accept it. He pleads long and earnestly. How magnificently the Midrash voices his craving for life. At first, Moses argues with God and brings forth every argument in his arsenal. He challenges God's justice, he questions His mercy. But to no avail. He then supplicates God, "Let me enter the land and grant me two or three more years." His plea goes unanswered. Moses, in desperation, then addresses himself to the stars and the planets and invokes them, "Go and beg for mercy for me." He appeals to the sea, the hills and the mountains and the heavens, "Go, I beseech you and beg for mercy." But his plea goes unanswered. In that moment, says the Midrash, Moses wept.

How penetratingly true! In the end, Moses is unreconciled. For a long lifetime he had been God's faithful servant, fulfilling every divine decree without question and without murmur. But the decree announcing his death—this he will not accept.

This is the problem for which I have been seeking an answer in Israel's wisdom. If I cannot be reconciled to the inevitable—and I surely cannot change it—what am I to make of the fact of my mortality? The last work of wisdom in life is supposed to be: change what you cannot accept, and accept what you cannot change. Here, however, I can neither change the fact that at some turning in the road I must part company with life, with all that is sweetest and dearest to me, nor can I, or any man, really accept it.

What then am I to do? I must do a seemingly paradoxical thing. I must put the fact of my mortality out of my mind, forget it and go about living as if I were going to live forever and, on the other hand, I must remember to count my days for they are speedily gone. This is what the wisdom and the piety of Israel teaches me. You ask, and rightly so, is not that self-contradictory? Am I not affirming on the one hand what I deny on the other? No more contradictory, I answer, than man himself. No more contradictory than life itself.

Do I not walk upon the earth and with my mind reach for the stars, am I not dust and ashes and at the same time a child of the living God? Am I not driven like the lower animals by the passions of hunger and thirst but at the same time am I not stirred by love, fired by beauty and inspired by truth? In sum, am I not both mortal and immortal?

And what of the contrarieties of life? Koheleth summed them up. "There is a time to be born and a time to die; a time to weep and a time to laugh; a time to mourn and a time to dance; a time to keep silent and a time to speak." To his summation, we now add, a time to forget the inevitable day, hold life lightly, use it and spend it without reckoning the cost, and a time to be mindful that man born of woman is but for a few days and his candlelight is brief.

This is no superior original wisdom of my own, it is what I have learned by pondering Israel's ageless wisdom.

This very man Moses, who argued and pleaded and

cried for a few more years; there were other times and other circumstances in his life. There was the time when the children of Israel had worshipped the golden calf and so angered God that He was about to destroy them. Moses threw himself into the breach and pleaded with God, "Wilt Thou not forgive their sin? If Thou wilt not, then pray blot me out of the list of the living." Moses was ready to fling his life away. Without his people, his existence would be meaningless. There ought to be something of Moses in all of us: the spirit of expending our lives recklessly, if you will, in behalf of that in which we believe.

I do not know of any good or great thing that ever came into this world except through people who did not stop to reckon the cost to themselves. How do you think great books are written, great music composed, great pictures painted? Men poured out their life blood and went through mental and physical torment. How did freedom ever come into the world except by men who threw away their lives in what must often have seemed a hopeless cause? How did America win its freedom and how did Israel become a State? Not too long ago, on a windswept hill overlooking Jerusalem, I saw the graves of sixteen, seventeen and eighteen year old Jewish boys and girls, who laid down their lives that Israel might be free. How did truth ever come into the world except through men who refused, no matter what the cost, to acknowledge falsehood. The Church had Galileo thrown into prison for teaching that the earth moves around the sun. And when they had done their worst, Galileo, emerging from prison, exclaimed: "*E pur muove.*" It still moves.

So then, there is a time to forget that the deepest thing within us is the will to live; the time when we must stop counting our days as children count and hoard pennies. But give ourselves to the great calls that come to us, to the call for a better world, a nobler Jewish community, aye, even the call to a single soul in distress.

My friends, all men must die. Let us die for something and not of something. Let us expend our all on the things without price.

And then there are times when we ought remember that our days are as a fleeting shadow, that they are speedily gone and we fly away. Oh, how I wish I could shake some people out of their willful forgetting of the day when they too will join the innumerable caravan to the land from which no traveler returns. I would like to say to them, "What are you doing with these all so few precious years? What are you spending yourself on?" Alas, how true it is of all of us that forgetting the inevitable day, we live as if our little schemes and our little plans will last forever. It often takes the fact of death to give us a new perspective on life; a perspective in which we see ourselves frittering away our days and years on the trivial and inconsequential. How ridiculously petty some of our strivings must seem when viewed under the aspect of eternity. Ah, if we could but pause now and then to contemplate our mortality, would we, I wonder, so extravagantly spend ourselves in the mad rush for the things that are but of the moment.

The Rabbis in the Talmud said it a long time ago, "If a man sees the evil inclination overpowering him, let him remember the day of death." And the great *Yezer Harah* (evil inclination) that afflicts so many of us, is the relentless drive for just a little more.

So then, out of Israel's wisdom, our problem has been answered. Spend life recklessly and extravagantly on the great and good things, on truth, on beauty, on goodness. Give it away for friendship and love. Fling it away on your devotion to the great ideals of our people.

Forget the point of no return.

And then remember that your time is running out, swifter than the weaver's shuttle. Shake yourself loose from the mad desire for position and possession, recalling with Job that naked you came forth from your mother's womb and naked you must return to the earth.

We are tightrope walkers treading a rope stretched across the abyss. Always we must remember to keep our balance, but we cannot move lightly across the rope unless we look ahead towards the goals that beckon us and forget the abyss below.

14

No Retreat From Sinai

Rabbi Solomon D. Goldfarb

THE SINAI CAMPAIGN will long be remembered as one of the most miraculous events in the first decade of Israel's rebirth. The 100 hour lightning-like drive toward Sinai that shook the world, will inspire admiration in the hearts not only of military students, but of all men, for a 100 years to come. Here, an infant army displayed amazing Napoleonic strategy and agility!

Unfortunately, that brilliant victory ended in a withdrawal of the Israeli forces. Although the overwhelmed and defeated Egyptians were crushed, the combined pressure and threats of the *big two* compelled Israel to yield. The decisive victory was converted into a forced retreat from Sinai.

On the festival of Shavuoth, we recall another march of the children of Israel toward Sinai. That dramatic move constitutes the most decisive event in our history. Indeed, that Sinai event shook the world for thousands of years, and its effects have changed the spiritual and moral face of Western civilization. The greatest miracle of all, is that the Jewish people have never abandoned their stand at Sinai.

Selected from *Best Jewish Sermons 5719-5720*.

We have not retreated from this sacred mountain, nor have we withdrawn from its awesome hold upon our lives. Throughout the ages, the Jew has clung to his position at Sinai and no amount of pressure exerted by *great powers* succeeded in forcing him to yield his spiritual conquest. Threats and torture, pogroms and "persuasion," did not avail; he would not turn his back from Sinai.

The question that we have to ask ourselves is this: Where do we now stand in relation to Sinai—to Torah? Are we as determined, as were our forefathers, to continue to hold our position at the foot of the mountain of the Lord? Are we prepared to put up resistance, equal to that of our ancestors, against those forces and pressures which by no means spent themselves? Do we possess the loyalty and stamina to defend the positions which our people occupied in the "wilderness?"

What is the meaning of *mamad har sinai* in our lives? It assumes a staunch faith in the God of Israel and a love of Torah. It implies a loyalty to our people and a dedication to ethical and moral values. It involves a life of holiness and goodness. It calls for adherence to the tradition and ideals of Judaism.

Let us face the fact that our stand at Sinai will continue to be open to pressure and force: the majority cult, the drive toward conformism, the "natural" *powers*, poised to dislodge us from our forward positions. Every generation produces forces which seem intent on our retreat from Sinai—from Judaism. It is at such times that we are called upon to muster the faith of our unintimidated spiritual giants of past ages—from Abraham, the father of Isaac to Rabbi Abraham Isaac Kook, and declare: *lo nazuz mipoh*—we shall not retreat from Sinai.

That this is by no means an easy task is underscored by our sages. They observe that when the people perceived the thunder, the lightning and the mountain smoking ... they trembled, that is *they withdrew a great distance from Sinai*. However, that was only a temporary retreat, for the ministering angels came and helped them return from their rightful position. (*Ha-yu nirta-in l'achorehen ... umalachai ha-shareth ba-in umsa-yin olan l'hachziron*).

This message likewise does not fail to reckon with the hardships and trials entailed in taking up a non-yielding stand at Sinai. These are often sufficient to frighten the uninitiated and to cause trembling in the camps of those unprepared for an enduring and costly campaign. Both physical and spiritual pressures are often at work to weaken the morale and to undermine the faith of the hesitant and halfhearted Jew. Thus, for instance, the young engineer who is the only Jew among non-Jewish men in a "big outfit," finds himself under terrific, almost terrifying, pressure to conceal his identity and to withdraw from Jewish life. Or the young man in love with a non-Jewess needs more than a lecture to help him hold fast to the faith of his fathers. In such cases—and there are many—there is a crying need for "ministering angels," dedicated leaders, to help our young people resist temptations and threats (however veiled) which make for retreat from faith and fold.

There are, of course, those who plan a deliberate withdrawal from Judaism, and who, of their own choice, beat a retreat from Sinai. They are willing to abandon positions taken up a hundred generations past, and held by valiant men and women through the centuries. Concerning that type (alas, not so rare in our history!) the prophet Isaiah said: "They have forsaken the Lord ... they have turned away backward (*nazoru achor*)."

This message, however, is intended for those men and women who do not run away from their inheritance of their own accord, but who find it beyond their power to retain their stand at the foot of Sinai and slowly yield to the pressures (the tyranny) of the majority. To them we say, let the spirit of their forefathers and the true ideals of democracy serve as "ministering angels" to encourage them to fulfill themselves in the tradition of their people.

It is for us, teachers and parents, rabbis and communal leaders, to serve as "ministering angels" to our sons and daughters who are often caught in the dilemma of "whither?" under modern pressures of mass psychology. Let us stand ready to offer these bewildered young people the wisdom and inspiration of our sages and the benefit of the experiences of our own generation. Even the Israeli army, which was forced to pull back from Sinai, felt a sense of defeat. Only when they realized that the fact of their existence in this post-Hitlerian era was a reality, did their retreat take on the aura of victory. It was living testimony to the eternality and vitality of the Jewish people.

American Jews have the opportunity to advance peacefully on the path leading to Sinai, to the mountain of religion and moral life. If we understand our position in the world, namely, that it is only through our loyalty to Torah and adherence to tradition that we have become a universal people and an eternal people; if we realize our great potential, as sons of prophets and children of idealists, we shall cling to Sinai all the days of our lives and bequeath this heritage to generations yet to come. We shall then move forward—toward the mountain of the Lord—and advance from strength to strength.

15

Reopening Old Wells

Rabbi Morris S. Goodblatt

MOST OF THE weekly portions in the Book of Genesis deal with the lives and achievements of the patriarchs Abraham and Jacob. Only one *Sedrah, Toldot,* is concerned with Isaac. As the Torah unfolds the careers of the patriarchs, Isaac appears to be the least important of the three patriarchal luminaries and is entirely overshadowed by his illustrious father and his equally distinguished son. He was, someone said, the son of a great father and the father of a greater son.

Isaac's fate resembles that of Abraham Mendelssohn whose great father, Moses Mendelssohn, is far better known than himself and whose distinguished son, Felix, similarly overshadowed his father as one of the most gifted musical composers of our time.

It was not the intent of the biblical narrative to distinguish Isaac's stature nor portray him as a mediocrity. On the contrary, the Torah and the sages of Rabbinic literature stressed his saintly qualities, his piety and his unquestioning submissiveness to do God's will even when it entailed a supreme sacrifice. Yet, a careful study of Genesis leads one to the inescapable conclusion that

Selected from *Best Jewish Sermons 5714.*

Isaac was not as great as his father nor as his son, lacking their dynamic and colorful personalities. Unlike Abraham, he was no epoch maker or trail blazer; and unlike Jacob, his personality lacked ruggedness and venturesomeness.

Yet, with it all, Isaac emerges from the ancient world of the Bible a heroic figure, since he has performed a most necessary and significant duty: he served as a faithful guardian and transmitter of his father's teachings and traditions.

The Torah tells us how a famine in the land of Canaan compelled Isaac to travel southward and to settle in Gerar. There he prospered; but his prosperity evoked the envy and hostility of his Philistine neighbors. Affluent Isaac, however, was not one to be satisfied merely with material success. He was drawn on to higher goals and moved by nobler motives. Prominent among these was the determination to reclaim, restore, and safeguard the accomplishments of his father. The biblical narrative records that Isaac reopened the wells of water which had been dug in the days of Abraham, for the Philistines had stopped them up after the death of Abraham; and he gave them the same names as his father had given them. Isaac, surrounded by envious and hateful enemies, devoted himself to the reopening of the wells which the Philistines had stopped up and filled with earth. Isaac did not dig *new* wells but considered it his duty to uncover the wells which his father had dug in former times.

The lesson to be learned from this biblical episode lies upon its very surface. It is simple, yet profound. There are eras in human history that witness the emergence of great personalities, personalities of the stature of Abraham. These men are divinely endowed with extraordinary mental and spiritual powers. Such men, in a symbolic sense, dig *new* wells. They blaze *new* paths; they unfold *new* visions to mankind. These giants of the spirit, appearing at rare intervals in the annals of civilization, promulgate *new* moral principles and crystallize *new* concepts of right and wrong that illumine the lives of people for ages to come. When Abraham formulated the belief in one God, he dug a new well for the benefit of mankind. When Moses brought the Ten Commandments from the heights of Mt. Sinai, he opened up a new fountain of living waters that enriched civilization and nurtured its future destiny. When Israel's prophets in the name of God pronounced the eternal principles of justice and mercy, brotherhood and peace, they released invigorating streams from new wells and fresh springs of the spirit that have nourished and sustained men in their resolve to build a better and more decent world. When the Maccabees rebelled against the Syrio-Greeks and valiantly fought for their right to practice the beliefs and traditions of their fathers they uncovered new fountainheads from which flowed the blessing known to modern man as freedom of worship.

All who hewed new and uncharted paths to human freedom, all who crystallized for men the concepts of human rights, all who struggled to realize the democratic way of life throughout the centuries were "diggers of new wells." They uncovered clean, sparkling waters that nourished hearts of a parched humanity. To this category of epoch makers belong the Founding Fathers of America, those who framed the Bill of Rights and the Constitution of our country, and all who translated their immortal principles into patterns of human conduct. Releasing new energies of the spirit, they made America the greatest democracy in history.

But in every age there are evil people. Their poisoned minds and hate-ridden hearts emulate the Philistines in their destructiveness. The historian Toynbee maintains that a recurrent pattern is found in human history. That pattern is one of progress and decline, moral growth and deterioration. An era that witnesses the digging of new wells is often followed by an age of foul passions poisoning the wells which power-mad tyrants seek to stop up.

Mt. Sinai was momentarily darkened by the golden calf. The French Revolution, proclaiming liberty, equality and fraternity was perverted within two decades by the enemies of freedom into an era of black reaction. This reactionary tendency to neglect, to disregard, and to destroy the spiritual achievements of preceding generations emphasizes the far-reaching significance of Isaac's role as a restorer of ancient wells. The appearance on the stage of history of men of the moral stature of Abraham is a rare occurrence. But Isaacs, who are far more numerous, also have their role to play, a role that dare not be underestimated. These Isaacs may not unfold new visions, create new values and open new wellsprings of the human spirit, but they serve the indispensable purpose of being zealous watchmen and guardians of the spirit. The spiritual reservoirs which evil men maliciously seek to conceal, they uncover and safeguard.

Who can evaluate the role played by the Isaacs among the Jews who lived during the Middle Ages when Europe was a vast religious empire, monolithic in form, formidable in strength. These plain people, unarmed and unsung, refused to bow to the Christian majority and to be swept away by its powerful currents. The Jew, like Isaac of old, by his determination to remain loyal to his faith and to adhere to his group, though few and weak, kept open the neglected wells of religious freedom which the Maccabees had dug long before him.

Similarly in our own day when the bestial hordes of Nazism conquered Europe and ruthlessly stopped up and polluted the wells of human freedom, valiant Isaacs arose to cleanse these wells and preserve them for posterity. Eternally must we be grateful to those intrepid companions of freedom who in the underground movements of Europe assumed the dangerous role of Isaac and with their lives protected the wellsprings of freedom and justice. Nor will future historians fail to record the saga of heroism and deeds of self-sacrifice performed by noble Christians, especially in Holland, Denmark and Norway, who dared to defy their brutal conquerors and frustrate their evil designs to degrade and torment their Jewish fellow citizens. These modern Isaacs in days of suffering and dark despair restored our faith in human decency.

America today also stands in need of modern Isaacs to safeguard and keep pure the traditional wells of American liberty which our Founding Fathers had dug for us. Waves of hysteria and unprecedented intolerance threaten to inundate our country. Self-seeking bigots and malicious demagogues are determined to poison the fountains whence flow our cherished liberties and free institutions. These modern Philistines conspire to stop up the wells of free speech and thought, the right to differ and hold unpopular beliefs, the very essence of American democracy.

In the history of every people moments arise when it needs the leadership of an Abraham, a Moses, a Benjamin Franklin, a Thomas Jefferson, who hold up new visions to their people and lead them to hitherto unscaled heights. There are also times when national welfare demands a different caliber of leadership—a leadership such as Isaac's These men, valiant in their own way, are indispensable. They are the dedicated guardians of their people's institutions and spiritual treasures. They are the preservers of the national reservoirs. America today must have such fearless and faithful Isaacs who will save its spiritual wealth from being polluted and defiled by our modern Philistines.

When one views the American Jewish scene, the need for modern Isaacs is equally evident. The Jewish people, more than other religious groups, has been distinguished for its precious wells of moral teaching and religious truth whose living waters nourished and enriched western religions and civilizations. Yet the fountains have become completely hidden from the sight of the American Jew. Like Hagar, mother Sarah's maid, who was overcome with personal anguish and failed to see the well of water which was beside her, many of our young people today are unaware of the availability of rich and satisfying wellsprings of our faith. Among those whom we label intellectuals, many are often led astray in their search of spiritual sustenance. They resort in the end to alien cults and worship before the altars of false ideologies which ultimately fail them.

How timely and applicable to our own generation is the outcry of Jeremiah the prophet: "... my people have committed two evils: They have forsaken Me, the fountain of living waters, and hewed them out cisterns, broken cisterns, that cannot hold water."

Pitiful and tragic it is that so few Isaacs are available to rescue these misguided ones, to unveil their eyes and enable them to see the ancient wells of their own religious heritage standing close beside them. When so many of our people today thirst from a drought of the spirit, these wells need to be reopened. Their unfailing waters will more than quench their thirst; they will renew their spirits, clear their eyes, and enable them to find new meaning and purpose in their lives as Jews.

The story of Isaac lends deep significance to the efforts of those who labor in behalf of synagogues and religious schools. Every man and woman who helps maintain a synagogue and participates in the task of disseminating Jewish learning is an Isaac redigging the neglected but life-giving wells of our people. Every parent who seeks to introduce religious observances and ritual into the home, who maintains the serene and radiant Sabbath atmosphere on Friday night and the Sabbath day is uncovering the stopped-up fountains of religious inspiration which will revive and refresh the parched souls of our age.

The role of Isaac may seem to be undramatic, unspectacular, unrewarding. Ultimately it will prove itself to be a quiet but a glorious adventure, a modest but an enriching experience. Those who assume this role enlist in the ranks of the faithful and honored guardians of our ancestral heritage, the redeemers of Israel's faith. Few of us can be Abrahams. But if we play the role of the Isaacs of history with skill and sincerity we too shall merit the love and everlasting gratitude of future generations. Others will say of us what was once said of an actor whose destiny it was to play only minor roles: "He was great in small parts." Let us too serve our religion greatly, though in the minor role of Jewish history.

Isaiah, the Prophet, called on our ancestors to look to the rock whence they were hewn and to the pit whence they were dug. Similarly, let us look to our father Abraham and seek out the wells he dug. But let us look also to Isaac for inspiration when the times demand that we reopen the precious wellsprings of Israel's spirit. Then the reward assured us by this same prophet, Isaiah, will be ours and our children's after us. "... I will pour water upon the thirsty land, and streams upon the dry ground; I will pour My spirit upon thy seed, and My blessing upon thine offspring."

16

Leave a Little to God

Rabbi Robert Gordis

IT IS MAY 24, 1884. A bearded scientist with a group of colleagues is seated at a table tapping out some sounds on a little instrument before him. Moments later, forty miles away in Baltimore, the message is received— "What hath God wrought!" The world stands jubilant and thankful before a modern miracle. The telegraph has been invented and a new era of human communication has dawned.

It is September 13, 1959. The news is flashed around the world and banner headlines in the newspapers announce— "Russians Land Rocket on the Moon, Time Calculated Within Eighty-four Seconds." Before this extraordinary achievement of man's intellect, the free world stands frightened and dismayed. A new era of possible human annihilation has dawned, and some are even tempted to murmur, "What hath Satan wrought!"

The brave new world for which men prayed and hoped for centuries has been ushered in, but it has left us prematurely old and frightened by the prospects. If we seek a refuge from the international scene by turn-

Selected from *Best Jewish Sermons of 5719-5720*.

ing to the domestic front, we find no peace. Corruption, crime, delinquency and fraud seem universal. Massive problems create crises and the massive crises threaten us with catastrophe. No wonder hope and confidence are fled and everywhere there crouch anxiety and foreboding, if not terror and despair. On the threshold of the New Year how can we muster both the energy and the will to face the future?

A century and a half ago, the French tyrant Napoleon was master of Europe. In Spain an embattled English army under the Duke of Wellington was trying to resist his advance. One day a young lieutenant came into the British general's tent with a map clutched in his trembling hands: "Look, General, the enemy is almost upon us!" "Young man," the General replied, "Get larger maps, the enemy won't seem so close."

If we wish to understand the shape of things to come, we cannot be satisfied with the headlines of today. We need the perspective of history, the full record of man's past struggles, defeats and achievements. We are accustomed to speak of the path of human history as though men advanced on a straight highway. Actually, man's progress is best compared to a pendulum, for it is characteristic of human nature that we do not go forward in a straight line, but fluctuate from one extreme to the other. To borrow the language of the physicists, men go from one action to an opposite and almost equal reaction.

When our primitive ancestors first emerged upon this planet, they were animals—with one difference. They were intelligent enough to be frightened, to feel helpless before a vast and unknown world filled with countless dangers lurking everywhere. Hence man, and man alone, peopled the hills and the valleys, the seas and the skies, the rivers and the trees with invisible beings, with spirits, gods and demons, fairies and witches, who were powerful and could determine man's fate.

As time went on and man began to organize his ideas, the gods were now assigned special spheres of sovereignty, given different functions and arranged in families, with elaborate rituals created to win their favor. But in ancient religion, as in primitive times, man saw himself as helpless and dependent on the whims and caprices of the spirits, their favor or their displeasure. Man was the plaything of the gods. The ancient Babylonians, for example, who were kinsmen of the Hebrews, had a tradition about the Flood similar to ours in the Bible. But while the Torah tells us that it was man's colossal wrong-doing that impelled God to visit that catastrophe upon the human race, the Babylonians ascribed it to the fact that men on earth were making so much noise that the gods could not sleep! One can well sympathize with their outraged feelings! The Greek myths in which we take delight today were not legends to the Greeks. The tales of the gods of Olympus, using human beings as the instruments and the victims of their greed, their jealousy, their lusts and their quarrels, constituted religious truth in the Greek world.

When the great religions of the Western world arose out of the bosom of Judaism, man's position underwent a change, but not as radically as is sometimes thought. To be sure, he was no longer a plaything to capricious and unpredictable gods. Man was now the creature of a God of Justice and Mercy. But man's position of total dependence did not change. To accept this total surrender became the mark of piety. The mightiest religion of the West, Christianity, taught, "Believe in Me and ye shall be saved." The most militant religion of the East, Mohammedanism, declared that man's destinies were totally predetermined by Allah and the only course for man to adopt was Islam, total submission to Him. For most teachers of religion, man, being a creature of God, was nothing, and God was everything.

But whether or not, as the song-writers tell us "love is a many-splendored thing," it is true that man is a many-faceted being. In their churches and cathedrals, men continued to echo the idea that man is nothing, but in their laboratories and plants, their factories and fields, men were acting on the contrary theory that man is everything. The ancient Greeks, who were the architects of our civilization, had a phrase for it: "Man is the measure of all things." The advancing tide of science kept strengthening man's confidence in his own powers. Cynics and disbelievers now whispered that instead of God creating man it was man who had created God. As technology progressed and blessings without numbers poured forth from the cornucopia of invention, man could hardly be blamed for regarding himself as the Lord of the Universe, creator and monarch of all he surveyed.

Few stopped to ask, "Whence came man?" who obviously did not create himself; or "Whence came the green earth?" which existed before man; "or the planetary system?" which existed before the earth; "Or the universe?" which antedated our planetary system. Who could blame the German biologist, Ernst Haeckel, for announcing triumphantly that he had solved "The Riddle of the Universe." Napoleon once met the great French astronomer, LaPlace. "I understand, Monsieur LaPlace, that you have written a seven-hundred-page book on the origin of the planets without once mentioning God." "M. L'Empereur," was the reply, "God is a hypothesis I can do without."

Exactly a hundred years ago in 1859, Charles Darwin published his *Origin of Species*. Many men were persuaded by the evolutionary theory and other scientific achievements that science had dethroned God as Creator and enthroned man in His stead. From the generous treasure house of science came not only ships and cars, planes, radio and television, and millions of gadgets and instruments of all kinds. The scientists broke down the barrier between matter and energy. They pierced the mystery of the hitherto unbreakable atom. They peered into the very constitution of the world and fashioned new elements at will. Was it not true that man was the prime creator in the universe? The only hymn that still made sense was:

> *"Hail to thee, great Science,*
> *From whom all blessings flow."*

The pendulum had swung from one extreme to another. First God was everything and man was nothing. Now man was everything and God was nothing.

But the oscillation of the pendulum was not ended. As man's intellect through technology was bringing him one rich gift after another as homage to a king, man's intellect through science was undermining his position on the throne. Psychology declared that man was a bundle of primitive instincts and his reason merely a false front, an empty facade hiding irrational impulses. Anthropology suggested that there were no moral standards, only varying customs among different peoples, and these could be discarded at will. The rise of industry in the nineteenth century had led to the mechanization of man and made of man a tool, a hand, a cog in a factory. The twentieth century brought the human race to the brink of a far more horrible fate—the manipulation of man. From being a tool of production, man became a tool of domination. He could be sold anything—a toothpaste, a candidate for public office, or a new fascist or communist order of society, not on the basis of any intrinsic merit or rational evidence, but under the spell of the new technique. There are levels of manipulation. It began, more or less harmlessly, with advertising, went on to "public relations," and reached its highest point—or its lowest—in organized brainwashing, in propaganda and the mass hysteria on which dictators have climbed to power.

Suddenly man discovered that he could do everything, but he himself was nothing. His powers were limitless, but wherever he turned he was helpless. When, toward the end of the nineteenth century, Alfred Nobel invented dynamite, he joyously reported that fact as proof positive that with so horrible a weapon available to the nations, war could never take place again. Now, two World Wars and fifty smaller wars later, we know that we can wipe out the human race completely through nuclear bombs. We can plan the exact place and moment of total annihilation, yet no one is sure that men will not take the fatal step.

If we avert our gaze from the world stage and look about us, we find everywhere else that man is helpless. There always have been criminals in society and malefactors in public office. Today the tragedy does not lie merely in the quantitative increase of wrong-doing. Today we take it for granted that there will be widespread breaches of trust in government, in the corporations, in labor unions, in public institutions, in the press and on television. The breakdown of the American family is highlighted by the fact that one out of three marriages in the United States now ends in divorce courts. Illegitimacy, abortions and adultery are increasing alarmingly, bringing in their wake a staggering burden of human misery and degradation.

Our moral crisis goes far deeper than the spiraling

rise of juvenile delinquency, vandalism and crime, which is by no means limited to underprivileged minority groups, but has infiltrated into the so-called better homes and finest "white" communities. The crisis is qualitative. In the past, society as a whole and the offenders in particular, recognized the moral standards against which they had sinned. To use the common legal term they knew right from wrong. Today the criminal derides the judge before whom he stands. He did it for "kicks," or for gain, for "dope," or out of sheer viciousness, and society, deep down in its heart, does not know right from wrong either. That is the essence of the tragedy. In the words of the Psalmist, *Ki hashatot yeharesun, zaddik mah paal*. "For the very foundations are destroyed, what can the righteous man do?" If Oliver Goldsmith were alive today he might be tempted to lament:

> *"Ill fares the land to hastening ills a prey,*
> *Where science accumulates and man decay."*

Doesn't that mean that the human race is the end of the road? Haven't we exhausted all the possibilities? First man was nothing and God was everything. Then God was nothing and man was everything. Now, God is nothing and man is nothing. Behind the alternating bluster and blandness of Khrushchev, the ineptness and ignorance of our own leadership, behind the wealth of science and the spiritual poverty of man, are we not hearing a voice of doom, "Nothing art thou and unto nothing shall thou return." This is the agonizing question confronting mankind.

There is, however, a sound more powerful than the blast of atomic explosions and the noise of jet planes roaring over our heads, a still small voice, first heard on

Sinai. Judaism, which first revealed the one Living God to a world steeped in paganism, still has a message in this hour of imminent catastrophe for mankind groping in darkest despair. Against the fear which has gripped human hearts that we stand at the end of the human adventure, stands the authentic message of Rosh Hashanah, which is the birthday of the world.

Judaism has its own view of man's role in the universe. For the Torah, man is not a plaything of divine caprice, nor seen as a helpless and corrupt creature at the mercy of an omnipotent Power. On the other hand, man is surely not the prime creator of his world, the total master of his fate. In the profoundest teaching of the Jewish tradition, man is neither a helpless plaything, nor a worthless creature, nor a self-creator—he is, in the words of the Talmud: *shutapho shel hakadosh barukh hu bemalaseh bereshit.* "The co-partner of God, the Holy One, in the work of Creation." This great cosmic partnership rests upon the profound Biblical concept of man set forth in the opening chapter of Genesis, which declares that Man was created *beselem elohim* "in the image of God." What does this vivid Hebrew phrase mean? Obviously, it does not mean a physical resemblance between God and man, because God has no form and man's body has much the same attributes as the animals around him. It means that man possesses part of the nature of God—the gift of reason and thought, the love of beauty manifest everywhere in the world, the unconquerable yearning for righteousness which never dies in the human soul, and above all the capacity to create, to mold and fashion the world, which is the hallmark of God Himself. Man is the only creature that can conceive of a past and a future. In Hazlitt's words: "Man is the only creature that can laugh and weep, because he is aware of the gulf between what is and what can be."

What are we doing here in God's world? The hymn of the Daily Prayer Book has the answer: *Barukh elohenu shebara'anu likvodo.* "Blessed is our God who has created us unto His glory."

The Midrash boldly spells out the meaning of this cosmic symbiosis, this partnership of God and man. Basing itself on a great passage in Isaiah (43:12) *atem edai, neum hashem, va'ani el.* "Ye are My Witnesses and I am God"—the Midrash (*Shoher Tob* ed: Buber 255a) interprets, *Kesheatem edim ani el, ukeshe'ein atem edim eini el.* "When ye are My Witnesses, I am God, and when you are not of my witnesses I am no longer God." As surely as man cannot build the world without God, God cannot build without man. In Robert Browning's poem, Antonio Stradivarius, the famous violin builder says, "God cannot build a violin without Antonio."

What does it mean to recognize that God and man are partners? What practical consequences flow from this insight into man's relationship to God? I find the answer in an utterance which the great Solomon Schechter, first President of The Jewish Theological Seminary, was accustomed to repeat, "Leave a little bit to God." Note what he did *not* say. Not, "leave it all to God," for then man becomes nothing. Nor "leave nothing to God" for then man is doomed to failure. "Leave a little bit to God,"—that is the counsel we need. We must do our share and know that God will do His. *Action and faith both must be our watchwords. To work and to wait must be our program—passion and patience, both are needed for life.*

With this insight we can confront the major crises of our age and conquer. With the threat of worldwide annihilation posed by the cold war hanging over us, two clear-cut alternatives exist. We may choose to surrender to Communism or wage an all-out war against it and run the risk of blotting out the human race. There are siren voices urging one or another of these courses upon us. But there is a third possibility, slower, more painful, far less simple, making greater demands upon us—the effort to co-exist on this planet even with those whom we cannot wholly trust. To this end, we must use the United Nations and direct diplomatic negotiations, trade relations and cultural exchanges, all as instruments for preserving the peace. But this course of action requires high intelligence and firm resolution and above all patience without end.

Whence shall this patience come? It can only come from faith, the assurance that if we do our part, God will do His and the painful process of "peaceful co-existence" will lead to a happier state of affairs. This faith is no mere whistling in the dark. For God has taught us through His prophet, *Lo tohu bera'ah lashevet yetzarah* (Isa. 45:18). "He created the world, not for chaos but for human habitation." Mr. Khrushchev's denials notwithstanding, our social and economic system has undergone vast changes in the last hundred years. So, too, far-reaching changes are taking place in Soviet Russia, and we can be certain that the tempo of change will increase. What will emerge will be in accordance with God's purposes for the world, not Mr. Khrushchev's, nor Mr. Eisenhower's, nor yours, nor mine, but something different and something better than what either our adversaries or we possess at present. *Lo tohu bera'ah lashevet yetzarah.* "God created the world not for chaos, but for human habitation." We must work and wait and leave a little to God.

Or let us turn to our homes and our families. How often do we see the children we have loved and nurtured wander off into new and perilous paths, apparently becoming strangers to us and all that we hold sacred? Across how many of our homes might we inscribe the title of Shaw's play, *Heartbreak House*. All too often we are tempted to feel that all our efforts in rearing our children, in setting before them standards of reverence and responsibility and in inculcating loyalty to truth and goodness, have been wasted. We know we did not do a perfect job, for perfection is with God alone, but we did the best we could and behold the consequences! Here again Schechter's words have a message for us, "Leave a little bit to God." Action and faith, passion and patience, are needed in this cosmic partnership. In the words of Koheleth, *Baboker zera et zarekha uva'erev al tanah yadekha*, "In the morning sow your seed and in the evening do not let your hands be idle. For you cannot tell which of them will prosper or whether both of them will be good." From faith in God comes patience. If we wait, we shall discover that the seed we have planted has not fallen on fallow ground. Our plowing and planting of the field have not been wasted, because God's sunshine and rain also have been working from above. What will grow in our children will be new, and it may be different from what we are accustomed to, but we can hold fast to the faith that the best of what we have known and loved will not be utterly lost. The good and the true are immortal.

"Leave a little to God." Do your share and He will do His, for He created the world not for chaos and destruction, but for human habitation and joy.

Hayom harat olam. "On this day of Rosh Hashanah the world came into being." The majestic Musaf Service in its three-fold structure, proclaims the life-giving truth of man's relationship to God as co-partner in creation. The *Malkhuyot* proclaim the sovereignty of God—God rules the world as our Father and our King. Nor do we not have to go it alone. For the *Zikhronot* recall that God is mindful of man's struggles and agonies, his weaknesses and frustrations, his capacity for goodness and greatness. And out of the sovereignty of God and the significance of man comes the third section of the service, the *Shofarot* paying tribute to the Shofar which was sounded on Sinai at the giving of the Law and will be heard again proclaiming the Messianic age.

The Shofar is symbolic of the cosmic partnership of God and man. On Mount Sinai it was said: *Moshe yedabber vehaelohim ya'anenu bekol,* "Moses spoke and God answered him with a loud voice." Let us speak and act for the right and then leave a little to God, knowing that He will not fail us. Together we can go forward to build a world worthy of God's greatness and man's hopes.

17

Covering Our Sackcloths

Rabbi Sidney Greenberg

IT WAS A PERIOD of profound crisis for Samaria, the capital of the northern kingdom of ancient Israel. The King of Aram and his armies had besieged the city and its inhabitants were being starved to death. So intense had the hunger become, that mothers began to devour their young. When this news reached the King of Israel, the Bible tells us, "he rent his clothes ... and the people looked and behold he had sackcloth within upon his flesh."

What a shock that sight must have been to the people! Each citizen knew of his personal troubles and tragedies. But how amazed they all must have been to see that beneath his royal robe, even the king was wearing a sackcloth—the symbol of personal sorrow and misfortune.

A deep truth speaks out to us from this incident—one that we ought to keep steadily before us especially in time of trouble. "Why did this happen to me?" people frequently ask the Rabbi amidst sorrow, as though they alone were singled out by a malicious destiny as a

Selected from *Best Jewish Sermons of 5715-5716.*

target for its bitter shafts. We rarely stop to realize that even kings wore sackcloths.

The better I get to know people, the more impressed I become with this one fact. Rare indeed is the individual without a sackcloth. Some of us wear the sackcloth of a deep frustration—a career to which we aspired but did not attain, a heart we sought but failed to win. Some of us wear the sackcloth of a haunting sense of inadequacy, or a deeply bruised conscience of an aching void left by the passing of a loved one. Blasted hopes, unrealized dreams, anguish and grief—is any life unfamiliar with them? Is not the sackcloth the common garment of all men?

There is a second significance to the Biblical incident. The King wore his sackcloth *underneath*. He did not make of it his outer garment. He did not display it too prominently either to others or to himself. Here was an act of wisdom we would do well to emulate.

Fathers and mothers have sustained grievous losses during the past few years. Ours has been the tragic generation of which our Sages spoke—the generation where parents bury children. Doubly tragic are those afflicted parents who have not learned to cover their sackcloths, who have made of it their outer garment.

In this matter, the rituals of Judaism concerning mourning contain an excellent prescription for emotional recovery from misfortune. Judaism prescribes a terminus to mourning. Just as it is a law that the Kaddish must be said for eleven months, so is it a law that the Kaddish may not be recited longer than eleven months. The Shiva period may likewise not be prolonged beyond seven days. After Shiva, the mourners must leave their sorrow-laden homes and go out into the healing sunshine of human society. After the prescribed period of mourning, the sackcloth must become an undergarment.

Some time ago, the widow of Colin Kelly was remarried. To some, her remarriage appeared as an act of disloyalty to the memory of her husband. In defense of what she had done, she said quite simply: "Of course you can never forget the past and the past will always color the present. But I do not think that you should let the past affect the present so much that there can be no future." This is an attitude which can usefully be applied to every sackcloth that life imposes. We must never let the past affect the present so much that there can be no future. If life is to be lived at all, we must learn to cover our sackcloths. But with what shall we cover them?

The first thing we can use to cover our sackcloths, it seems to me, is the Robe of Understanding. We tend to regard trouble as an intruder and interloper who has no place in life's scheme of things. In the words of a popular song, we often think that the world was made only for fun and frolic. Nothing makes the wearing of life's sackcloths more difficult to endure than the fact that we are not prepared for them.

If we would learn to wear life's sackcloths properly we must cover them with the Robe of Understanding. We must realize that, as the Bible puts it, "Man is born to trouble." Trouble, far from being a gate-crasher in life's arena, actually has a reserved seat there. Human life is attended at its beginning by the piercing cries of the infant and at its end by the agonized wailing of the bereaved. In between, there are sadness, heartbreak, disease. For that reason, the great tragedians of literature have not wanted for themes. All they had to do was to observe life carefully and report it faithfully and the tragedy spelled itself out. "Man is born to trouble."

I know that many will feel that such a gloomy view of life leads to pessimism and despair. Actually, however, the reverse is true. If we accept realistically life's somber backdrop then the manifold blessings we enjoy will emerge in bolder relief. The love which nourishes us, the friendship which warms us, the beauty which inspires us, the health which sustains us—all these, and the countless blessings which are ours, will be all the more gratefully welcomed.

God grant us the Robe of Understanding to cover our sackcloths.

But the Robe of Understanding, beautiful and becoming as it is, is not enough. For at best it can only teach us the spirit of resignation to our troubles, and it is not enough to merely *accept* trouble; we must do more. We must learn to *use* trouble and convert it into a stepping stone to triumph. For that we need the Robe of Wisdom.

In the 48th chapter of the Book of Isaiah, there is a very remarkable verse. The prophet is chastising his people and among other things he says to them, according to Moffat's translation: "I purged you, but nothing came of it, testing you in the furnace but all in vain." Here the prophet is rebuking his people for having been through the furnace of affliction and having learned nothing from the experience. "What," he is asking them, "have you to show for all the suffering you experienced? The tragedy is not that you endured pain; the tragedy is that your pain was wasted, leaving you none the wiser, none the better."

Yes, the prophet expected his people to do more than *accept* trouble. He expected them to *use* it. The fact is that some of life's most valuable lessons can be, and have been, learned precisely in the crucible of adversity. We discern most clearly many a basic truth of life when our eyes are dimmed by tears. Robert Browning Hamilton expressed a common human reaction when he wrote:

I walked a mile with Pleasure
    She chattered all the way
But left me none the wiser
    For all she had to say.

I walked a mile with Sorrow
    And ne'er a word said she
But oh the things I learned from her
    When Sorrow walked with me.

We speak very often of *"victims* of circumstance" —
people whose souls are crushed beneath the wheels of
unfortunate events. We would do well to start thinking
of *"victors* of circumstance"—people who use even negative circumstance and distill from it some new insight
into life, keener understanding or more beautiful character. We often speak of people who were successful
because they knew how to take advantage of good
"breaks." We would do well to start thinking that people can be successful if they have the wisdom to capital-
ize on their bad "breaks." It is possible to be like Wordsworth's "Happy Warrior":

Who doomed to go in company with Pain
And Fear, and Bloodshed, miserable train!
Turns his necessity to glorious gain.

Or as this Psalmist puts it:

They pass through a valley of tears and
convert it into a life-giving fountain.

God grant us the Robe of Wisdom to cover our sackcloths.

Thirdly, may I suggest that we cover our sackcloths
with the Robe of Service. There is a legend of a sorrow-
ing woman who came to a wise man with the heart-

rending plea that he return to her the only son whom she had just lost. He told her that he could comply with her request on one condition. She would have to bring him a mustard seed taken from a home entirely free from sorrow. The woman set out on her quest. Years elapsed and she did not return. One day the wise man chanced upon her, but he hardly recognized her for now she looked so radiant. He greeted her and then asked her why she had never kept their appointment. "Oh" she said in a tone of voice indicating that she had completely forgotten about it, "Well this is what happened. In search of the mustard seed, I came into homes so burdened with sorrow and trouble that I just could not walk out. Who better than I could understand how heavy was the burden they bore? Who better than I could offer them the sympathy they needed? So I stayed on in each home as long as I could be of service. And," she added apologetically, "please do not be angry, but I never again thought about our appointment."

Here is a most profound truth to remember when life makes us don a sackcloth. Trouble and sorrow naturally make us think only of ourselves. But after the first impact of the blow has worn off, our emotional recovery depends upon our ability to forget ourselves. And there is no better way of forgetting about ourselves than by thinking of and serving others. Human experience every day confirms the truth of the legend. He who can do no better after sorrow than engage in the futile search for the mustard seed to restore the loss which is, in fact, irretrievable, is destined to spend years of avoidable heartache. But happy is he who can rise from his mourner's bench and so lose himself in the service of others that he finds himself unknowingly climbing the mountain of healing to which the road of service inevitably leads.

"Man like the clinging vine supported lives:
The strength he gains is from the embrace he gives."

God grant us the Robe of Service to cover our sack-cloths.

The last and most significant robe with which we might cover our sackcloths is the Robe of Faith—faith in the immortality of the souls of our beloved.

The Yizkor prayer which is recited four times every year makes a bold affirmation about the human soul. It declares that death has no dominion over it. "May God remember the soul of my mother. . . ." "May God remember the soul of my son. . . ." The soul survives to be remembered. It does not perish with the death of the body. This same faith is echoed in the "El Mole Raha-mim" prayer where we speak of the soul as being bound up in "the bond of life everlasting." Thus Judaism, like all great religion, teaches that "Death is not a period which brings the sentence of life to a full stop. It is only a comma that punctuates it to loftier existence." Here is the most comforting of all robes to cover the Sackcloth of Bereavement.

To be sure, like all daring affirmations of Judaism, the belief in immortality cannot be scientifically demon-strated. It is as the philosopher Santayana correctly called it "the Soul's invincible surmise." But if it is a "sur-mise" it is one of mankind's most persistent surmises. From ancient man in his primitive beliefs down through the long corridors of time stretching into the present most sophisticated faiths, men have always held the human soul indestructible. Nor has this belief been lim-ited to religious thinkers alone. Philosophers, poets, physicians, scientists, all answer "present" when the roll is called among the believers that death is not the end. How the soul *survives* is, of course, a mystery. It is no less a mystery, however, than how the soul *arrives*. It originates with the Source of all Life and flows back to its origin.

When death robs us of a loved one the pain of parting can be assuaged through our faith that the essence of our beloved lives on not only in our hearts and in our memories but more especially with the Author of life Himself. It is faith which burst forth out of Emerson after the passing of his little son. "What is excellent," he wrote in his "Threnody," "as God lives, is permanent." It is this faith which James Whitcomb Riley sumed up in his beautiful poem, "Away":

> I cannot say, and I will not say
>> That he is dead! He is just away!
> With a cheery smile, and a wave of the hand,
>> He has wandered into an unknown land.
> And left us dreaming how very fair
>> It must be, since he lingers there.
> And you—O you, who the wildest yearn
>> For the old-time step and the glad return.
> Think of him faring on, as dear
>> In the love of There as the love of Here.
> Think of him still as the same, I say:
>> He is not dead—he is just away.

God grant us the Robe of Faith to cover our sackcloths.

The story of a king introduced our problem. The story of another monarch will sum up our solution. Alexander the Great, it is told, once commissioned an artist to paint his portrait. He gave him only two conditions. It was to be an exact likeness, unfalsified. Moreover, it was to be handsome and attractive. The artist had not an easy task, for over his right eye, Alexander had a prominent battle scar. The artist was thus confronted with a painful dilemma. To omit the scar would be a violation of the first condition. To include it would be a violation of the second. Finally, the artist came up with the solution. He painted Alexander in a pensive mood, his face supported by his right hand with his forefinger covering the scar.

We cannot eliminate life's scars upon our souls for we would not be true to life. Nor can we permit them to be prominently viewed, for they would then make life ugly and unlivable.

We must learn to cover the scars upon our souls, the sackcloths upon our flesh. With the Robe of Understanding which teaches us to accept trouble as part of the price we pay for being human; with the Robe of Wisdom which helps us *use* trouble, and convert it into triumph; with the Robe of Service which enables us to recover our own strength while at the same time bringing strength to others; with the Robe of Faith which whispers comforting assurance that the soul is mightier than death; with these robes, let us cover our sackcloths and thus make the portrait of our lives beautiful and inspiring to behold.

18

Miracle of Jewish Survival

Rabbi Leon A. Jick

SOME YEARS AGO, archeologists went to work excavating a deserted mound of sand at a place near the Jordan River called Tel-El-Amarna. Among the relics which were recovered was a clay tablet containing a report from an Egyptian governor of Canaan to his ruler. The date was about 1500 B.C.E. and among the messages was one which said: "Israel is destroyed."

History does not record the event which led the governor to his premature conclusion. Undoubtedly his report reflects a military defeat or act of repression which had painful consequences for our ancestors.

But to us, their descendants, very much alive and filling this sanctuary on the eve of Yom Kippur 3,500 years later, the archeologist's discovery comes as a reminder of something other than defeat. For us, this information serves to intensify what all of us must already feel on a night like this: awareness of the miracle and the mystery of Jewish survival.

Think of the miracle represented by our presence here—

3,500 years after the Amarna letter reported the end;

Selected from *Best Jewish Sermons of 5721-5722.*

2,547 years after Nebuchadnezar, the King of Babylon, destroyed the Temple of Solomon;

1,691 years after Titus, General of the armies of the Roman Empire, conquered the second Jewish Commonwealth and burned the second Temple, declaring "Jerusalem has perished";

900 years after the blood bath of the crusades;

500 years after Torquemada and the Inquisition;

44 years after the execution of Nicholas II, the last of the Czars of all the Russians;

16 years after the demise of Hitler and his Third Reich;

7 years after the unmourned death of Stalin, Hitler's competitor in ruthlessness—

We are here, living amidst a Jewish renaissance unparalleled since antiquity. American Jews and American Jewish life are bursting with creativity.

There is a State of Israel and a modern Hebrew culture.

There was an Einstein and there is an Oppenheimer.

There was a Brandeis and there is a Ben-Gurion.

There is a Bernstein and a Buber, a Chagall and a Salk.

We are here, and we are accounting for ourselves, and this is a miracle.

It almost seems less incredible that man could have developed from an amoebae in two billion years of evolution, than that you and I should be here tonight, 3,500 years after the first announcement of the news that "Israel is destroyed." The first miracle, the miracle of biological development, is a fulfillment of natural process. The second, Israel's survival, is defiance of natural process.

Like every real miracle—this one is a mystery. No attempted explanation really accounts for it, and on this Yom Kippur Eve, it would be sacrilege even to try. Let us stand in awe before this mystery and try rather to understand what it means to us. What is the message to

Jewish experience? What is the truth which this survival, without parallel in all history, presents to us and to mankind?

Before we can understand the message, we must correct our misconceptions about Jewish history. Very few of us have more than the most superficial acquaintance with the facts of Jewish history—and yet, however little we know, we invariably think of Jewish history as one long bloodbath, an unbroken succession of misfortunes and afflictions. We review the history of our people in the same perspective that the *Daily News* reports the life of our country: as a collection of calamities. The more bloodcurdling they are, the more memorable. This is the approach to history which remembers everything and learns nothing, which sees everything and understands nothing.

But when we read *all* of our history, when we read the record of Jewish existence in meaningful perspective, we discover a pattern of immeasurable consequence. From the moment of its birth in the liberation from Egyptian slavery, to the day of the resurrection of the State of Israel and to this very day, the experience of the Jewish people has demonstrated the power of the human spirit to prevail over material obstacles. More than any other human experience, this survival reveals that the power of an ideal is more durable than the ideal of power. Jewish history is an unbroken affirmation of a Power in the Universe which makes for salvation.

From which period in Jewish history shall we choose illustrations? We could go back to the beginning and observe how our ancestors remembered the God of Abraham, Isaac and Jacob amidst the degradation of slavery in Egypt and burst upon the stage of history in an act of liberation which proclaimed that freedom is indestructible.

Or we could choose an episode from yesterday—
from the generation which, on the ashes of Hitlerian
barbarism, built a state which is a model of democracy
and social justice and a light unto the new nations of
the world.

We might look to the Maccabean period and observe
how a people fought against insuperable odds for the
right to differ, to pursue its own destiny, to preserve its
own ideals and culture, and won. Or we might learn
from the Middle Ages how this same people, deprived
of the power of physical resistance, fortified itself from
within and defied the whole world for the sake of
integrity and truth, and prevailed.

I do not wish to overlook the great price our ancestors, through the ages, paid for their defiance. Tyranny
cannot tolerate differences and tyranny has always singled out the Jews as its first victim. Nonetheless, each
day our people recited a prayer in sincerity and joy,
thanking God for the privilege of being a Jew. By their
willingness to stand fast, to say "no," when the whole
world said "yes," they kept open the gates of freedom
and dissent for all men. They paved the way for the
Reformation and the Renaissance. They kept alive the
right to be different. In darkest times, the burden was
never so great that it crushed their sense of worthy self-
identity or their spark of creativity.

When they lived in their own land, our ancestors
produced prophets and sages, from Joshua son of Nun
who led them in settling the land, to Joshua of Nazareth
whose teachings spread the spirit of Judaism throughout
the world.

In Babylonia they produced jurisprudence and law,
the wit and wisdom of the Talmud. In the Moslem
world, they produced philosophers and poets. In medieval Europe they produced pietistics and mystics. Even

in the aridness of Eastern Europe they produced a way of life—a language and a literature. In the hell of World War II, in garrets and ghettos, they poured forth poems and dramas and memoirs and songs, affirming and reaffirming that even this hell was not the end, that even if they perished, their destruction would not be the end. *Zog nit keinmal as du geyst dem letzten veg* . . . sang the Jewish partisans. "Never say that you go on your final way, however dark the skies, however bleak the days; our longed-for hour will come at last, the pounding of our footsteps will proclaim we are here!"

Thus people perished, but the people survived, creatively, triumphantly affirming once again that tyranny does not prevail and brutality is not the end—this is the people you and I come from. This is the history of which you and I are a part.

Jewish history in its totality "is the epic of a noble people transcending its troubles, capable of pitying its persecutors, preserving its power of love in the midst of evil, and seeking to serve God from wherever it might be. Jewish history is the story of a people that not only stayed civilized but sane, not only sane but creative, not only creative but holy!" For this, history has no parallel.

This history of our people is more than glorious—it is a living testament of the power which dedication to God brings to men. It is a history which is not only worthy of study, but also worthy of continuing.

It is true that our commitment to continue Jewish existence involves a price and a risk. The price is that we will not be invited to the Holly Ball at the Scarsdale Country Club and that some real estate agents in Greenwich will not sell us a house. A few other similarly dubious privileges will be denied us. Some of us act as if the price were high, but it is very small.

The risk is much greater. The risk now, as it ever was

and always shall be, is that if tyranny rises again, we will again be singled out to be its first victims, we will again be on the side of the Einsteins against the Eichmanns.

If we are men and women, let us glory in this role. Let this understanding goad us into the front ranks of those who oppose tyranny. Let it bring us back to Jewish knowledge and to Jewish observance, so that we may acquire the indestructible strength and integrity which flow from self-knowledge and self-respect. Let us communicate to our children this sense of mission.

Let our understanding enable us to embrace with joy the destiny of our birth which assigns us to the group which is the most exciting, most puzzling, most turbulent, most productive, most demanding, most rewarding, most indestructible group in all history—the eternal people, Israel.

This is the eve of Yom Kippur. According to our tradition, it is the anniversary of the day when Moses came down from Sinai with the second set of the tablets of the covenant, his countenance aglow with the light of God's presence.

It is the anniversary of the day when our ancestors confirmed their commitment to the covenant—to become a kingdom of priests and a holy people—saying, "*Na'ase v'nishma* . . . We shall do and we shall hearken." May this covenant be renewed through us this night.

Let us hearken and let us do—so that in the future as in the past the steps of the people of Israel will resound, proclaiming: "*Mir zeinan doh* . . . We are here."

19

Three Dimensions of Humanity

Rabbi Benzion C. Kaganoff

THE MAIN THEME of the season of the High Holy Days is best summed up by the words of the liturgy, *"us'shuva us'filah utz'dakah ma'avirin es roa hagzayrah—* penitence, prayer, and charity," these are the three dimensions of the religious life within which man must place himself if he is to become the higher being of creation for which he was intended.

Penitence means that man *can* lift himself by his own bootstraps out of the rut of listlessness, out of the pit of moral lethargy and out of the mire of wrongdoing. Judaism firmly maintains that man need not live with a feeling of guilt under a burden of eternal damnation. This is a basic difference between Judaism and Christianity, between the teachings of the synagogue and the doctrine of the church. For man, asserts Judaism, was created to be a little lower than the angels. But being possessed of human frailties, it is almost inevitable that man will make mistakes. In fact, the Bible portrays all life as a choice in the hands of man—a choice between that which will lead to good or to evil, between right and wrong.

Selected from *Best Jewish Sermons 5717-5718.*

Life has been described in many ways. It has been described as a ship upon the high seas. Mark Twain described life as a tough battleground, a struggle "from which very few of us come out alive." Judaism sees life as a series of crossroads, with highways leading to moral blessedness and self-fulfillment or to wickedness and frustrations of the spirit. Man is placed at these crossroads, and he must make his own choice. And very often it happens that we err and take the wrong road in life. We are then temporarily lost; we become perplexed and dismayed. The divine image in which we were created becomes jarred out of focus; the spark of our soul becomes dampened, sometimes even almost extinguished.

But God has given us the greatest of divine blessings—*penitence*. In fact, the Hebrew word for penitence is *t'shuvah*, and it means *return*. The entire High Holy Day period, beginning with the New Year, *Rosh Hashanah*, and culminating with the Day of Atonement, *Yom Kippur*—this entire period is called the season of penitence; it proclaims: *"Return, O Man, to your God!"* Find your way back again to an elevated and more lofty concept of humanity. Even if you have become lost and have gone astray on the highways and byways of life, now is your opportunity to return, once again, to the *right* way. Now is the chance for spiritual stock-taking, for finding your place, once again, with your God, with your family, with your community, with yourself!

Penitence, then, is the first dimension of humanity. It permeates the very depth of our souls, constantly admonishing us that all is not lost, that there is a great deal of salvaging to be done, that things can be set aright, that wrongs can be rectified, if we will it.

How is this penitence to come about? The second element of our three-dimensional scheme, *prayer*, offers one possibility.

Prayer proclaims that *man is not alone in this world.* There is a great Power which rules over us, a power Who, in His infinity, incorporates every striving and every aspiration of finite humanity. Man, however, must learn to pray properly. If we do not pray in the right way, then we have missed the entire meaning of prayer and shall have failed to communicate with our God. Here, again, the genius of Judaism expressed itself. The word *prayer* comes from the Latin *precare*, which means *to beg, to ask.* Many of us, unfortunately, look upon prayer only as an occasion for asking things of God, for making promises to Him in return for gifts which we expect from the Almighty. The Hebrew word for prayer is *t'filah*, and it expresses a higher motivation. It is derived from the word *his-palel*, which means *to judge oneself.* This is the true purpose of prayer. Rather than an occasion for us to seek favors from God, prayer is the opportunity for us to judge and examine ourselves before Him, to see whether we, by our conduct, have measured up to the standards set up by God and by His law. Once we attain this higher concept of prayer, we can come to realize that faith is reciprocal, that while we rely upon God and His goodness, we must endeavor to prove to Him that He can rely upon us and upon our loyalty to Him. This, then, is the second dimension of humanity, that through prayer— the right kind of prayer—we measure our *own* spiritual stature and come to understand that we are never alone in this world.

And finally, the entire High Holiday season stresses not only the need for man to maintain a close bond with God; it emphasizes that which is the entire goal and purpose of religion—that man must maintain a closeness with his fellow man. If prayer teaches us that man is not alone, the third dimension of humanity, *charity*, points out that man cannot *live* alone. Man by himself is nothing; he is not even man. Together with others, he becomes mankind, and it is through the concept of mankind that he attains his most exalted state. If penitence is the *depth* of the spiritual life and prayer measures the *height* of our religious motivations, it is charity which gives us the dimension of religious *breadth*.

With regard to the idea of charity, too, let there be no misunderstandings. Many people have been moved by the cry of distress to feed the hungry, clothe the naked, heal the sick and bring joy to the unfortunate. But such kindness, as praiseworthy as it may be, is not always the most constructive. It may relieve the conscience of the giver rather than be of greatest benefit to the receiver. Religion demands that we deliberately and consciously include the less fortunate into our own plan for happiness. We are to care for them, not only in accord with their needs, but also with their self-respect.

Our gifts to the needy and the fashioning of closer bonds with our fellow human beings, Judaism stresses, must come as a natural and self-evident social duty, as obvious and as important in our own eyes as the promotion of our own welfare. For in the Hebrew there is no such word as charity. What we translate as charity, *tz'dakah*, means *justice!*

In the eyes of Judaism, then, the rights of the poor, the rights of the underprivileged, the rights of the downtrodden, the rights of the enslaved, the rights of the Jew, the rights of the State of Israel, the rights of the Negro in the South—all this is not charity, but justice. Charity interpreted thus, as a sense of justice, blesses the giver, too. It promotes his ethical welfare; it refines and ennobles his character. For he who understands charity as justice will give of himself, of his possessions, and of his good will out of love; he will give regularly, intelligently, constructively. This kind of *social interac-*

tion becomes in the long run *tz'dakah, social justice*; it is a kindness bestowed by the receiver upon the giver.

God grant that every one of us be blessed with the attainment of our higher moral and ethical self, so that we may be able to measure our life within the three spiritual dimensions which we have outlined.

May all of us, during the coming New Year, be inscribed in the Book of Life, Happiness and Peace.

20

Open the Gates

Rabbi Robert I. Kahn

ONE OF THE MOST beautiful services of the Day of Atonement, really one of the most moving services of the whole Jewish year, is the *Neilah* service. Yet it is also one of the least known. Coming as it does at the end of a long hard fast, it is neglected by the average Jew.

But Neilah is not only neglected by laymen, but by rabbis too. Almost no one preaches about it. Therefore I should like to make it up to this neglected service this evening with my sermon.

The prayer which sets the whole tone of the service is a little Hebrew poem, now hundreds of years old, which the congregation recites and the choir sings:

> *P'sach lanu shaar, b'es n'ilas shaar,*
> *ki vo hayom.*
> *Hayom yifneh, hashemesh yavo v'yifneh,*
> *navoah shaarecho.*

> Open to us the gates in the time of the
> closing of the gates.

Selected from *Best Jewish Sermons of 5715-5716.*

> The day is ending, the sun is setting,
>   let us enter Thy gates.

Can you hear the pleading tone in those words? Do you feel the sense or urgency? I never hear them but I am reminded of a memory of years and years ago; the memory of a little child, shut out for some reason or other banging his fists against a closed door; on his face the streaks of tears, in his gestures panic, in his voice an almost hysterical note as he cried, "Open the door!"

Over the years, other memories have attached themselves to that original. I recall the young man who came to my office before the war. He wanted to be a doctor more than anything else in the world. He had applied to medical school after medical school, and all had rejected him. He was desperate. On his face was the same expression as on the face of that little child: *P'sach li shaar*, open the door. Then one day on a penal farm down near Sugarland (near Houston) a prisoner sat and talked to me behind bars—he wanted a parole, and in his voice was the same urgency as in that child's voice: Open the door.

And then I remember a mother sitting on the edge of her chair in a hospital corridor, her eyes on a door marked "Surgery," and although her body was rigid, I could visualize her beating against that door; open the door, open the door and let me see my child!

P'sach lanu shaar, Open to us the gates. Who among us has not known this feeling? Who has not come up against some closed door? Who has not had a gate slammed in his face? Or, even if the gate may open, who has not known the uncertainty and trepidation of approaching a closed door? A young man rings the bell and waits for a blind date to appear. On both sides of the door, there is a quickening of the pulse. Could this, perhaps, be it? We sit in an outer office waiting to be interviewed—this may be the opportunity of a lifetime. We carry a bride over the threshold of a new home—what will the future hold for us?

It was in this mood, friends, that we knocked on the door of the New Year, 5716, just ten days ago. If you recall, on the very first page of our Holy Day prayer book, the very last paragraph began: "Open to us in mercy the portals of the New Year." We said it in the midst of the congregation, we whispered it by a sick bed, we cried like a child beating its fists against the door—*P'sach lanu shaar*, open the gates! Open the door, dear God, to a good New Year.

And from the other side of the door, there comes a voice, the voice of God, asking "Who's there?" Who's there? Who knocks? Because whether the door opens and to what it opens depends on the kind of person who knocks, upon the kind of character and the kind of personality that stands at the door. . . . Tomorrow is not like some formal garden behind a gate, which looks precisely the same to anyone who peers through. Tomorrow is not like some individualized road map you get back when you write to a touring service. Tomorrow is uncharted territory, unexplored; its landscape and its road conditions depend upon who enters the gate.

Let me explain what I am driving at. Much of the time, too much, we think of life as what happens *to* us. We think of our own lot in life as the result of good or bad breaks, good or bad luck. And, of course, to a certain extent, this is true. We live our lives against a backdrop. Economic conditions, world tension, hurricanes, floods, do all have their impact upon our lives. But to a large extent, much larger than we usually imagine, our life is our own, to make or to break. The greatest factor in our fates is not fate, but character and personality.

The kind of tomorrow we will have depends on the kind of yesterday we have lived, the kind of today we have prayed. Open the door, we ask, and the voice replies, who's there.

Now this is very obvious in our human relationships, in our homes and our businesses. The test of happiness and success in life is how well you get along with people, how much consideration we have, and tact, and sympathy, and understanding and cooperation. These are the factors that make for good luck, in every field. Engineering, for example, even this highly technical way of life. Now it may be better luck to be graduated in 1955 than in 1935, and fundamental ability makes a difference, but everyone who knows the engineering field will tell you that success in this profession is still largely due to a man's ability to cooperate, to get along with, to work beside, understand and work with other people.

Of course, all of us recognize that this is true about the other fellow, but we do not like to accept this truth for ourselves. Have you ever had anybody tell you that he was fired because he didn't measure up to the job? No, there's always an excuse, someone else slammed the door. I have yet to have a wife or husband come to me and say: "I have been a poor husband, or I have been a poor wife, and I have wrecked my marriage and I want help in putting it back together again." But always, "my wife has, my husband has ruined our marriage. . ." We make our own happiness. We build our own tomorrows.

And this is true not only in the obvious sense; it has some very subtle and far-reaching implications. We ask God for a year of health, yet more illness than we have ever imagined is the result of our own character, our attitude and behavior. Whether a well man gets sick, whether a sick man gets well, depends upon the kind of spiritual life we lead. Unhappiness, worry, hatred, envy, fear, anxiety, failure to love and be loved, can and do cause a whole variety of illnesses; they make well people sick, and sick people die. In a way, we *do* literally catch a cold. Psychologically, we chase it. Do you want a healthy year? Build a healthy soul.

And even in the realm where luck would seem to be the largest factor in life, in the realm of accidents, even here fate is not all just fate. The statisticians have discovered that some people seem to be accident prone. They get into more trouble than they have a right to, statistically. The psychologists have an interesting explanation—there seem to be certain factors of personality that *drive* some people into accidents. Even accidents, you see, are not accidental. We make our own future. We create our own tomorrow. When we knock on the door, God asks who's there.

This is precisely what our prayer book tells us, very plainly in that most magnificent prayer in the afternoon service, the *Unsaneh Tokef.* It begins by saying that God passes us under His crook, as a shepherd his sheep— this one to go to the market, this one to stay home, this to be fed, this to be sheared. So does the Almighty write of each man his fate: Who shall grow rich and who grow poor, who be well and who be sick, even *Mi yichyeh u-mi yamus,* who shall live and who shall die. But then it goes on to say: "Yet prayer and repentance and charity can change the evil decree." Life is not fated. We knock on tomorrow's door, "Open to us in mercy the portals of the New Year," and the voice replies, "Who's there? Have you repented, have you prayed, have you done deeds of lovingkindness? What changes have you made, will you make, in the direction of your life, in the quality of your character?" Because you and you alone can change your tomorrow.

And surely one of the tests of the character of the

person who stands at the door would be the way in which he acts when he is the doorkeeper. All of us are in the position of being able to open the door at the plea of others. As parents, employers, neighbors, citizens, we are besieged and beseeched by those who cry, *P'sach lanu shaar*, and if we slam the door in their faces, how shall it open to us?

There is a patient in the Old Hernan Hospital tonight who stands at the gate of death. His only chance is by way of transfusions, lots of them. The Jewish Family Service advises that no one is helping, he has no family, no friends. Who will open the door of health to him? (The congregation will be happy to know that five donors appeared at the hospital the day after this sermon.)

In Huntsville tonight, in the penitentiary, a young man sits with this prayerbook in his hand. Perhaps at this moment he is reading the prayer, *p'sach lanu shaar*, open to me the gates at the time my gates are closed. Five years behind him and twenty years ahead, unless someone puts faith in him and gives him a job that will help him get a parole. Who will open his gates? (A man in our congregation has offered a job.)

Do you remember those terrible years after 1933, and particularly those awful months after November 1938, when the plea came to us: open the gates, sign an affidavit for me, for my wife, my brother, my father, my cousins, my friends. There was a lady standing in the harbor then, with her arm lifted high, and the door was open, at least a little bit, and we signed affidavits and opened the gates and waved in welcome, before the concentration camp doors closed behind them.

Today, the light in that lady's hand has almost been put out. It is truly an *es neilas shaar*, a time of the closed gate. The McCarran Walter Immigration Act has practically closed the door to any immigration, to refugees from behind the iron curtain, to the poverty-stricken of southern Europe. Anyone who wants tomorrow's gates to open to him should surely do anything he can do, as a citizen, to open the gates of America again to the "tempest-tossed, yearning to breathe free."

And so, too, for our own people, for the waves of persecution are beginning to lap at the shores of North Africa. The tide of prejudice is rising. In a struggle between colonialism and nationalism, between Arabs and French, the Jews, as always will be the buffet. There is a door that will open to these people, but we have the key, the golden key, in our hands and our pockets. Dare we ask that the door be opened to us unless we give to the United Jewish Appeal, and buy Israel Bonds, and do everything in our power to hold the door open for them. *P'sach lau shaar b'es neilas shaar*, this is the plea of our people.

This is also the plea of our God. For He, too, knocks at the portals of our hearts and asks to be let in. We usually think of God as a remote power, someplace far off. And we go begging to Him, go praying to Him, pick up the phone and ring Him. We forget that as much as man seeks God, God seeks man. He knocks on every door and whispers into every ear.

Whenever we feel ashamed of ourselves, not just of one wicked or foolish act, but of our whole souls, God is knocking. Whenever we sense something of the glory of life, and our failure to achieve that glory, He knocks. Whenever some natural beauty seems so lovely that it hurts inside, whenever something in life, a poem, a song, a story, a face, grips us by the throat and makes us ache with longing for something better than we've ever known, this is God knocking at our hearts.

But we've got to let Him in. Just hearing the knock,

just knowing He is there is not enough. For to many of us religion is a sentimental experience rather than the doorway to a new life, a flirtation rather than a marriage, religiosity rather than religion. We go through some experience as deep as Isaiah hearing the angels sing Holy Holy. Our hearts are filled, and then we hear His voice saying, "Who will go, and whom shall I send?" and that's when we take our hand off the knob and turn away—"Not me, Lord. I'm busy, I've got a wife and children, I don't want to stick my neck out, wouldn't it be all right if I just sent a check?"

P'sach lanu shaar, God cries to us. Let Him in, for when we let Him in, life changes and doors begin to open to new life. We need only to read the record. Who was Abraham but a desert sheik, living comfortably in Haran, and then God said *Lech l'cho,* Go thou, and he went. Who was Joseph but the spoiled brat of a father too old and feeble to spank him? And God knocked at his door, and he answered and became a prince among men. Who was Moses but the son-in-law of a wealthy rancher—then God spoke out of a burning bush and he replied and became the symbol of freedom for all the world. Who was Moses ibn Ezra, author of so many lovely prayers in this very Neilah service, but a youngster with a talent for versifying, writing songs about wine and about women; and then God knocked and from his answering lips came some of the most beautiful religious poetry of our people. Who was Israel Baal Shem Tov, but a *belfer,* an assistant teacher whose main job, like a modern school bus driver's, was to see that the children got safely to and from school? And then something happened inside him, and he founded one of the great movements in Jewish life that has enriched our music and our prayers. Who are you and I but ordinary people? But if God knocks and we let Him in, our little lives are made large and meaningful. *P'sach lanu shaar b'es neilas shaar.* He shouts it in the thunder, whispers it in the breeze, echoes it in the cry of a child beating on a door, Open the gates.

You might well ask, friends, why so late? Why do they wait until five o'clock on Yom Kippur afternoon with this urgent call? There's a reason. Have you ever watched children on a playground, during recess, and the teacher will say: "Children, come now, it's time to come in." And all of them lift their heads, and some of them start toward the building but for most of them, one more throw, one more slide, one more swing—and then the bell rings and oh what a scurrying and a scampering.

We, too. We go through the holiday services. We gather in unprecedented numbers, but inside nothing happens. We are spectators more than participants. God calls us through the blast of the Shofar, He calls us through the *Avinu malkenu*, through the Kol Nidre, through the *Al chet*. He calls and calls. We lift our heads, then go back to our absorptions. And then . . . that's why at five o'clock in the afternoon, as the doors begin to close, there suddenly appears this urgent plea before it is too late! *Make the day mean something. Make it mean a real change of life; a real Teshuvah.*

Open to us the gates, at the time of the closing of the gates. Open the gates of your heart to your fellowman. Open the gates of your heart to God, that you may walk through tomorrow's gates to a year of happiness, of health, of service, of Godliness. Amen.

21

Adding Life to Our Years

Rabbi Abraham J. Karp

WE OFFER UP many prayers these High Holy Days. We pray for pardon and for forgiveness, health and bodily vigor, security, good sustenance, salvation for Israel, peace for the world. There is one prayer, a short and simple supplication that we breathe with added fervor, *Ribun ho-olom zohrainu l'hayim aruhim,* "Lord of the Universe, Remember us for a long life." We pray and we long for a long life. We turn our thoughts to length of days, anxious to add years to our life.

I well recall a discussion on this matter with the oldest man I ever met, my great-grandfather, Ha-Rav Shmuel Yehudah, rabbi for more than sixty years of the community of Adelsk. Great-grandfather was the family patriarch and a family legend. His age at the time of our meeting was reckoned to be well over a hundred. No one knew his exact age, and no one dared ask him. Before our family left for America, I was taken to him for his blessings. He sat, as I recall, at a small table near the window, a folio of the Talmud before him, studying. With the boldness of youth, I asked him: "Grandfather, how old are you?"

Selected from *Best Jewish Sermons of 5713.*

He replied with a smile: "I've long since passed my allotted years of three score and ten."

I made bold to ask again: "To what do you attribute your length of days?"

"You ask me? The Talmud contains a section devoted to just this matter. When you'll be older, you'll study and learn."

I have recently studied that extremely interesting and informative portion of our lore. Students ask their teachers: "Through what merit have you reached old age?" And the sages give their formulas for longevity. It is one of these formulas that I would discuss with you this morning.

R. Nehunia b. Hakonoh was asked by his disciples:

"In virtue of what have you reached such a good old age?"

The sage replied: "Never in my life have I sought honor for myself through the degradation of my fellow man, the curse of my fellow man has never followed me to my bed, and I was free with my money."

Psychosomatic medicine, which has shown that many physiological ills are caused by psychological disturbances, would tell us that the human failings, which the sage carefully avoided in his own living, could actually take years from a man's life. Unprincipled ambition to get ahead; using human beings and human misfortune as stepping stones to success; worry, continuous and growing, over the acquisition and retention of money—a person beset by these shortcomings, one who surrenders his being to their service, such a man actually subtracts years from his life.

So, R. Nehunia's answer is a true answer, and a good and valid lesson for life. But not a full lesson! There is another side to the coin! The Talmud records an interesting addition to this discussion, a comment, which must have occurred already to many of you. The sage Rava is quoted as saying: "Long life depends not so much on merit as on fate." How right he is! There is little we can do to make long a life that is destined to be short. There isn't much we can do to add years to our life. But the Talmud teaches: *Yaish shanim shel hayim, v'yaish shanim she-aynon shel hayim.* "There are years which are filled with life. There are years which are empty of life." Now, we can fully understand the words of R. Nehunia. Nay more, we can live them! We may or may not be able to add years to our life, but it is fully in our power to add life to our years.

The formula of the sage is to be viewed not merely as that which takes years from life, but that which takes life from our allotted years. The life of a man who raises himself on the misfortune of others—is that a life? You've heard these boasts: "Did I give him a licking. If his business survives, it'll be a miracle!" Or, "I'll make good, and no one is going to stand in my way." Such people can't "make good." They can only make it bad for their associates and employees, a bad name for themselves and families, a bad life—that really is no life. What is the life of a man, who labored a lifetime, only to merit this description: "He's the wealthiest and loneliest man in town." No, the life of a man, who views fellow man as a rung on his ladder of success—to be stepped on in order to reach the next rung—is no life at all, for it is bereft of all friendship, serenity, true accomplishment.

The story is told of a wealthy Jewish manufacturer, who was the most beloved man in town. He was especially admired for his wonderful relationship with his employees. Particularly beautiful was his friendship with the old superintendent of his buildings. He often spoke of him as, "the man who saved my life." But no one knew what he was referring to, and the superintendent swore that he never did anything to merit that praise—nor would the man explain. The rabbi of the town, intrigued with the matter, finally took courage and asked for an explanation. He heard this reply:

"In my early days, when I was first starting out, I was the toughest and the most hated employer in the whole town. I once needed a janitor, so I put an ad in the paper 'Hand Wanted' and waited for the applicants. A man came in response to the ad. I had to put him in his place immediately. I was rough with him and gruff to him. I was trying to beat down his wage by beating down his spirit. I kept referring to him as a 'hired hand, a hired hand.'

Suddenly he interrupted me: 'I don't know whether I'll get this job, and what's more I don't care, but don't call me a hand. I am a man. I have a name. In me, as in you, there beats a heart, there's a mind and a soul. If you want a man—I'm available. If you want a hand—good day!'"

"That day, he saved my life!" continued the manufacturer. "He caused me to see men not as tools, but as individuals, human beings, co-workers, associates. Had my life continued as before, I would have been hated and despised, without friends and without honor. He saved my life. He showed me how truly to live."

R. Nehunia tells us that a life of strife is no life at all. To live with a curse against your fellow man always in your heart is not loving, for it is a life that causes curses to be heaped upon you, that makes people hate you.

But people will question: "What can I do about it? If he hates me, if he curses me, what can I do?"

It once happened that two newcomers to a community were visited on the same day by the local rabbi. During the course of the conversation, the first new resident asked the rabbi:

"What kind of people live in this town?"

The rabbi answered with a question: "What kind of people live in the town you came from?"

"Oh," replied the newcomer, "they were wonderful people. Friendly, neighborly, real, genuine people."

"You'll find," said the rabbi, "the same kind of people in this town."

During the rabbi's conversation with the second newcomer, the same question was asked of him, and he gave the same answer. The new resident replied:

"The town I came from was a horrible place. The people were unfriendly, disagreeable, the worst sort of gossips, always feuding!"

The rabbi replied: "You'll find that this town has the same kind of people."

In truth, it is our own actions and attitudes that bring out the good or the bad in people. To live a life that brings out the evil in people—why that's no life at all. To live so as to bring out the goodness in fellow man, that's putting life in our years.

Finally, R. Nehunia admonishes us that the life of the grasping miser is no life at all. Years spent in merely gathering, those are years bereft of life. The lust for money is a progressive disease. The more you accumulate, the more you grasp for. You and I have seen men, whose whole life is grasping for more and thirsting for yet more.

Such a person was Takom, a peasant, who worked hard upon his land, and then bought more land and was thus able to live in comfort. But he was stricken with the disease of wanting more. He heard that across the Volga land was being given away free. He went there and found that it was indeed so. There was but one stipulation. A man was permitted to retain only the land he could cover before sunset. So, at the break of dawn, Takom began to walk. As he surveyed the vast stretch of land that was to be his—he began to yearn for yet more. So he hastened his pace, and began to run. He was getting weary. His heart was beating heavily, his feet were aching. But he wanted just a bit more, just a few acres more. The sun began to set and he began stumbling in utter exhaustion. Still he had to have just another bit more. And as the last rays of the sun were sinking behind the horizon, Takom fell. Exhaustion had taken its toll.

Takom got his land, six feet of it!

How many do we know who spend their lives always trying to grasp for just a little more—who end up like Takom? Men who don't pause to use their gains for the benefit of their community, for the welfare of others, or even for themselves! Is that life?

The question that life asks is not: "How much have you made?" It is rather, "What are you doing with it?"

We add years to our life and life to our years, if we respect man, and call him fellow-man; if our life brings out the best in people about us, in "scattering" and not in "gathering."

A truly effective prayer has a two-fold message. It is a plea to God. It is also an admonition to the one who utters the prayer. On this day of Rosh Hashonah, as we pray for *hayim aruhim*.

We petition God to add years to our life.

We must also admonish ourselves—to add life to our years!

22

Our Minor Sins

Rabbi Morris N. Kertzer

ONCE AGAIN THE strange and mysterious magnet of *Kol Nidre* draws us warmly into its embrace, and all the children of Israel everywhere stand in silent awe of that which is holy in life.

Yes, this is a Holy Hour. What compelling force gathers us together in one mighty congregation?

Is it fear ... undefined, disquieting fear? Perhaps the ancients are right, and Yom Kippur is truly the Day of Judgment, when the Supreme Judge examines each of us, saint and sinner alike, and marks our cards "pass" or "fail."

Is it reminiscence that beckons us ... family memories of small, crowded, airless synagogues, where fathers wrapped themselves in prayer shawls, and mothers dropped their tears on old and tired prayerbooks, while they pleaded with a merciful God to be good to us, their children? For many of us, *Kol Nidre* night is a lump-in-the-throat occasion.

Or do we come here this night because there is a matchless peace, a serenity we can capture in no other place and at no other time in our prosaic chaotic lives?

Selected from *Best Jewish Sermons 5721-5722*.

The shining white of the Torah scrolls and pulpit covers, the white robes we wear—how comforting is the almost bridal quality of the evening's song and prayer!

Into this mood of pensive quietude, I should like to inject some thoughts about what I choose to call our minor sins. As you know, we Jews have our confessional, a confessional just as meaningful and spiritually moving as that of our Roman Catholic friends. In some ways, the Jewish rite of confession is similar to the Catholic. Jewish tradition dictates that a man recite the formal catalogue of sins in public, and, to quote an old source, "when he knows that he has committed one particular sin he ought to cry as he mentions it, and confess with particular emotion." If there is an unlisted sin of which he is guilty, he ought to confess it from the depths of his heart. "If his sin is well known, he ought to confess it loudly."

This custom is not too different from that of the ancient and medieval Church. As the church historian, George Foot Moore, describes it: "Restoration (for the sinner) was possible only by way of public penitence solemnly undertaken in the presence of the church, and proceeded only by slow stages."

Both Jew and Catholic are required to express their penitence before their fellow man, but there is a crucial difference. Since the year 1215, when the Church made it an obligation for all the faithful, Catholicism has held that a man's sin is against the *Church itself*, and can only be forgiven by an official of the Church. But the object of the Jewish confessional is never to convey information about one person's weakness to another. For the Jew, sin is a private and personal matter, a relationship between one man and one God. In Catholicism, the Church is the representative of God on earth. *The synagogue, whether traditional or liberal, is God's home, not His office.* All spiritual contact runs directly from man's heart to God's presence.

I have always been impressed by the fact that the transgressions we list in these Yom Kippur prayers do not include the major sins. We do not beat our breasts and declare: "Forgive our sins of killing, of stealing, of adultery." We speak only of disrespect, of stubbornness, of evil meditations. Why? Is our prayerbook too squeamish, too gentle, too circumspect? I don't think so.

The transgressions of which most of us are guilty are not the cardinal ones, the once-in-a-lifetime, twice-in-a-lifetime sins. What corrodes our spirit, what nibbles away at our souls are our tiny, almost imperceptible faults. It is these little sins that are most destructive, for we live and work and play in a society which sanctions, indeed encourages, *petty* larcenies, *petty* cheating, *minor* breaches of good taste.

An ancient talmudic law declares that when you pass your neighbor's house, you may not pick a single picket off his fence on the theory that he will not miss it. For if all his neighbors did the same, there would soon be no fence. How often do we, in casual conversation, scratch a trifle of our neighbor's reputation in a passing snide remark, a seemingly innocuous comment. And how strangely inconsistent we are. Any gossip in which *we* indulge is, we are convinced, minor, casual, merely a passing of the time of day, but when we become the *objects* of these same comments, those who speak of us are vicious, malicious creatures who use their tongues to destroy a fellow human being.

Our society looks askance at anyone who insists that principle is principle; that truth cannot be bent; that honesty has no exceptions. In our culture, such a person is regarded as overly fastidious, probably a candidate for the psychiatrist's couch. In high school, it's the sissy who won't allow his neighbor to glance at his examination paper. In business, the approximate truth is often all we demand of ourselves. Yet the fact is that a society built on 95 *percent* truth, on 95 *percent* integrity, inexorably destroys itself.

We are all quite clear about this when it comes to the world of sports. Among those who take their golf seriously, how long would a player last who moved the ball surreptitiously, who stopped counting after he reached 6? And woe betide the bridge player who earns the reputation of calling signals. Without scrupulous honesty and unimpeachable fairness, it just isn't worth holding the cards in your hands. Our harsh standards are based on an elementary principle . . . cheating destroys the very fabric of the game so that it no longer makes any sense.

Yet in the greatest game of all, the game of life, how often we rationalize about our departures from truth, from integrity, from fairness!

As a tourist in Italy, I walked through the magnificent ruins of ancient Pompeii. On the main street is a drinking fountain that stood in the middle of the thoroughfare centuries before the Common Era. The guide pointed out where the water had gushed forth, and, amazingly, the spot on the marble where people placed the four fingers of their hand to lean over for a drink. There, etched in the marble, are the deep indentations of a human palm and four fingers. Incredible? It is hard to imagine that a hand leaning on a piece of marble would leave a mark. But when done for 400 years the hand might as well be a chisel.

Our souls are very much like that marble: A little bit of cheating, a tiny grain of gossip, the mere suggestion of larceny, may seem to leave no imprint. But the accumulation is a corrosion of conscience, an eating away of character, so that each time another Yom Kippur comes around, and we catalogue our minor frailties, we are lesser persons than we were the year before.

This is a solemn night of resolutions. Our hearts are softened, our minds directed toward the hope that in the coming year, we may fashion our lives a little closer to the image of God. Again, most of our resolutions deal with little things: a promise to curb our tongues of hurtful words; to be a little more patient with our children, more forbearing with our brothers and sisters. We know that these are the minute deficiencies that make or break our relationships with those nearest and dearest to us.

Finally, there are resolutions concerned with our Jewish pattern of living. This year, we say, we will truly seek to become well informed as Jews. We will participate in Adult Education, work with Sisterhood and Brotherhood, bring our family to worship.

The Holy Season passes, and with it our mood of resolution. But the dissipation of our resolve is not dramatic and sudden. We do not decide in a moment to free ourselves of our *Kol Nidre* vows. What actually takes place is little more than a trial. One Friday night the movies beckon; on another, friends invite us to their homes, and we haven't the courage to say, "It's *Shabbat*, and we'd rather be at Temple." By the time Chanuka comes, most of our earnest resolutions have been washed down the drain, and the season's habits are fixed in a way we had not intended.

Is Yom Kippur, then, nothing more than a dramatic spiritual interlude, a momentary dream that we are capable of becoming better than we were? No. I feel, with all my heart, that we can climb to new levels of aspiration and fulfillment.

Have you ever looked up at a hillside peak and said

to yourself: If only I had the energy to scale its heights! You begin, and as the trail becomes more precipitous, your breath is shorter, your knees a good deal more uncertain. You reach a plateau, and how much wider the vista, how much more glorious the view. Finally, you stand at the peak and you discover mountain-tops which were not even visible in the valley.

I firmly believe that we are capable of making such ascents in the quality of our lives. We are not lifetime prisoners of our ignoble impulses. If we purge ourselves of the minor temptations to move backward, and forge ahead without waiting for every one of our fellow climbers to reach our level, each Yom Kippur eve will find us slightly closer to the spirit and the image of God.

23

God's Fier Kashes

Rabbi Herman Kieval

AT THE BEGINNING of Passover, we ask *Fier Kashes*; at the beginning of life we have all sorts of questions, requests and demands to make. At the end of Passover, however, we no longer ask the questions; as life goes on and approaches its end, questions are asked of us.

Who asks these questions? God asks them! What are God's "Four Questions?"

Rava, the sage of the Babylonian Talmud, said that when we stand before the Almighty Judge to render an accounting of the life that has been granted us, God asks us these four questions (Shabbat 31a):

> First — "Have you engaged in honest business dealings, in honest labor?"
> Second — "Have you set aside time for Torah study?"
> Third — "Have you helped to build family life?"
> Fourth — "Have you kept your trust in God's power to save?"

A Jew once came to the Belzer Rebbe and asked, "Rebbe, tell me how I can die as a good Jew should!" The Rabbi answered: "Don't worry about how to die;

Selected from *Best Jewish Sermons 5727-5728*.

just live as a good Jew and you will die as a good Jew!"

So it is with us. Many have come into the synagogue with thoughts of death uppermost in their minds, as we recall our dear departed. But Judaism tells us to concentrate on life. Then death need cause us no excessive fear or concern. As Rabbi Joshua Liebman wrote, "Only those who have an unlived life are morbidly afraid of death."

How should we live that we may answer "Yes" to God's "Four Questions?"

The first question is: Have you engaged in honest labor? Have your business dealings been faithful?

This question is addressed to us all: it applies equally to the big and the small businessman, to the worker, to the professional, to the housewife. Every person must have a vocation in life—a systematic and persistent performance of needful work. We are born into the world with a job to perform, and normal people are never happy unless they are busy doing that work. Ethical religion requires that we do this work as satisfactorily and honestly as possible.

It was a favorite saying of the Sages of Yavneh: I am a creature of God, and my neighbor is also His creature; my work is in the city and his is in the field. ... As he cannot excel in my work, so I cannot excel in his work. But you may say, "I do great things and he does small things." We have learned that it is of no weight whether a man does much or little, so long as he directs his heart to heaven.

A story is found in one of our great ethical books about a tailor who left instructions that at his death his coffin should be made out of his work table. Why?—so that the very wood might testify on his behalf when God asked him the "first question"—Have you done your work faithfully?"

How many among us can make this statement? Will

the automobile manufacturers be able to face God and say that they have honestly done everything they can to prevent the frightful slaughter on America's highways?! The list could be extended indefinitely to those who make careers and fortunes out of misleading the consumer. But, dishonesty is not the monopoly of the business world. It is rife in the professions. It is commonplace among workers who fail to give their best, and students who cheat their way to graduation. It is proverbial among taxpayers who fail to live up to their responsibilities as citizens of a great nation which has given us so much to be thankful for.

The excuse that "everybody is doing it" may salve our bad conscience, but it will not satisfy the ethical demands of Judaism. The teachers of old warned against the temptation of fragmenting life between God and business: "Whoever says that the words of Torah are one thing and the words of the world another, must be regarded as a man who denies God!"

The second question is: Have you set aside time for the study of Torah?

What can this mean in our modern world? Torah, in the classical sense, meant learning the books of the Bible and Talmud, the codes, studying the ethical teachings of Judaism. We freely admit that these studies do not teach us everything we need to know in order to live adequately. But they do tell us who we Jews are, they spell out our spiritual purposes; they indicate the goals we seek and the method to follow.

For us today, "Torah" would also include such secular knowledge as will help us to understand our world and man's place in it. This is called normative knowledge. Why is normative knowledge so important for the world in which we live? The former President Griswold of Yale gave the answer: "We are the best informed generation that ever lived, with the most primitive ideas of what to do with our information. We know how to blow up the world but we don't know how to govern it." One of the most urgent needs of our time is that every man and woman acquire not only technical and professional skills, but also a spiritual orientation that will tell us what to do with the specialized information taught in our schools and colleges, acquired through our books, magazines, radio and TV.

We Jews should recognize this need more than anyone else, because it is so basic to our pattern of meaningful, moral living. "Thinking," said the late Professor Louis Ginzberg, "is as characteristic a trait of the Jew as suffering, or—to be more exact—thinking rendered suffering possible. For it was our thinkers who prevented the wandering nation ... from sinking to the level of ... vagabond gypsies."

For the Jew, to live meant to learn. Torah was the "elixir of life"—*sam ha-chayyim.* "He who increaseth his knowledge increaseth life." It is this quest for knowledge, this restless urge to learn, that has made the Jews a great force in human history! Professor Solomon Schechter used to tell the story of a Catholic saint who was beheaded by his pagan persecutors. But, like a good saint, he took his head under his arm and walked off. "You smile," he used to say, "and think it perhaps too much of a miracle; but a Judaism without a Bible is even a greater miracle. It would mean a headless Judaism. ..."

When shall we realize that it is a contradiction to try to live a meaningful Jewish life without a head? No program for Jewish life in this country will be valid or effective unless it will give due prominence to Torah, unless it acquires a learned leadership and an informed laity. "A Jewish community that has ceased to learn—no matter how active and busy it may seem—has ceased Jewishly to live" (Morris Adler). Only when we, as individuals, will accept upon ourselves the practice of Torah study as a requirement of Jewish citizenship shall we be able to answer "yes" when God asks us His "second question."

What is God's "third question?" Have you built the structure of family life?

If the first two ingredients of a meaningful and moral life are learning and labor (normative knowledge and faithful work), the third is love. The Greeks and Romans—indeed all the pagans, both ancient and modern—have believed that love is a Goddess who makes her own rules! Judaism, however, does not recognize love as an autonomous force that makes its own laws, but as a force that builds and creates the structure of society. Judaism does not agree that "all is fair in love."

Today we are face to face with a new paganism which excuses all sorts of private arrangements between the sexes on the grounds that "it's all right as long as you are in love!" We Jews also recognize that love is a powerful life force, but Judaism always insisted that it must be directed and channeled if it is to help men and women build lasting meaning into their lives. This channel is marriage and family. If there is one aspect of life that we Jews are supposed to be experts in, it is the harnessing of the love force into the creative structure of the family, instead of allowing it to run wild to waste and destroy human happiness.

Things have changed a great deal, however, in recent generations. The Jewish family today has been riddled and battered by all the destructive forces of our troubled society. Today, Jews, like Gentiles, suffer from the curse of that immoral doctrine of our time known as "self-expression." This means: do whatever you wish in order to have "fun out of life." Let the family, let the Jewish

people, let America, suffer—as long as you express yourself without inhibitions.

We would not be here today honoring our beloved
parents if they had yielded to this pagan doctrine. If we
want our children to remember us as we remember our
parents, let us so live that we may answer "Yes" to God's
third question.

What is God's fourth and final question? Have you
believed in God's power to save?

Over the generations, this *bitachon*, this trust in
God's power to save became a characteristic of Jewish
existence. It was an upsurge of this classic Jewish faith
that led Jews in the Warsaw ghetto and death camps to
sing in their darkest hour, "Say not that this is the end
of the road." (*Zog nit keinmal az du gehst dos letzte veg!*) A
familiar phrase was turned by these martyred heroes
into a triumphant hymn, as they sang unto death, "*Ani
Maamin, Ani Maamin,*" (I believe, I believe in the coming of Messiah, and even though he be delayed, nevertheless I shall wait!) The State of Israel which has enriched our lives as Jews with enormous dimensions of
meaning would never have come into existence without
this conviction that God will not abandon His faithful
ones.

Perhaps this is the most important contribution we
Jews can make to our fellow men in this critical hour of
history. Judaism asserts that there is a grand design for
history by which men and nations move toward truth,
goodness and unity. There are frequent setbacks on this
road to a better world. The decent people are defeated
again and again. But the direction is eternally there for
those who do not lose hope that mankind shall yet
reach its goal of a world free from war, ignorance, cruelty and terror. There will always be questions that baffle
the mind, sorrows that pierce the heart, frustrations

that challenge the stoutest, most intelligent spirits. *But the Jews never surrendered their trust in God's power to save!*

"It is our heritage as Jews to maintain an unhysterical and unpanicky mind, to do what our ancestors did when war was to the north of them and persecution to the south, and hunger and plague to the east and the west. They kept on writing, teaching, and praying and working for a world beyond their little day on earth" (Joshua L. Liebman). So shall we today teach and think and pray.

Now that we know God's *"Fier Kashes,"* what will our answers be?

Can we dare respond, at this sacred hour of memorial, with anything less than the prayer of our hearts:

> O God of our Fathers!
> Show us how we may build up our
> little lives with meaning and purpose
> through *labor* and *learning*
> through *love* and *faith*.

Then shall we be liberated from fear in this imperfect world, and continue to trust in Thy mercy for the better world that is sure to come.

24

Requirements of Happiness

Rabbi Gilbert Klaperman

ONE OF THE freedoms that has not yet been achieved by man has so aptly been termed "the inner emancipation from the corroding sense of futility." By this is meant the passive, supine, and submissive acceptance of the blows of life. When life's difficulties are received without hope, they shatter the human personality, rob it of all opportunities for happiness and destroy the delicate recuperative mechanism that is brought into being by initiative. We know full well that the ability to mold and to fashion the directions of our lives and to choose the path upon which we will travel, is what elevates man and distinguishes him from the animal kingdom. Man has been blessed with the opportunity to say: "Today *I* will be better. Today will be different." The animal can only hope—if hope he does—that his lot will be bettered.

And yet, my friends, we know so many men and women who are corroded by futility, who are caught up in the stream of existence, and who, instead of themselves shaping their lives, squeeze or stretch themselves into a Procrustean bed of convention—a pattern that

---

Selected from *Best Jewish Sermons of 5715-5716.*

others have made for them. In self-pity they lament and cry "Who am I and what am I to change the course of destiny." Few, if any, of these helpless people are ever aware that, if they but willed it, life would indeed be different.

In theology this spiritless yielding to conditions is called predestination. In psychology the debilitating fatalism and bowing to conditions has been attributed to the restrictions of heredity. And in the study of history this human sluggishness has been explained by the overpowering influence of the "zeitgeist"—the conventions and spirit of the times.

Regardless of the name that we give it, accepting the decrees of life as final without a struggle and without an effort to improve and refine our lot leads only to further despair and frustration. This is true not only of the poor but of the rich as well, not only of the unsuccessful but of the successful as well. The race with the Jones's on any level is just such a symptom of the lack of initiative which ends in being swept along with the tide. The successful man who drops the friends of his early days is, in effect, in another way, also bowing to his fate. "What can I do?", he shrugs, implying that he has no alternative in betting against the results of his own success.

Ah, my friends, the struggle for the maximum good that life has to offer must be constant and continuous. For the first moments of submission have a cumulative weakening effect on the spirit of man. The athlete who breaks training the first time finds it hard to resist the appeals of his sweet tooth the second time and has forever ruined his diet the third time. And one who has been conditioned into accepting the justification of the endless frustrations can only arrive at the one inevitable and pessimistic conclusion of Ecclesiastes, who said: "There is no man that hath power over the wind to retain the wind; neither hath he power over the day of death; and there is no discharge in war." Such a man loses hope. He is convinced that nothing can ever be changed and he firmly believes that he plays no part in the control of his destiny.

Thomas Hardy, who was a master at describing man as the plaything of fate and ascribing his consequent misery to the unfeeling, relentless, and crushing web of destiny, epitomizes this surrender to the inevitable when he concludes the history of the pitiful Tess of the D'Urbervilles with the epitaph: "The President of the Immortals had finished his sport with Tess." For, the timid and the fearful lose not only the hope of carving out a productive and fulfilling way of life, but they deny the very Being that makes all of life possible. For them, even God becomes a giant conspirator in the plan to confound their existence.

This call for unqualified capitulation to destiny pictures man as the unavailing product and the unwilling subject of circumstances who journeys alone and without hope, along the unfriendly and unfeeling road of life. Judaism has never accepted this debasing of the human intellect and the creative power in man. On the contrary, rather than subscribing to the theory that man was little more than the beast of the field, it has always submitted the challenging, but hopeful, alternative that man was little lower than the angels, a partner with the Almighty Himself in the miracle of creation and a happy adventurer in the science and art of living.

Rabbi Akiba, one of the greatest of Israel's teachers and sages, recognized in this eternal dilemma of man's existence the elements of truth in both alternatives. "Everything is foreseen by God," he taught, "yet the freedom of choice remains with man." Properly viewed, he would say to our confused generation, "man is not a slave of circumstances or destiny. On the contrary, he dare not yield for the freedom of untrammeled action lies with him!"

The fallacy of the counsel of surrender is humorously demonstrated in the tale of the philosopher's son who struck his father on the cheek, saying, "It was ordained that I should do this." The philosopher replied with equal aplomb as he dealt his son an even severer blow, "And it was ordained that I should do this."

While there may seem to be circumstances that are beyond man's control, man can learn to make peace with them and thereby rise above their restrictions. For humanity will never be free and life will never be worth living until we have learned that we can adjust to the arbitrariness of nature, the despotism of events, and the tyranny of fate. If primitive man had not learned this elementary fact of life and mastered the circumstances that seemed to be beyond his control, we would still be cowering in abject fear in the darkness of a miserable cave, startled by every untoward sound and at the mercy of every sulking beast.

There are ways in which we can come to terms with our surroundings and make ourselves so free and independent, so strong and able, so spiritually tranquil that we can face almost any kind of distressing situation and not crumble under the strain.

The first thing that we must realize is that there are and always will be problems that man must face in his constant struggle to attain a happier life. It is only those who are lulled by a dream of perfection into expecting a world of untarnished idealism that are shaken to their very soul at its absence. Justice Holmes once declared that his greatest sense of relief came when he recognized this truth—that man is not called upon to be God. Certainly there are human frailties and unmanageable events of nature that man will never be able to face adequately, and there will always be a wide discrepancy and a vast divergence between "what is" and "what ought to be." Yet this realization should not bring on a hopeless pessimism and a frustrating disillusionment that urges a retreat to the hermit's cave, on the one hand, or a gnawing, biting cynicism, on the other hand. For both of these deprive even the good things in life of the pleasures they bring.

Intelligently understood, life should be recognized as an unending series of tests, problems, experiences and challenges—some of which can be met and others of which are too great for us to solve at the moment, or possibly, even at any time. But never should we despair of living life and striving for progress.

The broadjumper does not expect to better the established record with every jump, nor does every runner hope to achieve the perfect mile, nor does every golfer hope to shoot a "hole in one"—but because he recognizes his limitations, the sportsman continues to play the game and finds enjoyment in it, rather than frustration.

This brings us to the second great point. With awareness of the difficulties placed in our way by what appears to be an unfeeling nature and a complexly developed world, must also come the courage to face these problems and wrest from them whatever little measure of happiness or comfort that they possess. There is no man who has not employed at one time or another his instinct to fight, to rebel or to become pugnacious. These are the weapons with which we carve our freedom. We have to learn to make natural use of these instincts every single day, to regain lost opportunities, reclaim lost talents and liberate ourselves from a self-imposed slavery to events and conditions.

Many more of us, my friends, could profit by emulating the decision of Louisa May Alcott, beloved by all children for her great legacy of books for little people. When experiencing hard times, rather than to yield, she wrote with constructive fury that she had "resolved to take fate by the throat and shake a living out of her." This kind of courage and refusal to accept the inevitable guided Pasteur through innumerable tests, that taxed his patience and strength, to liberate the world from a dread disease and open new horizons for the students of science. It was this kind of courage that infused Emile Zola to fight the inhumanity and social scourge of anti-Semitism in France against the advice and counsel of his friends and in opposition to the conventions of his day. It was this kind of courage that strengthened Father Abraham to rise head and shoulders above his contemporaries to battle idolatry and bring the knowledge of God to the people of the world.

The man who recognizes that the course of his life is in his own hands has already taken the first step towards improving it. The alcoholic who says, "I will master my impulse"; the crippled body who shouts out, "I will overcome my infirmity"; the weak soul who repeats, "I will resist temptation"; these are the men and women who will never grovel, who are not vanquished by life, but are shaping it instead to the ends they seek.

The third great point is the conviction that there is a God above to help us in our battle. Many of us, when tragedy strikes, are prone to throw up our hands in helplessness as if God has left us completely. I am constantly moved by the story of the legless World War veteran who was observed at a shrine of his faith. As he hobbled up to the shrine someone remarked: "That silly man! Does he think God will give him back his leg?"

The veteran overheard the comment. Turning around

he replied: "Of course I do not expect God to give me back my leg. But I am going to pray for God to help me to live without it."

From King David who, in his distress, called unto the Lord from out of the depths in the most expressive prayers of man's literature, to the veteran who called to his God for aid in adjusting to a handicapped life, man, when he willed it, has been able to "take fate by the throat" and shake it.

There is no man living who, at one time or another, did not have the opportunity to do this. Any crossroads brings the need for a choice; any venture forward or plan for the future requires a decision. The men and women who face the challenge of life fearlessly are those who are ready to take the new step, to try—to try to make the change for the better.

We peoples of the free world are beginning to appreciate with every passing minute the precious political and social freedom that we have, and that equally precious freedom, the freedom from futility. We are not mere cogs in the wheels of state. We are not an inarticulate, driven mass; we are individuals, men—free men!

Let us then know our blessing and fulfill its promise. Let us, like the countless heroes of the battle for better living throughout the age, "take fate by the throat" and shake her, like a Pandora's Box, to bring forth the many bounties and benefits that life has to offer. We must have the courage to recognize the test and the strength to face it. As Shakespeare put it:

> Men at some time are masters of their fates
> The fault, dear Brutus, is not in our stars,
> But in ourselves, that we are underlings.

25

The Legacy of Jacob

Rabbi Isaac Klein

THERE IS ONE kind of literature which is definitely unique with the Jews. A few years ago the Jewish Publication Society issued two volumes entitled *Hebrew Ethical Wills*. It is a collection of admonitions which fathers left to their children as a last good-bye. One reads with a feeling akin to awe the last words that some people leave to their children. Today the word "will" brings to our mind a legal document drawn up by a lawyer. The two books contain wills that are very removed from such documents. The wills there consist of legacies that fathers leave to their children telling them which is the righteous path that they should choose. One father urges his children to exercise the virtue of kindness to all human beings and never to grow angry at anyone. Another admonishes them not to neglect prayer and study which are the greatest glory of mortals.

I believe that no other literary expression could indicate so clearly the ethical sense of a people. One is bound to tell during his last moments that which he deems the most important. A few years ago a volume of

---

Selected from *Best Jewish Sermons of 5715-5716*.

sermons was published entitled, "If I Had Only One Sermon to Preach." When one writes a will, he feels as the minister who has only one sermon to preach and he will put in that which is closest to his heart and soul. When one's last words to his children is that they be God-fearing, we need not guess very long what his ideals are. Peretz, the great Yiddish writer, indicates that in his sketch, "Four Generations—Four Wills."

The pious father tells his sons not to forget that wealth comes from the Lord and that, therefore, they be generous in their giving. He also tells them of the value of prayer and study. The one who is more interested in his business enterprises instructs his successors about the ways of conducting a business successfully. The last one leaves a will in which he tells that since life had no meaning to him, he has nothing to tell to posterity. From the wills they leave, one can judge very well what people value most.

It will, therefore, be of interest to see the first Jewish will which is found in the Scriptural reading of today. When Jacob was about to die he called his children together, blessed them, and wished to speak to them about the future. The Bible does not record a will by Abraham, nor by Isaac. There is a reason why of all the patriarchs, only Jacob left a last Will and Testament. He was the first patriarch who died in exile amidst a foreign civilization and culture. He came from Canaan, a land of nomads with a primitive civilization, to Egypt which was then at the height of its power and the peak of its culture. Jacob saw the danger that was lurking in this power and splendor. On the one hand he feared that the magnificence of this new civilization may lure his children away from their humble heritage. On the other hand, he surmised that all this pomp and glitter was made possible by the enslavement of the people. He

feared that the enslavement may also lead them to forget the faith of their fathers.

The Talmud has a poetic comment on this event.
Jacob was about to reveal to his children the end of
days but the Divine Presence departed from him and
the future became dim. He feared that this departure of
divine inspiration was due to the lack of faith of his
children. His family noticing Jacob's perplexity said,
"Hear O Israel, the Lord our God the Lord is One," and
assured him that just as he believed in one God, they
too believed only in Him. Jacob was consoled and said,
"Blessed be the name of His glorious Kingdom forever
and ever."

Yes, Jacob feared that the heritage he kept alive at
such great sacrifice would die with him. When he saw
the new generation grow up in Egypt, speaking a new
language, following new customs, he feared that it may
result in a departure from the truth and light started by
Abraham. The future which he wished to reveal to them
became dim as a result. What future could there be if
the children would depart from the truths he cherished? He was reassured when the children all told him
that though their garb and their language were different, yet they upheld that which Jacob delivered to them
and would continue to forge the chain that linked them
with the past and with the future generations of Israel.
It was only then that the mist cleared and Jacob again
had a clear vision of the future.

I wonder how many a father in our own day shares
the fears and the anxieties of Jacob. How many a Jewish
father today who has suffered and sacrificed to have a
Jewish home and to give his children a Jewish education, does become sad and perturbed when he views the
ways of his children. How many of them see how their
children trample upon those observances and practices

which he cherished and which to him were dearer than life. He weeps when he thinks of the future of Israel. He thinks of the great Jewish culture, of the beautiful Jewish home life, of the sacredness of the festivals, of the devotion to learning—all of which will now fall into desuetude and oblivion. A great literature, a heroic history, a glorious tradition will pass out of the life of mankind.

Lincoln Steffens, in his autobiography, tells one of his experiences as a reporter on New York's lower East Side. He saw how on Yom Kippur, while the elder people spent the entire day in fasting and prayer in the synagogue, the young people would stand outside, smoke and laugh at them. Steffens remarks: "The tears hurt, the weeping and the gnashing of teeth of the old men, who were doomed and knew it. Two, three thousand years of heroism and devotion, and suffering for a cause lost in a single generation." Many a dying patriarch has that thought when he breathes his last.

It is not very often, though, that the children can give the answer that his children gave to Jacob. They cannot say that though they may speak a different language and follow different customs, they still will weave the glorious tapestry of Jewish history. Two, three thousand years of Jewish heroism and devotion and suffering, lost in a single generation.

Today, in our skeptical generation, we are bound to ask what would have been the harm had the children of Jacob merged with the great Egyptian people. Historically speaking, the civilization of Egypt was far superior to that of Canaan whence Jacob and his sons came. Why do we make so much ado about Jacob desiring his sons to adhere to the ways he taught them rather than those followed by the Egyptians? Was not the grandeur of the Egyptian civilization to be preferred to whatever Jacob had to offer?

Our answer will be the well-known incident in the life of the Prophet Elijah. While in the desert as a fugitive from the wrath of Queen Jezebel, the Lord was to speak to him. At first there was a great wind that rent the mountain and broke the rocks into pieces. Surely, thought Elijah, the Lord will appear from amidst the august manifestation of nature. But the Lord was not in the wind. Then there was an earthquake. Then there came a fire. But the Lord was neither in the earthquake, nor in the fire. After the fire there came a still small voice from where the Lord spoke to him.

Our interpretation about what constitutes a civilization runs parallel to the phenomena in which Elijah expected the glory of God to appear. At first we have the wind, the earthquake and the fire. These natural phenomena catch the eye with their visible manifestation, their size, and their destructiveness. It is these qualities that we have often used as the measuring rods for our civilization. When we talk of the monuments of ancient civilizations, we think of the pyramids, the great cities, or the vast empires built on conquest. In modern times, we speak of the advances made in technology which create the power that does man's work for him. We boast of the machines that do work which before required thousands of people. We boast of our industrial plants and organizations. Yes, we boast of the destructiveness of our arms which have reached unprecedented proportions. All these advances that the past few generations witnessed created in man a certain self-satisfaction. He thought that he found the secret of everything, that he uncovered the mystery behind creation. If there were some questions still left unanswered, man was confident that in time science would find the solution.

Today, man's arrogance has been humbled by the

events that are now transpiring. We have found out that technology is not the answer to all problems. A civilization that is built on technology, solely, is a body without a soul, a Frankenstein that eventually destroys its creator. The voice of the Lord does not speak from it. It is from the still small voice of just human relations that the Lord speaks. Real civilization expresses itself in moral maturity. The sooner our generation comes to recognize that, the likelier it will build a stable society.

Our father Jacob brought with him a heritage that preached the Fatherhood of God and the Brotherhood of Man. In Egypt, he found a great civilization, wealthy in material manifestations. It attracted the eye. It had grandeur and splendor. Our Father Jacob, however, was not deluded by appearances. He knew that the huge structure rested on slavery and oppression. The walls of the great cities were built upon human misery. The bricks were cemented by mortar mixed with the blood and sweat of the masses.

Jacob preferred his brand of civilization and was anxious that his children should adhere to it too. That was his legacy on his deathbed. Today, we may repeat the words of Jacob to our children. Our young men stray away from the heritage of their fathers attracted by the tinsel and glamour of the world around them. The words of the prophet still apply:

> Thus saith the Lord:
> Let not the wise man glory in his wisdom,
> Neither the mighty man in his might;
> Let not the rich man glory in his riches.
> But let him that glorieth, glory in this,
> That he understands, and knoweth Me.

26

Supremacy of the Torah

Rabbi Benjamin Kreitman

THE GREATNESS of a people is often mirrored in small events. In the arid stretches of statistics we meet with in the opening chapters of the Book of *Bamidbar*, relating the census taken of the children of Israel during their sojourn in the Wilderness, we see the promise of the spiritual greatness of the Jewish people.

Though taking a census is a simple act, it nevertheless presents a problem. With whom should the count begin? It would seem that one particular person or one particular family has a natural or logical precedence over the others and therefore it is with these that the count should begin. The normal procedure, in ancient days, was to begin the census with the first-born son—the *bekor*, because the first-born, according to the ways of the ancients, ranked next to the parents in familial responsibilities and duties. He took precedence over all his brothers in both the privileges and the duties of the household. The Torah recognizes this rank by granting the *bekor* a double portion of the inheritance. Accordingly, the general census began with the descendants of Reuben, who was Jacob's first-born (Numbers 1.20).

Selected from *Best Jewish Sermons of 5714.*

A different order, however, was followed in the census taken of the families of the Tribe of Levi, the tribe consecrated to the ministry of the Lord's sanctuary. Instead of beginning the count with the first-born son of Levi, Gershon, as was to be expected, the count began with the middle son, Kohoth.

The Sages of the Talmud, noting that in certain unusual situations the Torah does alter the usual order of precedence, sought the reason for this change in the assigned duties of the families of the Tribe of Levi. *Lamah hikdim ha-kathuv le-Kohoth le-nesiath rosh ve-ahar manah le-Gershon?* "Why does Scripture give precedence to Kohoth and then turns to counting Gershon, the first-born?" And they answer: *le-fi she-Kohoth hayah me-toanei ha-aron;* "Because Kohoth carried the Ark of the Law (Ba-midbar Rabbah 6)." For the Tribe dedicated to the service of the Lord, the rank of Torah supplants the ranks of birth, caste or position.

From its infancy as a people, the Jew has had only one true nobility, the nobility which came to him as the bearer of the Torah. This eminent position is within the reach of all; we need but to study and sustain it. There is a striking statement in the Talmud which gives expression to this deep-rooted attitude of the Jew, *Haham kodem le-meleh, meth haham ein lo keyotzei bo, meth ha-meleh kulam reuyin le-malhuth,* "The wise man, the one skilled in the knowledge of the Torah, outranks the king. Should the wise man die, there is no one like him to take his place. Should the king die, anyone can replace him." (Horayoth 13a)

In the statistics recorded in the Torah readings of these Sabbath mornings, we find, therefore, the seed thought of the intellectual and spiritual development of Judaism throughout the ages; the pre-eminence of Torah and of those scholars who sustain it and transmit its teaching. In the era of the Second Commonwealth, the Rabbis, lay teachers of the Torah constituting the Pharisaic party, wrested the leadership of the Jewish people from the Priests, who had degenerated into unschooled, ignorant Temple functionaries. Their battle slogan was: "The Torah is greater than the priesthood and the royalty!" (Pirke Aboth 6.6) Rabbi Meir, a teacher of the second century, went so far as to place a non-Jew, who was engaged in the study of Torah, in the same class as the high priest. *Afilu goy ve-osek ba-Torah ke-kohen gadol,* "Even a gentile who is occupied with the Torah is like unto a high priest." (Sifra Ahare Moth)

This devotion to the study of Torah became the salient characteristic of the Jewish people. The principal ornament in the Jewish home was the bookcase filled with sacred books. The *Talmid Haham,* the scholar, was the most respected and honored man in the community. To be counted in the company of scholars was to achieve life's greatest ambition.

The love of Torah-study gave intellectual impetus to the pursuit of knowledge in the arts and the sciences. The great luminaries of the medieval era, such as Isaac Israeli, Yehudah Halevi and Moses Maimonides, were profound students and interpreters of science and philosophy, but the Jew gave unmistakable priority to the Torah and its students. In the Jewish hierarchy of values, philosophy and science were considered handmaidens to the Torah.

Emerging with these thoughts from a review of the past, we are led to the painful observation that for the modern American Jew the Torah has been dislodged from its position of eminence, and the traditional Jewish love for learning has been transferred to science, technology and the arts. The scientist and the philosopher have replaced the *Talmid Haham* in the affection and esteem of the Jewish people.

This changed attitude was recently stated by the venerable Yiddish journalist, Sh. Niger, in an interview published in one of the Anglo-Jewish magazines. "A large number of American Jews," he wrote, "choose intellectual pursuits and professions. This is simply a transmutation of the ancient Jewish love of learning, which today manifests itself in altered forms. Instead of the Talmud, the modern Jew studies law or medicine or nuclear physics. The link is different but the chain continues." Does law or medicine or nuclear physics belong to the same chain as the Talmud? From the perspective of history, to place these studies in the same line of succession is a misreading of the meaning of the Jewish love for learning.

This changed attitude towards scholarship is not confined to the intellectuals. It is manifested in the financial support given to various Jewish institutions of higher learning. During the past few years we have witnessed the spectacular growth of Brandeis University, which is under Jewish auspices but non-sectarian in policy. Being non-sectarian it must necessarily subordinate Jewish religious studies to the secular subjects. I am certain that the great majority of American Jews acclaim the development and prosperity of this new university. And this is as it should be. What grieves me, as it does many who are concerned with the future of Judaism in this land, is that American Jewry has given priority to a university avowedly secular and has left great academies like the Jewish Theological Seminary, Yeshiva University and the Hebrew Union College, which are devoted to the study and transmission of the Torah and our religious tradition, to struggle for their meager budgets.

The radical shift away from Torah and its study imperils the future of Judaism in this land. It is incumbent upon us, committed as we are to the perpetuation of our faith and tradition, to seek the root cause of this change and restore the Torah to its position of supremacy in Jewish life.

I recall a conversation with a young Jewish physicist that suggests the basic reason for the dislodgment of Torah from the summit of Jewish esteem. The chat turned to a discussion of the American Jew and his need for religion. This young physicist spoke with more than ordinary knowledge about his religion and his people's history, having attended in his early years one of the prominent yeshivas in New York. He aligned himself immediately, as was to be expected, with what he chose to call "the scientific approach to life and thought." Those who did not share his view he considered benighted souls. After arguing back and forth about the relationship of science and religion he finally admitted his great admiration for the insights into human nature and the human predicament found in the Bible and Talmud, the wholesome outlook of the Scriptures on life, and their regulations for the good life. Then he hit upon the crux of our problem. "We can arrive at these Biblical ideas, attitudes and regulations through our present-day knowledge of psychology, the social sciences and the whole complex of modern scientific thought. The only difference is that the Torah has a strong emotional appeal to some people because around it cluster sacred memories. Our modern resources of wisdom and knowledge give us the same conclusions." He sealed his argument with a spirited declaration: "Modern man is emancipated. We no longer need to depend on Divine revelation or inspiration."

The young scientist had revealed a crucial point of view, one that has disturbed many Jews, particularly the young people. At issue is not the hackneyed conflict

between science and religion; the now threadbare arguments over the contradictions between the scientific
conception of the origin of the cosmos and the Biblical
account of the creation, or the opposition of the natural
laws to the miracle stories. Both the religionist and sec-
ularist of today are too sophisticated to insist on the
Bible being accepted as the definitive text book on science. The real conflict between science and religion is
the belief that we possess the means for the good life in
the resources of modern science, as well as in the Torah.
For a modern person it would seem logical to look to
science or modern philosophy for guidance to a happy
existence rather than to the Torah.

I can imagine a father asking his college student son
to join him in the synagogue and the boy saying: "Attending synagogue, praying, reading the Bible and listening to the Rabbi's sermons may serve your needs
admirably, but I find the same satisfaction in listening
to my professors' lectures, and even in studying my
textbooks. I have no need for the beliefs and disciplines
of the Torah."

Let us not mistake the thoughts of our imaginary
college student as being peculiar to the twentieth century. Rabbi Johanan, one of the great sages of the Talmud,
expressed the same thoughts even more forcibly, albeit
for different reasons. *Ilmahleh lo nitnah Torah hayinu
lemeidin tzniuth me-hathul ve-gezel me-nemalah ve-arayoth
me-yonah vederek eretz me-tarnegol,* "If the Torah had not
been given us we could have learnt modesty from the
cat, honesty from the ant, chastity from the dove and
good manners from the cock." (Erubin 10b). Observe
the instinctual behavior of these animals, Rabbi Johanan suggests, and you will derive from them the laws of
proper human conduct.

Why then were we given the Torah? Why this need

of a Divine revelation of a code of laws regulating human conduct? The answer is implied in the words of Rabbi Johanan and in the collective thoughts of the Sages, if one looks deeply into them. There is a grave danger that man might learn from the wrong animal—honesty from the cat, chastity from the dog, regimentation from the ant and ferocity from the tiger. Left to his own devices, depending only on his own resources, man may take as his model the cruelest laws of nature, the laws of the jungle. And this has happened in modern times. Thomas Hobbes, the progenitor of the totalitarian state, inferred from natural events that the primary condition of nature, including human nature, is one of collision, conflict and war. With this observation as his major premise he came to the conclusion that the most suitable government is an absolute monarchy or, to use a more modern term, a dictatorship. Prince Peter Kropotkin, studying the laws of nature, particularly the evolutionary process, discovered in the animal world the law of mutual aid, which he hoped would become the natural basis of a noble human community. On the other hand, the German philosopher Friedrich Nietzsche, learned from the natural laws of evolution an opposite principle—the law of the survival of the fittest. He proclaimed as the end product of the human evolutionary process Superman, who would reach his exalted height by crushing the weak and the helpless. Nietzsche gave the German people the philosophic impetus to run amuck as the "super-race" among the nations of the world. Or, to take an immediate example: Karl Marx and his disciple, Lenin, derived their economic and political programs from what they considered the natural laws of economics and history. In the name of the "natural" law of dialectical materialism, the peoples of Russia and of the satellite countries are being cruelly regimented by a "dictatorship of the proletariat," with terror and bloodshed the law of their lands.

It is the great tragedy of history that in this era, when man has turned to his own resources of knowledge and wisdom, he has discovered that he cannot rely on himself. Jeremiah's prophecy has been nigh fulfilled: "Because you trusted in your works and your treasures, you also shall be trapped."

The Torah, being the embodiment of the Word of God and the disclosure of His Will, proclaims the dependence of man on the Divine. Whatever way this revelation is conceived or interpreted, be it in the orthodox or modernist manner, it is a profound recognition of our human need for Divine guidance and inspiration. Though our human resources of knowledge and wisdom be sufficient for the moment, ultimately we must rely on God and His guidance.

To restore the supremacy of the Torah in our lives means the rejection of the belief that man is the measure of all things in the universe—a notion that has placed man on the brink of self-destruction—and the declaration that man before God is the measure of life. The scripture reading this morning summons us to reaffirm the supremacy of the Torah; to become the spiritual heirs of the family of *Kohoth*, the bearers of the Ark in the Wilderness.

27

The Eloquent Silence

Rabbi Harold S. Kushner

PART OF THE greatness of the Bible, which is its ability to reach and move and instruct different kinds of people across so many ages, lies in the essential humanity of its characters. These are real people to whom real things happen: Abraham and Jacob and Joseph, Moses and Aaron, David and Jeremiah. ... On one level they are the magnificent heroes of another age, reaching heights of accomplishment at which we can only marvel. But on another level, the Bible shows us these same people as private citizens, at home with their families, their problems, in circumstances to which we can readily respond. And if we can learn something from seeing these people as great leaders and pioneers, we can perhaps learn even more from seeing how they react to problems as private individuals. And it's such a lesson that comes out of this morning's *sidra, Shemini.*

In the course of bringing a sacrifice before the Lord, two of Aaron's sons, Nadav and Avihu, somehow desecrate the altar. They introduce a strange and improper fire to the sanctuary, and the awesome Holiness embodied there bursts forth and kills them both. In a flash,

---

Selected from *Best Jewish Sermons of 5725-5726.*

they are struck down for their desecration. And Aaron, the High Priest, Moses' brother, is stunned by this double tragedy. Suddenly, he is no longer the High Priest, an exalted public official, he is now only a father who has been bereft of two of his children.

Moses tries to console him by saying, "This must be what God meant when He said *bik'rovai ekadesh*, I expect holiness from those closest to Me," but no words of consolation could really be adequate to the situation, and we are told, *vayiddom Aharon*, "Aaron remained silent."

It is perhaps the most eloquent silence in the whole Bible—those moments when Aaron refrains from speaking. You realize that the Bible, with its compact narrative style, doesn't usually make a practice of telling us that people keep quiet. If a person isn't saying anything, the text usually just ignores him. And so, when it makes a point of saying that "Aaron remained silent," it must be to emphasize that there was something he might have said that he didn't—some outcry, some protest, some lament. But he never utters anything of the sort. And we are never told explicitly what was in his mind at that moment, no long soliloquies of the sort that you might find in a modern novel, no articles for a national magazine on "How I Felt That Day," or "What I Now Believe." All we know is that in the very next chapter, just a few days later, Aaron is back functioning as High Priest, sharing with Moses the job of teaching Israel to distinguish between pure and impure, clean and unclean.

It certainly couldn't have been easy. Here was a man who had every reason to complain, to rail against heaven and never set foot in the Tent of Meeting again. He had served God loyally, taking responsibilities and restrictions onto himself for the sake of heaven, and now he had this happen to him. Yet somehow Aaron's faith survives the test, and he is able to go back to ministering to God as *Kohen Gadol.*

I do not think it was a matter of blind faith, of saying, in the face of tragedy, "We're not meant to understand it, and we're forbidden to ask questions. We just
have to go on believing." One might have thought that
was Aaron's answer, were it not for that moment of silence, for that little hint of hesitation and doubt, of
searching for something deep within himself. But I cannot help feeling that out of that silence came an answer
much more profound.

During those first moments when he kept still, Aaron
was searching for something within himself—and he
found it: the capacity to go on believing in God and to
go on serving him, despite what had happened. He
learned something that day that he could never have
known before, and something that is very important for
a religious person to discover about himself: he learned
that he could go on believing in God and worshipping
Him even if things do not always go his way. He learned
that day, what he could have hoped was true, but never
knew before, that "I believe in God, not only because He
takes care of me, but because He is God, because that is
the way I give my life meaning and am able to make
sense of the world." He traded in his belief in a God who
would strengthen and comfort him, and give him something to live for, even when sorrow struck.

Earlier this morning, we recited the 30th Psalm, *Miz-
mor Shir Chanukat Ha-bayit,* "A Song at the Dedication of
the Temple," and after we recited it, those in mourning
joined in the *Kaddish.* I've always felt a certain regret
that this particular psalm comes so early in the service,
when not too many of us are present to read it, because
it makes a profound and beautiful point.

It was apparently written, thousands of years ago, by
a man who had been close to death, and promised that

if he recovered, he would devote the rest of his life to singing the praises of God and teaching others what this experience had taught him. And this psalm is the fulfillment of that vow.

"I was a man," he says somewhat more poetically than I am putting it, "who believed that nothing bad could ever happen to me. God had always been on my side, protecting me from misfortune. I used to say in my days of security, I shall never be disturbed; the Lord has ringed me about with mountains of strength. And then one day, God turned away from me, and I was terrified." We are never told just what happened to him, whether it was bereavement or illness or business failure, or a blot upon his reputation—but something destroyed the illusion he had been living with all his life, the illusion that nothing bad could ever happen to *him*. And the author then goes through a very difficult time, when the whole world seems pointless and chaotic; when God seems to be no help and life doesn't seem worth living. Then, from this low point of despair, he comes to a new realization: that he can go on believing in God and affirming and accepting this world, *despite* what had happened to him; that it's really the same world that he thought was so wonderful a few days earlier. And if he made the mistake of overestimating its perfection before, because tragedies had always happened to someone else, and not to him, he wasn't going to make the mistake now of underestimating its goodness. *Ba'erev yalin bechi, v'laboker rinah,* "Weeping may tarry for the night, but joy comes in the morning." God's displeasure may be for a moment, but His favor lasts a lifetime. That is to say, there are so many good things, and so many good days ahead, that we are making the day of sorrow disproportionately large when we let it outweigh all those days of joy.

By now the author of the psalm has replaced his simple, almost childish faith, which was based on the impossible assumption that nothing sad would ever happen to him, with a much more mature and realistic faith. He has gone through the same process that Aaron went through, and he has discovered something about himself that he couldn't possibly have known before the disaster: that he has the strength to go on believing in God even if God isn't always blessing him. If God is real, God doesn't become less real because misfortune happens to me instead of to somebody else! And so at the end of the psalm, having attained this insight, he says: *L'maan y'zamercha kavod v'lo yidom, Adonai Elohai l'olam odekha,* "Let my soul *continually* sing Thy praise, and not be silent; O Lord my God, I will give thanks unto Thee at all times."

The path the author of that psalm traveled, from his sickbed to the Temple where he proclaimed his psalm of thanksgiving, the path that Aaron the High Priest traveled the day the strange fire caused the death of his two sons, is a path down which a great many people have traveled since. All have sought the answer to the question: Can I go on believing in God and serving Him even if His world doesn't always conform to my wishes? And, it seems to me, one of the purposes of religion is to prepare people for the time when they will be asking that question, and to try to prepare them to answer it.

Some weeks ago, a man at a Bar Mitzvah reception identified himself to me as belonging to an orthodox *shul* in a nearby community, and told me of something very sad that had happened in his family. And then he went on to say, "Rabbi, I go to *shul* every week. I'm there at nine in the morning, and I don't leave till the end. I never miss a *Shabbos*. My next door neighbor never goes, not even on Yom Kippur. And if something like this could happen to me, and not to him, tell me, what have I been going to *shul* for?"

I said to him, "I don't know what you've been going to *shul* for. If you've been going so that God would owe you something, so that your family would never know sickness and your business would prosper, then you've been going for the wrong reasons. We'd like to be able to guarantee that, but we can't; no religion can. I would hope that you've been going to *shul* for the faith and the strength to be able to survive and overcome a tragedy like this, so that if it happens to you, you don't go to pieces and give up on the whole world because of it. We can't guarantee that nothing sorrowful will happen to you; all we can try to do is to give you a few beginning lessons in how to cope with it if it happens."

But, of course, you can't prove to anyone, intellectually, philosophically, that tragedy and misfortune shouldn't undermine his faith. There are only two ways he can be brought to that conclusion. One is the hard way, to undergo that sort of experience, and then look deep into himself to see if he still has the capacity to believe. And the other is to be confronted with examples of people who have been hurt, but have gone on believing, and to be moved by their example, saying to himself, "If they can do it, I guess it *can* be done."

Last week I attended a tribute to the memory of the late Rabbi Milton Steinberg, on the occasion of his fifteenth *yahrzeit*. And one of the speakers recalled an incident that happened when Steinberg's book *Basic Judaism* was published in 1947. One prominent critic, a Jewish agnostic, attacked the book, asking how its author could go on believing in God after what had happened in the concentration camps and after what we had learned about the world in the Second World War. And Steinberg replied, "Would I be better off if I stopped believing in

God because of that? Will the world be a better place if I stopped believing? Will I honor those six million dead if I give up my faith because they died believing in it? Where else will I be able to turn to find the strength and the moral determination to go on fighting evil and alleviating sorrow, if I give up my belief in God? Before I learned about the camps, I knew there was a lot of evil in the world, but I believed that there was a God behind this world, nonetheless. Now that I've learned just how deep the roots of that evil are, how pervasive that misery is, I need an even stronger faith than ever before."

That, perhaps, has been one of Judaism's greatest contributions to the world of the spirit. The Jews of an earlier age gave the world the Bible and the idea of believing in one God. But the Jews of medieval and modern times, the Jews of Spain and Poland and Russia, the Jews who rose from the ashes of Hitler's Europe to rebuild Israel and gather in the homeless, they deepened and redefined that belief. They gave the world a lesson in man's capacity to go on believing despite tragedies and misfortune.

Anyone who has read even one page in Jewish history knows that the purpose of our religion isn't to guarantee you protection against tragedy, but to teach you how to live with tragedy, and not lose faith. Those generations of Jews gave the world an example of man's ability to save himself from meanness and pettiness of spirit by not letting persecution and suffering undermine or embitter the grandeur of their faith.

Some people are permanently embittered by tragedy. They never forgive the world for not having treated them better. And there's no way of reasoning with them to change their position. Once they've lost their innocent faith that God will never let anything bad happen to them, they have nothing with which to replace it.

But then, there are people who can turn an ordeal into an occasion for refining and deepening their faith. There are people like Aaron, who was able to return to his duties as High Priest; people like the author of the 30th Psalm, who chose to devote the rest of his life to trying to teach people what he had learned from hard experience—that even if sorrow lingers for a night, joy comes in the morning. Our childish faith is then replaced by a more mature and realistic one, by a belief in God that doesn't depend on God's reciprocating and doing us favors. Such are the men who, after reading the 30th Psalm, rise to recite the Mourners' Kaddish, to proclaim before the congregation that "despite the fact that something sad has happened to me, I'm still able to come to *shul* and praise the name of God, and affirm the goodness of the world He created."

If I were compiling an anthology of great quotations from the Bible, on one of the pages I'd leave a blank space—for Aaron's silence which we read about today. That silence, that moment's pause, during which the God of childhood and naiveté was being replaced by a God of mature understanding, that silence that was followed by a new determination to continue serving this God whom, for the first time, he understood, is one of the most eloquent comments ever made on the subject of faith and suffering. What Aaron didn't say that day, the words that tragedy couldn't force him to utter, the example he portrayed for all Israel—of a man who could go on believing despite the fact that the world's evil had touched him personally—was more eloquent than a thousand words.

28

Ancient Temper/ Modern Tantrum

Rabbi Maurice Lamm

"EVERYTHING NAILED DOWN is coming loose." That is the way Marc Connelly, a popular playwright, described the crisis of contemporary society. The philosopher, Alfred North Whitehead, generalized to the same effect: "Every great age is unstable." The inevitable conclusion that begs to be drawn is that ours must be the greatest age of all, because surely it is the most unstable. An historian of note sharpens the fact of the crisis when he said, "More change has taken place in the last two years than in the previous 20"; and now in the moon age we might sardonically add: "in the last two months more than the last two millennium." There is no doubt that the furious pace of change has made itself abundantly evident in the transformed social values and the structure of American society and of the Jewish community, as well.

In the American society of the moon age, roles and goals are changing in a frenzy of movement. Students are not content to study; they want to change society.

Selected from *Best Jewish Sermons 5729-5730*.

Policemen no longer are merely protectors of the peace; they also must be social workers. Parents are no longer primarily guardians and guides for moral living; they must be participants in the young revolution, if they are to be considered "with it" and not themselves be rebelled against. Clergymen have learned that, like it or not, they must abandon their once hallowed ivory towers and descend to the street to practice their theology. Writers who traditionally reflected the agonies and beauties of man's soul, now reflect only his bedroom so that readers of popular fiction today have become the classic peeping toms of the country. All in all, the city, historically the cradle of civilization, has now become a hotbed of barbarism. In the city, technology has taken the place of theology. The computer today is an object of faith and provides the certitude that men once sought only from God and through religion. The old morality is abandoned, and in its place is a new morality which is not new and hardly morality.

At the same time, perhaps even as a vanguard, Jewish values have slid mercurially up and down the old scale. College education has become more important than religious commitment. Stop and think: if American Jewry were given the choice of one or the other, college education or religious morality, as thankfully it need not be given, might not the consequences be disastrous? Jewish morality is easily being traded for the great American way, whatever that is, so that the American dream might well become the Jewish nightmare. The precious and uniquely Jewish God is hardly recognizable on many major campuses and there is nothing particularly Jewish of a host of our Jewish students and faculty but their Jewish names. In terms of Jewish values, our youngsters indeed are growing up absurd. Inspiration today comes from neither the synagogue nor the religious school. It comes unfailingly from the tension, the courage, the individualism and idealism of protest. Great social welfare movements are magnificent and very valuable as a major *part* of life. Today they have become the total replacement for all religious idealism. The Peace Corps is marvelous, but it has become a substitute for the Prophets. Social service is magnificent. It is something that Judaism has always proclaimed. But it has become the *alpha* and *omega* of the religious personality. In the words of one astute observer, our people have become "social welfare giants and Judaic pygmies." *Shma Yisroel* bids fair to be replaced by "We shall overcome." Indeed, if matters continue this way for the Jewish community, the future may bring the sad refrain, may God forbid it, of "We *are* overcome."

In today's frame of reference, Judaism threatens to become obsolescent. In the face of cataclysmic events, Jews and Judaism remain largely passive. *Mirable dictu!* Whereas for centuries *faith* transformed *people* and interpreted historical *events*, today *events* transform *people*, while *faith* stands by as a spectator aghast.

Now the Jewish community has faced cataclysm before: philosophies have changed, societies have been turned upside down, and peoples have been chased and sometimes decimated. We have lived through many a revolution. In fact we have started some ourselves. We were threatened in every century by the possibility of being overcome by alien philosophies or fads.

But from Abraham to Elijah to Mattathias we were able to reject that which was abominable. We survived because we were able to say "No!" We were the ancient "nay-sayers" of civilization. We were as incredible in our "nays" as we were brilliant in our "yeas." The clue to our survival was that we were able to rebel against the major trends of the day. We were able to utter the "No" to that which we, as a minority, felt to be reprehensible.

No expresses thought, conviction. Yes, submissiveness.

No indicates rebellion, striking out against prefads. Yes means going along, adjusting.

No, in good conscience, means doing it yourself, far from the madding crowd.

Yes requires no great strength or courage. No is a symbol of great courage.

Yes is a nodding of the head. No is a flexing of muscles.

The two greatest documents of American society have rejected as forcibly as they have espoused. The Ten Commandments demand that there be NO other gods before you; that His name NOT be taken in vain; that man shall NOT murder; and NOT commit adultery; and NOT bear false witness; and that he shall NOT covet. The Bill of Rights of the Constitution has almost every article framed in the negative; it declares that NO law be passed to establish a religion; that NO rights of man be violated; that excessive bail shall NOT be required; that man shall be able to DISSENT, REPUDIATE, PROTEST. . . .

In a sharp insight into the power of the No, the Raisher Rav interprets the words of Kohelet: *Umosar haadam min habehemah ayin,* which is usually translated to read "Man is but little above the beast," but literally reads that "Man is above the beast in *ayin,*" which means "Nothing." Is he then above the beast in nothing? Says the Raisher Rav: Man is above the beast in *ayin,* the ability to say *ayin,* No! The beast says Yes to instinct; man must say No. The beast says Yes to killing, Yes to the satisfaction of every appetite. Man is human precisely to the extent that he can say *ayin,* No, and limit his desires and his baser instincts.

This interpretation accords with ancient philosophers who found many qualities of the essence of man which differentiates him from the beast. There is *homo sapien*, man the thinker; *homo faber*, man the toolmaker; but also *homo negans*, man who can say No and pursue his idealism even though it might militate against his very physical survival and adjustment to his environment. He is distinguished from other animals in that his No is an affirmation of morals, religion, love and truth and integrity even in the face of death itself!

Of course in our day the preachment of this solution is not comforting. You are so right if you are saying to yourselves: "Enough of No!" We are overwhelmed by No. Students say No. Negroes say No. Peaceniks say No. School parents say No. No is thundered by union officials and Black Panthers and university professors and children and government officials and women's rights lobbyists. Whole organizations are committed to "No, No, we won't go." "We are fed up," you must be saying, "with No. Give us some Yes!"

I agree with your feelings. The rebellion of youth and the rebellion of minorities is often purposeless and lawless and almost always arrogant. It is frequently an idealized uprising of spoiled, stubborn children whose demands are vague and who seem intent on only noisemaking: of minorities, some of whom would like to substitute the ease and vitality of rebellion for difficult, slow achievements.

But, whatever the outcome, whatever the motive, whether they are right here or wrong there, whether they are idealistic or merely ornery, they have taught us a profound lesson: *That we must express our conviction, no matter how far out, how different from society's prevailing opinion; that we have power as individuals to do our thing even if that thing is not acceptable to the majority; that we are truly and blissfully free men and that we have every obligation to use that freedom with courage.*

It is precisely here that we have failed as Jews. We have failed in expressing the genuinely Jewish No. Every No has been a secular No and it has been a No to civic tradition and to religious tradition. It is time for Judaism to raise its voice, to express its individualistic attitude. It is time to end our age-old apologetics and meekness, and to do and say what we genuinely feel to be right, if we have to say No a hundred times. For 3,500 years we have been out of step with the world, and we have therefore remained a repository of sanity in a mad, mad world. Abraham smashed idols and Moses defied Pharaoh and Akiba challenged Romans. Nay-saying, a Jewish Nay-saying is part of our tradition, of our character, of our history, of our very Constitution.

One element of modern life that calls desperately for a Jewish No is the post-modern pornography and sex explosion which has by now reached the stomach-turning point. Society today has come upon the "cult of utterness"—literature and film and theater which concerns itself with achieving the absolute and unimaginable limit of man's sexual imagination. It is this "utterness" which, only in the past few years, has come to devalue and depersonalize human sexuality. With utter disregard for the most minimal moral standards it has gone hog wild in presenting the perverse, narcissistic, brutal, and irrational. Who could have believed, only a decade ago, that some of our most liberal writers, such as D. H. Lawrence and Henry Miller, would be repelled by the new and ill-begotten liberalism in morality that, in the words of one great critic, has given pornography a bad name?

Now no one today can quarrel with healthy sexuality which makes of sex a citadel of privacy, a secluded area of life in which there is some kind of inviolate order and repose, which is infused with mystery and sanctity and devotion and sincerity and magnificence. But we must cry No when it is anything but healthy, when it is both a cause and a consequence of a sick, sick world.

True, we are living in an age of wide-scoped, far-reaching, progressive liberal thought. But *Jewish* morality must say that liberalism has a limit, that freedom is not free, that liberalism is not libertinism. We must counter-pose to the modern obsession with sex the Jewish concept of *tzni'ut*. More than two millennia ago Mattathias said No to the games and the violence and the naked-ness of decadent Hellenistic culture. Let us today say No to what has become the decadent American culture.

And let us not delude ourselves by saying that sex has been around for a long time. Historians assure us that we have sunk as low today as we have in any era in history and this should not be taken as merely another fad. What we can learn from history is only a parallel, a dilut-ed parallel, which teaches us the lesson that when soci-ety becomes obsessed with expressing its own sexuality, it begins to eat its own entrails and is ready to crumble.

In an era of Woodstock, when 400,000 youngsters from all over the country gather for rock, pot and pad, our foremost thinkers are impressed by the non-violence and the intelligence of the youngsters. But we have sunk so low that we are willing to accept the fact that more than one quarter of a million youngsters have lived for three days in a totally amoral condition. Our moral stan-dards have been so progressively lowered by each new wave of films and books that we are relieved to learn that our youngsters smoked only marijuana so long as they did not dip into LSD, that they lived in a communi-ty bedroom so long as they did not fight.

We have learned that legal censorship does more

harm than good. But we have become afraid to exercise even moral censorship lest our children be repelled by our old-fashioned morals, and do even worse.

It is time that we did our thing—that we exercised the Jewish No to the avalanche of filth and dirt that threatens to suffocate our beautiful society, even at the expense of sounding outdated.

This destiny is portrayed in the agonizing words of Ezekiel as they are amplified by the Talmudic teachers at the beginning of the common era (Ezekiel, Ch. IX and Tractate Shabbat 55a). Ezekiel has a vision of six men emerging from the gates of the city armed with swords and one other man in a linen robe with a quill and ink-horn. They all stood beside the altar of the Temple. And the Lord tells Ezekiel to send the men through the midst of the city to mark a letter *tav* in *ink* on the fore-heads of all the righteous who are *ne'enachim ve'ne'nakim*, who "sign and cry" for society's abominations, and in blood on the foreheads of the wicked who participate in evil. Said Rav: *Tav* for the righteous stands for *tichye*, "thou shalt live"; for wicked, *tav* stands for *tamut*, "thou shalt die."

But, the Rabbis of the Talmud noted, this was the only time that the Lord repented of a Divine decree to make it more severe. The principle of Justice appeared before God and asked, "Sovereign of the Universe: Wherein are these different from those?" Replied God: "Those are complete-ly righteous while these are completely wicked." "Sovereign of the Universe," cried out Justice, "they had the power to protest but did not." Hence, in the vision of Ezekiel, the Lord changed His decree and *all* men, begin-ning with the "sighers and criers" who served in the very Temple, were to be punished.

Ne'enachim ve'ne'nakim, "sigh and cry" is not enough in an age of abominations! We must protest! We must sound the harsh, unwelcome, Jewish No to that which is abomination. Every one of us carries a *Tav* on his forehead. If we will only "sign and cry" and let it go at that, it must stand for *tamut*, God forbid. If we sound the alarming No and stand for Jewish decency and Jewish religiosity, the *tav* will symbolize *tichye*. Today is Rosh Hashanah. Which will we choose: Life or death?

Let us apply the ancient temper to our modern tantrum, the hallowed No to some of our modern insanities, so that we may survive as persons, as a faith, as a nation.

29

Please Do Not Disturb

Rabbi Arnold A. Lasker

ON BROAD STREET in Newark, there is a church with a large bulletin board on which are painted the words, "Why worry when you can pray?" I recently read of a doctor who handed patients suffering from fear, inferiority, tension and kindred troubles a prescription reading: "Go to church at least once a Sunday for the next three months."

Ever since Joshua Loth Liebman, that brilliant warm hearted rabbi, wrote his famous book, the phrase "Peace of Mind" has been associated with the religious life. In this "Age of Anxiety," many people have seen in religion an antidote to conflict and turmoil. Again and again we are given the assurance that religion will provide us with tranquillity.

There is no question but that religious faith helps one to face the world with equanimity. It is true that we have the assurance of God's protecting care: "He leadeth me beside the still waters. He restoreth my soul." But there is a danger in the "peace of mind" approach—the danger of regarding ease and tranquillity as the goals of life,

Selected from *Best Jewish Sermons 5717-5718*.

with religion simply the means of achieving these goals.

Many people look upon religion as another form of sedation. They feel that by trusting all to God, they can cease thinking, and cease feeling—nothing will disturb them. It is as though they wanted the world to pass them by while they were in the protecting arms of a sheltering God. Several days ago, we read of a woman who wanted to take her vacation by remaining during that period in a hypnotic trance. To hear some people talk of religion one might imagine that it provides just such a trance for those who can no longer take the trials and tribulations of life.

It cannot be denied that such a form of religion has its attractions. Certainly large numbers of people desire to escape from the problems of life. This is what accounts for the phenomenal sale of tranquilizing pills—those tablets that leave one unperturbed by life's harsh realities.

In hotel rooms there is usually a sign that one can hang on the outside door knob to keep out bellhops, chambermaids and visitors. The sign reads "Please Do Not Disturb." Many people wish that they could have such a sign around them all the time. They would like to tell everyone, "please do not disturb me." They would like to ask of life not to disturb them, but to leave them alone in tranquillity.

Abraham, the first Jew, was told that in order to do God's will, he must leave the tranquillity of his home and family and journey to a new unfamiliar land. His was to be no easy life. Ten trials were imposed upon this father of the Jewish people, keeping him from having a constant unworried peace of mind. The most difficult trial was described in the portion of the Torah we read today. After many years of married love with his wife Sarah—a love that was marred by their lack of children—she finally gave birth to Isaac. Now Abraham was called upon to take "his son, his only son, whom he loved, Isaac," and offer him as a sacrifice to God. One can just about imagine Abraham's feelings at the time. He certainly did not feel that loyalty to God was resulting in a life of ease—nor apparently did he expect that it should.

There is another classic story told of Abraham—of how he pitched his tent in a spot where wayfarers of the desert would pass, and how he opened the tent to all sides so that he could see the weary travelers coming and be prepared to help them. He didn't hang a "Please Do Not Disturb" sign outside his tent.

The great prophets—Moses, Elijah, Amos, Jeremiah—gave up lives of ease and calm to accept the burdens imposed by God and to suffer under those burdens.

Karl Marx, in words engraved in stone at the Kremlin, called religion "the opium of the people." Is opium the symbol of religion? Or are tranquilizing drugs at this time to be regarded as the expression of religion's purpose?

Today we have heard the true symbol of the religious life. That symbol is the *Shofar*. The *Shofar's* sound is described by the Zohar—the basic text of Jewish mysticism—as a *kol hitorerut*, "a call of awakening." Maimonides pointed out that the blowing of the *shofar* is more than just the fulfillment of a ritual requirement. Its meaning, in his words, is *uru yeshenim mishenatkhem, venirdamim hakitzu*. "Awake, ye slumberers, from your sleep, and rouse you from your lethargy."

The *Shofar's* melody is no lullaby. Expressing in the *shevarim* the sighing of those who suffer, and in the *teruah* the weeping of those in distress, with the *tikiah* it serves as a call to action. The *Shofar* does not permit relaxation and calm. It calls us to a vigorous, mature religion—a religion that recognizes life's problems and attempts to cope with them.

The *Shofar* demands of us sensitivity and responsibility—sensitivity to the needs of others—responsibility to do our share to meet these needs. Sensitivity and responsibility—these are basic requirements of what I regard as a mature religion.

Such a way of life can be shared by the high and the low. The biblical Esther, queen of an oriental monarch whose whim was law, could easily have been beheaded for intruding on her royal husband. Yet, sympathetic to the plight of her fellow-Jews, she endangered her life to plead for them, commenting *ve-khaasher avadeti avadeti*, "if I perish, I perish."

Not long ago, many people of humble station evidenced the same kind of spirit. You undoubtedly remember how little Benny Hooper was trapped in a well-hole in Long Island. Volunteer workers finally succeeded in reaching him through an underground tunnel, bringing him to safety. They knew that this tunnel might collapse at any time and trap them all. What led them to risk their own lives to save the boy? The laborer who was credited with making the first contact with the child explained, "All of a sudden I got this funny sensation all through me. It seemed to me that God was saying: 'Sam, you must go and help get the boy out.'" He recognized a need and felt a sense of personal responsibility to do something about it.

Some time ago, right here in Orange, a rat was found gnawing at the foot of an infant in its crib. The slum where the child lived had long been unfit for human habitation, but too many respectable citizens had hung out on their own doors, "Please Do Not Disturb" signs. The *Shofar* calls upon us to be aware of conditions in our community and to feel a sense of civic responsibility to do our share in improving those conditions.

Despite the greatness of America, there is too much poverty, corruption, disease, vice and human suffering here. The problem of juvenile delinquency is not a single problem of bad boys and girls who need to be taught a lesson, but is the product of many different kinds of unfortunate conditions. It would be oversimplifying life to claim that even the most active concern would solve all the problems. But certainly the lack of concern of so many people who hide in their shells makes the situation so much worse and hinders any solution.

Throughout the world, there are hundreds of millions of men, women, and children who are rarely if ever free of the pangs of hunger. Yet our foreign aid program is cut down and is thought of, not in terms of helping fellow human beings but as strategy in the cold war. Isolationism has been dying, but it is not yet dead.

As we must remove the "Do Not Disturb" signs from the doors of our homes, so must we remove them from our country's borders. The *Shofar* calls to each of us to develop a sense of world citizenship.

I once knew a man who had a peculiar affliction of his eyesight. Most of us, while looking straight ahead, can see a considerable area to our right and to our left. This man could see only what was directly in front, as though he were wearing blinders. It was a dangerous condition, because he dared not cross the street without considerable care, lest a car coming straight at him would still be outside his range of vision. Physicians refer to this disorder as "tunnel vision."

Too many of us suffer from moral tunnel vision. We live in our own narrow world, insensitive to the needs of those about us. We are aware only of that which affects us directly, and are oblivious to the rest of the world.

It is understandable that we do not always bear in mind all the problems of the world. Life would, of course, be completely unbearable if we were to feel deeply the suffering of all others. Very likely Moses himself, raised as a prince and living as a shepherd, could never really feel the intensity of affliction that his brethren had to endure as slaves. Complete sensitivity is impossible. We cannot have all the ills of the world coming to our doorstep. But Rosh Hashanah is a time for widening our horizons, for opening our eyes and our hearts.

We can ask ourselves now, for example, how have we felt about the disgraceful situation in Little Rock? Are we distressed by the violence that has taken place, by the hatred that has been displayed, and by the injustice done to those children of darker skin? Little Rock is but a symbol, a tragic symbol, of the much deeper question of how Americans of all backgrounds are to live together in harmony and mutual respect. Are we hurt when we hear the words "dirty nigger" as we would be hurt to hear the words "dirty Jew?" Or, are we in favor of civil rights for Negroes only as long as they don't move too near to us?

You may remember Laura Hobson's book, *Gentleman's Agreement*, in which a reporter, Phil Green, made believe he was a Jew to get background material for a series he was writing on anti-Semitism. In this way, he found out the real impact of Jew-hatred. How many of us could, even in our imagination, experience the even sharper discrimination, contempt, and exclusion—let alone hatred—to which colored people are regularly subjected? Or do we prefer not to be disturbed?

The *Shofar's* strident call must evoke a response on our part—a response to work against bigotry and all its evil consequences.

We Jews have probably the longest experience of

what man's inhumanity to man can mean. We have had to endure expulsion, ghettoization, and pogroms, while so many good people among our neighbors could not be disturbed. During the rule of Hitler, we did see many cases of Christians risking their lives to help Jews, but the world at large was insensitive to Jewish suffering. The late President called a conference of thirty-two nations at Evian to see what homes might be provided throughout the world for Hitler's victims. Words of sympathy flowed, but genuine offers of help were few indeed. Six million Jews died, many of whom could have been saved if the nations of the world had but lessened their immigration restrictions.

The most disturbing thing, though, is that so many Jews are unconcerned about the future of our people. Each year, when it is time for the United Jewish Appeal, it is sickening to see how many Jews just cannot be bothered.

Ten years ago, a new chapter opened in the life of the Jewish People. After nineteen centuries of exile, a new Jewish state was born. No longer would Jewish victims of hatred and persecution have to grovel helplessly. The cold-blooded blockade of Palestinian shores by the British mandatory government was now at an end and a Jewish state was raising the banner of *be-rukhim ha-baim*, of Welcome, at every port for every Jew who wanted to share in the rebirth of the ancestral land. There is a sense of pride and satisfaction in the re-creation of a Jewish land rooted in the memories and traditions of our people.

One would imagine that every Jew would rally around the State of Israel and its needs. One would imagine that material and moral support would be forthcoming in abundance. It is true that American Jewish political and economic efforts have been invaluable to the State of Israel, but the amount of utter indifference we find on the part of so many Jews is appalling—and this at a time when Israel's future is at stake and tens of thousands of homeless Jews are on the move. Now is a time for every Jew to evidence sensitivity to the needs of his people and to develop responsibility for doing his share.

There is an old Yiddish expression: *"S'iz shver tzu zein a Yid"*—"It's hard to be a Jew." This is true not only in the sense that Jews have suffered but that Jewish religion makes heavy demands upon us. Micah said that God requires of us *"only* to do justly, and to love mercy, and to walk humbly with [our] God." But if we are to fulfill these requirements, a lifetime of dedicated effort is called for.

If Judaism imposes such burdens upon us, is its promised comfort a delusion? Do we not say, *bayado afkid ruhi,* "in God's hand I entrust my spirit?" Did not the psalmist call God a "shield and a buckler" and compare Him to a "high tower for the oppressed?" Faith assuredly provides comfort and consolation. It is true that "the Lord is nigh unto all who call upon Him," but God does not treat human beings as irresponsible infants. Man must live up to the challenge imposed upon him when he was created in the image of God.

Naturally, no man is expected to bring about the solution of all problems, since we are all limited in our capabilities. We are told *lo alekha ha-melakhah ligmor*— "It is not up to thee to complete the work." But the recognition of our limitations should not be an excuse for irresponsibility. *Lo atta ben horin le-hibatel mimenah,* "Neither art thou free to desist from it."

I said that the *Shofar* is the symbol of a vigorous, mature religion. It explains also how man achieves the sense of God's protecting care. You may remember that at the conclusion of the blowing of the *Shofar*, we said: *Ashrei ha-am yodei teruah, adonoy be-or panekha ye-halekhun.* "Happy is the people that knoweth the *Shofar* call, in the light of Thy countenance, O Lord, they will walk." If we respond to the challenge of the *Shofar*, we shall know God's presence. If we are with God we can feel that He is with us. For wherever we go, sensitive to the needs of the world, ready to fulfill our responsibilities, our path will be brightened by the light that comes from God.

30

The Restful Soul

Rabbi Moses Lehrman

THE SPIRIT of Chanukah is often missed even by those who apparently observe it. Thus, many of our strict adherents to the ritual kindle the Chanukah lights as prescribed by law. They are careful to light them from left to right; they pronounce the benedictions as commanded; they keep the details and they settle down into restfulness, so far as Chanukah is concerned, till the next time.

Among the detailed rabbinic regulations governing the lighting of the Chanukah lamp, there is a curious warning in the *Shulhan Aruch:*

Kol hatofes ner chanukah b'yado p'omed, lo amar klum. "To hold the Chanukah lamp in one's hand and remain standing is to accomplish nothing."

Certainly, the Rabbis did not envisage any Jew remaining stationary with lamp in hand while performing the *mitzvah*. Much more is implied in the halachic statement than meets the eye. Standing still is a grave violation. Nothing in life ever comes to a standstill. When it does, it is no longer life. The dazzling light of

---

Selected from *Best Jewish Sermons of 5714.*

the sun is in no way stationary. A terrific state of turmoil exists in its core as billions of atoms give up their energy to shower the blessings of God upon our planet. Life at its best is made up of continuous, turbulent, energy producing processes. The universe is in constant motion. This is how God created it.

The title of a recent article on "Words to Live," by Licia Albanese, Metropolitan Opera Star, reads: "Stop and Live." Such a contradiction in terms reflects the trouble in most of us. We stop and expect to live at the same time. Peace of mind in its literal sense is an anomaly and virtually non-existent. Despite all the literature on "Peace of Mind" and "Peace of Soul," the search for such a state of mind is vacuous and often tragic. Oddly enough, Dr. Joshua Liebman, the author of *Peace of Mind*, was the most turbulent, and restless personality one ever met. He was a living dynamo of spirit, possessed of the prophetic leaven, which moved, disturbed and lifted.

One has but to read the contents of his book to discover that the peace of mind he refers to is anything but peaceful. "This book attempts to distill the helpful insights about human nature, that psychology has discovered and the encouraging news from the scientific clinic about man's *infinite capacity to change* and *improve himself*," he says in his preface to the book, "as well as to correlate these latest scientific discoveries with the truest religious insight and goal of the age." There is nothing peaceful about goals in which man changes and improves in accordance with religious insights. Indeed, there is no salvation in a peace that is stagnation.

Men often speak of famous personalities as *having arrived*. Arrival seems to be the goal of success. They overlook completely the basic truth, underlying real success, that the creative soul never arrives. Toscanini in his eighties is still practicing and rehearsing for each performance, and Winston Churchill hasn't arrived as yet. He is still on the road of leadership and service to his people. Cervantes summed this idea up rather well in a brief yet complete statement—"The road is always better than the inn." These words convey a world of meaning. Worthwhile living never ends at some point along the road. It may pause at the inn only to resume its journey along the highways of achievement.

History discloses that most Jews enjoyed complete peace of mind during the pre-Maccabean revolt. Unconcerned with the spiritual decay that was consuming the vitals of Judaism, the restful souls lounged in Greek styled gymnasia and vegetated in public baths. Physically they were not harassed by the Syrians, so why be alarmed. Judas Maccabeus, recognizing the danger of a peace that is no peace, rose in revolt against the stagnating contentment of many of his own people, even as he struck out against the Syrian forces.

There is nothing peaceful about the message of the Chanukah lights. They arouse, stir, disturb and lift. They remind us that each inn along the road of Jewish experience is not a stopping place, but a starting point for some new and higher goal. They call to mind that the story of Jewish creativity and of vital contribution to mankind, through the long and weary centuries, is one of intellectual restlessness and spiritual disturbance. No peacefulness ever accompanied the great hours in Jewish achievement. Survival for the Jew was wrought in the heart of man's most violent storm centers. He never could have made it in the Shangri La of stagnating bliss.

In disappointment, we find that the deluding, sedative-filled ingredients of the standstill's formula has found its way into our religious observances and synagogue ritual.

To many of our people, Jewish ritual has become a

perfunctory, mechanistic business. The prayer book never stirs them. The synagogue never stimulates them and the Chanukah lamp never arouses them. They come three times a year to the House of God or on a *Yahrzeit* for good measure, to go through a stereotyped routine. They stop at the inn only to remain there. Even the *Bar Mitzvah* ceremony has been reduced to an arrival point in Judaism, marking the end of the journey. Against such violations of the spirit of Judaism, the Chanukah lights lift their voices: "To hold the Chanukah Lamp in one's hand is to accomplish nothing."

From time to time we hear of strange expressions pointing to accepted clichés. So many of us find comfort in the idea expressed by the phrase—"Life begins at—". Notwithstanding the TV programs enunciating this philosophy, life begins neither at 80, 60 nor 40. Life begins when it begins and never stops, until it reaches the end of the road, otherwise it is not life. Judaism stresses this unending journey of Jewish life in the eternal truth to which we give expression in our daily prayers: *Ki hem chayenu v'orech yamenu.* "For they are our life and the length of our days." Indeed, the essence of Judaism must fill our full lives, not a portion of it; the full length of our days, not a fraction thereof.

Some time ago, a young man attempting to show good faith in his Jewish intentions promised me that when he would reach the age of forty or forty-five he would attend synagogue services. Somehow, too many are of the impression that one must wait for middle age to begin attending services, until then—peace of soul. So they fall into the well formed mental rut—life begins at forty, oblivious to the unending road of Jewish creative living, and overlooking the one basic fact of life: that in life, at its best, there are neither stops nor arrivals. There are only starting points.

Studying the spiritual dilemma in Israel which manifests itself in uncompromising, irreconcilable and immutable fanaticism on the one side and total irreligion on the other hand, one is bound to view with concern the precarious position of the religious standstill. Here he finds himself in a dynamic land in which everything has changed since the Temple days. The economy of the land is different, his government has changed radically, his home life is not the same and the social structure of his community is new; and yet with respect to religion he remains unchanged and untouched by advancing centuries of progress.

Jacob's characterization of Issachar in his final days on earth is rather uncomplimentary. Comparing his life to a mere animal, he proceeds to explain: "For he saw a resting place that it was good; and the land that it was pleasant; and he bowed his shoulder to bear; and became a servant under task work." Quite an indictment! So it is with man who seeks only restfulness on this earth and is only desirous of harnessing life's pleasantness. He no longer is the master of his destiny. Slavishly, he rests, lounges and stagnates under the burden of ease. For no heavier burden is there than that of doing nothing.

While the ancient City of Pompeii was being excavated, a strange phenomenon presented itself before the archaeologists. Enveloped in a mass of hardened lava there stood erect an ancient Roman soldier as though defying the mad fury of lava rushing from Mount Vesuvius to engulf him. What a tragic symbol of man at peace with himself, when there is no peace; standing at ease while the fury of life's raging torrents are upon him!

31

The First Generation Gap

Rabbi Israel H. Levinthal

IT IS NOT EASY, my friends, for anyone to preach these days. There are so many problems facing us. We are living in a revolutionary age. The whole world is changing before our very eyes, and it is very difficult to find one theme that can serve as a common denominator of all the problems which confront us.

I have nevertheless selected one that I think is important, and I hope, on the other days of the holiday and festival, with God's help, to be able to discuss other significant topics with you. The theme of the sermon this morning what is popularly known as, "The Generation Gap"—the revolt of the young generation against the old.

I take as the text for my sermon the opening verse of Torah reading of Yom Kippur morning. This verse refers to a tragic incident in ancient Jewish life, the sudden and sorrowful death of Nadab and Abihu, sons of Aaron, the high priest (Leviticus, 16:1). The Bible tells the story of this affair in just two sentences; but the Rabbis of old wanted to know something more about what happened.

Selected from *Best Jewish Sermons of 5729-5730*.

All that the Bible says is that these two young priests brought an *aish zarah*, a strange fire, on the altar of the sanctuary, and that a fire emanating from God consumed them (Idem. 10:1,2).

The Rabbis were troubled by this incident. After all, these were not two ordinary young men. They were children from the finest family in ancient Jewish life—the sons of Aaron, the high priest. They were nephews of Moses, the prophet and law-giver, nephews of Miriam, the prophetess. The Rabbis wanted to know the nature of that *aish zarah*, that strange fire that they brought to the altar of the sanctuary.

Now, a number of traditions about this incident came down from ages past. One rabbi tells us as follows: Those entering the sanctuary marched in a procession. *Moshe v'Aharon mehalachin techilah*, the leaders were Moses and Aaron—they went first. *V'Nadab v'Avihu mehalchin achare-hem*. They were followed immediately by these two young priests; and after them came the Israelites. As they marched in that procession, each of these two young men said to the other: *Matai yamutu shney zeken-im halalu*, "When will these two old men die? *v'anu nohagin bisrarah al hatzibur tachtehem*—so that we will take the leadership of the community in their place" (Leviticus Rabbah, 20:7; Tanchuma, Achare Mot, 6). When God heard these words, He became very angry and a fire emanated from Him which consumed them.

My friends, I think you realize instantly how vividly this description applies to what we see before our very eyes today. The young generation is revolting against the old; and, while it does not wish the latter to suffer death, it certainly says to the old, "You just step aside. You have outlived your function, your purpose; let us take the leadership of communal life."

Now, there is really nothing wrong with a desire by

young people to play a leading role in the community. For too long a time we complained of the estranged younger generation. Its members, we observed, had little interest in anything except their own selfish lives. It is therefore good to see them now wanting to be active in solving the world's problems. The tragedy, however, is that they want to do it alone—without the aid of the old.

In speaking of the elderly, we recall from the Jewish tradition that when a man reaches the age of sixty—*ben shishim l'ziknah*, he is regarded as an old man; *ben shivim l'sayvah*—when he is seventy he has the hoary head, he is an aged man (Abot, 5:24). But these young people look upon a man of thirty as a *zaken*, an old man. At thirty, one is already an old fogey, he has outlived his usefulness, and ought to step aside.

As I said, it is good that young people should wish to play a leading part in fashioning life, but for them to seek to do it alone would simply be a calamity. It is true, youth does have many fine qualities and advantages— youth has strength, vigor, enthusiasm. But it must not forget that the old also have excellent gifts; they have the wisdom and the experience of maturity. To build a new world you need both, you need the qualities of youth and the quality of the old. Alone, the young can only destroy, not build.

In the pages of the Talmud, there is a beautiful epigram which says, *binyan yeladim sesirah*—"the building of young people is often just destruction" (Megillah, 31b; Nedarim, 40a), not construction. And it is true! When you ask these young folk, especially those of the New Left, "What is your program for the new world?" they readily admit—"We have no program. All we want to do is destroy the present establishment." That they can do! To destroy, that they can accomplish. But they cannot build a world by themselves.

Now, a second rabbi speaks of another tradition. He tells us: *Shenichnesu lamishkan shesuyeh yayin.* "They entered the sanctuary drunk" (Leviticus Rabbah, 20:6; Tanchuma), in a state of drunkenness. Mind you, they had to perform the sacred task of keeping the flame on the altar burning, but instead they entered the sanctuary absolutely drunk, soused with liquor.

I think you see here, too, a picture of what faces us today: the addiction of many of the young—and, I am sorry to say, of many older people who imitate them, to drugs—their extensive use of pot, heroin, marijuana, LSD. I am not speaking merely of the dangers of these drugs to their bodies and to their minds; but if you ask these young people "Why this addiction?" they will tell you that the world is filled with so much evil that they do not want to see it any more, they want to escape from it. And these drugs help them to enter "fantasy-land," a sphere of fancy where they see no evil at all.

But, again, my friends, they make a tragic mistake. You cannot rid the world of its evils and you cannot build a new world by trying to escape from it into a land of fantasy. If you want to purge the world of evil, you must plunge into the affairs of the world and work hand in hand with the old to eradicate the plagues that beset it. Simply escaping into "fantasy-land" will never achieve it.

Alas, many of these addicts are not just hippies and yippies, but students coming from fine homes, on the campuses of our leading universities. And unfortunately, too, it must be admitted that a large portion of these smokers of pot are our children—Jewish children. A recent study by a sociologist in California points out that from 30% to 40% of these drug addicts are Jewish young men and Jewish young women. This is a problem that ought to concern us directly.

A third rabbi invokes still another tradition. He tells us that the *aish zarah*, the strange fire, that they brought to the altar was this: *Shenichnesu mechosre begadim.* "They entered the sanctuary absolutely naked" (Ibid.). They cast off not only their sacred vestments, but also their undergarments, and they stood in the sanctuary in their nudity, flaunting their nakedness and flaunting their sexual organs, as if to say, "This is the new wave of life."

My friends, I think that this rabbi could have lived in our own day. He gives us an apt portrayal of what our very eyes behold—the all-important role that sex plays in the life of many of our youth.

Now, I don't have to tell you that Judaism, in contrast to classic Christianity, has a very wholesome attitude toward sex. In our Talmud, we have many pages in the tractates dealing with the problem of sex. Our sages recognized that sex is a very important phase of life; but they also recognized that it is not the only important facet.

The tragedy today is that these young people and, I may add, also many older people who try to be young in this respect, overglorify sex, as if it is the sole significant thing in life, so that today, with very rare exception, no novel can hope to be on the Best-Seller list unless virtually every chapter has a description of a sex orgy. In the motion pictures, no film will be popular unless the beginning, the middle and the end vividly present sexual debauchery. And we have reached the point when on the stage in legitimate theater—you see nude characters—*mechosre begadim*—utterly without garments, flaunting their nakedness. As one writer aptly noted recently, the current decade will go down not as the decade of the sixties but as the decade of the *sexties*.

Men and women, as I said, we do not minimize the

role of sex. What we object to is the deification of sex, its becoming a new religion, its worship as the paramount aspect of life.

And lastly, a fourth rabbi summarizes it for us. He tells us that in the sanctuary there were two bins with coal. One was an ordinary bin with coal—*mibet hakirayim*, to be used to feed the stove, the furnace, when heat was needed in the sanctuary. The other was a bin which was sanctified, and whose coal too was sanctified. It was only the sanctified coal which could be used to feed the flames on the holy altar. But what these two young priests, *Nadab* and *Abihu*, did was to take the ordinary coal from the ordinary bin and try to feed the sacred flame with it. That was the *aish zarah*, the strange fire—and they were consumed.

My friends, here in substance is the tragedy that we witness. We have fed the sacred flame on the altar of life with ordinary coals—the vulgarities current in the new day—instead of feeding the flame of life with the sanctified coals, the holy ideals that have come down to us from the ancient past. And if you were to ask me, "What is the function of Rosh Hashanah and Yom Kippur?" I would put it in just these few words: It is an appeal to us, an appeal to all mankind. Cease feeding the flame of the altar of life with uncouthness, coarseness and vulgarity, and begin feeding that holy flame with the sacred ideals of true religion, ethical religion, the ideals of the prophets and sages and saints of old. If we shall do that, then we shall at least have the hope of being able to build a world rid of evil and to build a life that will not be a curse but a blessedness to all mankind!

32

The Book of Life

Rabbi Philip Lipis

ON *ROSH HASHANAH*, we pause in the midst of our furious headlong living to meditate on the meaning of our lives.

To many people, life is a puzzle, a mystery. When a shocking tragedy occurs, when a new, strange and baffling situation arises, they say—"Well, that's life for you." By that they mean, "You must learn to take life as it comes. Don't be dismayed or crushed by any happening. Take things in stride. Life is full of the curious, strange, baffling, contradictory, paradoxical and unpredictable. Life is a mystery."

To those of more philosophical mold, life is a ceaseless quest to pierce the mystery. They are forever searching, hunting for data, reexamining their opinions, revising their conclusions. They are always reaching out more and more to the areas of the unknown and trying to bring them into the realm of the known. Yet, though the depth, breadth and height of their grasp and understanding of reality may be great, they too, frequently feel with Ernst Haeckel that they are up against "The Riddle of the

---

Selected from *Best Jewish Sermons of 5713*.

Universe," or with the "Mysterious Universe," of Sir James Jeans.

To Ben Johnson, of Elizabethan drama fame, life is a play. To Shakespeare, "All the World's a Stage" and we actors on it. Thus the dramatists.

To the Nietzsches and the philosophers of force and power, life is a struggle, an endless rivalry for power, for dominance. Do you recall Touhy, the demagogue in Ayn Rand's powerful novel, *Fountainhead*? Remember how he speaks. "All men," he says, "are born to rule or to serve—to be masters or slaves—to dominate or be dominated." And naturally, he chose to be among the rulers, if he could.

In Roger Martin du Gard's widely read novel, *Jean Barois*, the doctor gives expression to this philosophic notion when he says to a patient—"All existence is a struggle. Life is simply winning through." Rivalry, in this view, is the method of life, and mastery is the prize which goes to the victor.

To the pessimist, life is a joke, a farce, or as Alexander Pope suggests in his *Essay on Man*—a cruel jest.

Long before Omar Khayyam gave expression to his philosophy of futility, Koheleth was already saying: "Vanity of Vanities, all is vanity and chasing after wind. . . . What was, will be. . . . What happened, will recur; for there is nothing new under the sun. For grievous unto me is the deed that is done under the sun, for all is vanity and chasing after wind."

Schopenhauer, the philosopher of modern pessimism, writes in the same vein. "Our happiness is chimerical. Only pain is real." Elsewhere he says—"As the years increase, things look smaller, one and all, and life which had so firm and stable a base in the days of our youth, now seems nothing but a rapid flight of moments, every one of them illusory. We have come to see that the whole world is vanity."

Well, what do you make of these conflicting views of life that have been reaching out for the hearts and minds of people for centuries? Do you agree with the agnostic who says "Life is a mystery," or with the dramatists that it is a play, or with the philosophers of brutality that it is a struggle for power, or with the pessimists that it is a cosmic joke?

What you believe is evident not so much in what you say, not in the phrase you use, nor even in the beliefs you affirm with your lips. What you believe is manifest by your attitudes and behavior patterns. Rightly has it been said, "I can't hear what you are saying because what you are doing speaks in tones much louder than your words."

For many, life evidently is a stage and they are playing a part and they must always have the central role. How they go about in their posturing, the posing, panting for applause. The all-important thing in their life is "Do people like what I say or do?" For they are out to please even when it leads them into a pleasing absence of character. They dress, fix their homes, carry on conversation always with an ear cocked for audience reaction. The motivating factor in all their thinking and doing is "What will people say," and they are ready to sell their very souls to the mindless and soulless opinions of the vulgar mass.

Of course, there is such a thing as the decent respect for the opinions of mankind. It was Lincoln who wisely said, "It is good for a man to love the place where he lives. It is better that he live in such a way that the place loves him" Coupled with that saying must go the observation of Judah HaNasi, "Which is the way that a man shall choose for himself in life? One that is pleasing to God and pleasing to his fellow man." It must be pleasing to God first. Man must not seek to please man by losing his character, his dignity, his individuality, his integrity.

How many are there that make themselves slaves to the tastes and opinions of the marketplace. They think and act so that they will be popular. And how they thirst for the glory of being called a "good fellow," a "regular guy," at all costs.

Emerson is so wise when he says of such people that the trouble with them is that they tax their ingenuity to win applause, instead of taxing themselves in selfless service through which alone they can win genuine and grateful approbation. "Nothing," he warns, "can bring you peace but yourself. Nothing can bring you peace but the triumph of principles."

For others, life is a great contest for power. Who are the heroes to such people? Whom do they admire? Whose opinions do they quote most readily? Whose lives do they hold up as a model for their young? Why, the men of success! Those who are at the top of the heap—in money, influence, fame and power—how do they get up there? They never ask that. They are not interested, and even if they knew, it wouldn't matter much to them. They are so ready to forget and forgive shameful methods as long as they are successful. For them, dishonesty becomes cleverness and ruthlessness, strength and arrogance, superior wisdom. For to such, life is a struggle and victory belongs to the successful. Honor? Dignity? Truth? Justice? These are the corrupting devices of the weak to enchain the strong.

To those who hold this view, measures that seek to improve the health and welfare of all people in society meet their stubborn, furious and unremitting resistance. They want a society of rugged individualism which is often only another name for a system of society by which the strong and the clever few dominate and oppress the weaker and less clever many. They will resort to name-calling devices to discredit all reasonable steps that seek to place the ethics of social responsibility above the primitive jungle ethics of each man for himself. They will smear attempts to build a society on the principle of "let thy brother live with you." Behind scare words, they seek to intimidate people into a society of live and rule rather than live and help live.

As for the pessimists, if they are right that life is a cosmic joke, then on *Rosh Hashanah* we shouldn't pray for life, but for a speedy death. Indeed, Koheleth says, "I praise the dead who have already died than the living who are still alive." If we agree with this, we wouldn't be here. It is because we believe in life and trust it that we pray for it.

What has Judaism to say in this great debate on the meaning of life? It offers a striking symbol these days with the penetrating message that it brings. Life is not a mystery, nor a play, nor a struggle, nor a farce, but in its fundamental sense, it is a *book* and all of these other elements are secondary themes that run through the book. The controlling fact is that each man is the author of his life's book. "All your deeds are inscribed in the book of which you are the autobiographer," and on *Rosh Hashanah* we are summoned to write a great book—a classic. What are the criteria of a classic?

Surely, appearance is not one of them. A book must never be judged by its cover. Of course, there are shallow and superficial people who are taken in by appearances. They are attracted to tinsel and glitter. Sometimes, they don't even read, but select their book to match their wallpaper. The color scheme must be just right. They are not the ones whose judgment makes a book a classic.

Nor is a great book determined by its format and binding despite the most skillful craftsmanship that may go into it. Clever artistry cannot cover up shoddy and mediocre quality. So, too, a well-plumed woman and a well-groomed man cannot be substitutes for what's inside of them. Charm and social grace are assets as added gifts, but not substitutes for integrity and character. "Grace is deceitful and beauty is vain unless they are the mantles to inner reverence and inner dignity." Nor is a classic determined by the length of the story or the thickness of the volume. Thick, bulky volumes, impressive in size, may have their vogue, but they are soon gone with the wind. The book clubs will beat the drums and make them a best-seller, but in a short time they may fall into oblivion, and they are soon forgotten.

What then is the test of a classic? Does it have great timeless purpose and unity? A book that rambles, that's scattered and chaotic and whose theme runs in a variety of conflicting directions that never come together cannot hold people's attention and will not survive. So it must have great unified purpose.

How many of us have great unified purposes in our life? How many of us are linked with great ideals, great causes that master us and claim our whole-hearted devotion? For this is the road to unity and coherence in our living. For some, it is the synagogue; for others, Zionism, Jewish education, civic betterment, social progress, or some other commanding interest bigger than they are, that will survive after they are gone. Service to these gives meaning to their lives.

This is the season of the year when all kinds of calendars come to our desk. Broadly speaking, there are two kinds. There is the desk calendar. When the day is over, we tear out the sheet and toss it in the basket. At the end of the year the calendar is bare, nothing remains.

The days have gone off in all directions. But then there is another kind of calendar, the diary we keep. We record dates and events and keep them altogether at the end of the year. The diary full is far more precious than the diary empty. Well, a great cause to which we give ourselves pulls together our thoughts and actions and gives them a unity like unto the diary. To what services and to what causes will you inscribe yourselves for the coming year in the volume of life you are writing?

A second criterion for a classic is: does it have universal appeal? A great book is quickly translated into many languages for it generally deals with fundamental human needs and hungers. And so it will have appeal for all kinds of people in all sorts of conditions of life. That's what makes the Bible such a great classic, indeed the greatest of them all. That's why it was translated into over eight hundred tongues and dialects, and remains the best-seller year in and year out. The Japanese and Chinese, the Czech and Croatian, the Italian, Frenchman and American—white and black and brown—free man and slave—sick and well—all find messages in the Holy Book that touch and answer fundamental cravings and yearnings. So a classic reaches all varieties of people.

From this standpoint, what kind of a life story are you writing? Is it one of selfishness or one that touches and is involved in the lives of others? Does your book speak of isolated, ingrown withdrawal into self and immediate family only? Well, that's one way of life. But there is another way. To mingle with people, to work with them, dream and agonize with them and have your life involved in theirs. Which are you doing? Are you in the bleachers, issuing catcalls and jeers all the time, or are you in the arena mingling your toil and sweat, hope and aspirations with those of others?

It sometimes happens that the only time people get to know that someone had lived in the community is when this someone dies. Then an obituary notice appears in the paper. That is the first knowledge that the deceased had been on the earth. Does your life have width?

The third criterion for a classic is sincerity. Nothing repels the reader more than insincerity. If he feels the author is lying, if the theme is sloppy and careless or false and pretends to be one thing when it is something else, the reader will throw the book away. A book must have the ring of sincerity and integrity to win the confidence of readers. The shoddy, the counterfeit, the deceptive repels. The true, the faithful, the earnest, even when mediocre, attracts and holds. A sincere effort may not make a book a classic, but without it it is impossible.

How about the life story you are writing? Do you meet your neighbor with cheap, insincere flatteries and compliments? Do you say one thing and mean another, or are you of one piece, word and heart one?

We pray for life and we ask to be inscribed for life. What is equally important as this grant from God is what we are putting into the volume. "Remember us in such a way that we may inscribe our deeds in the volume of life so that it shall win the favor of the God of Life."

33

Balancing Our Lives

Rabbi Joseph Lookstein

THERE IS ONE PRAYER which, like a refrain, will recur throughout the High Holy Day liturgy. It is the prayer for life. We will address God as "the King who delights in life." We will implore Him to "remember us unto life." We will, of course, hope that He will "inscribe us in the Book of Life." All of our devotions at this season will, in effect, be variations on the general theme of life.

The desire for life cannot possibly be a desire for mere existence. It is true that man is in constant terror of the ultimate, that he is obsessed by a morbid fear of the grave, and that he would at all costs postpone the endless and dreamless sleep of death. He can understand a tormented Job cursing the day on which he was born, and a tortured Jonah crying, "it were better that I were dead than alive." Yet man seeks more than mere existence.

Man is not content to shuttle the threads of being back and forth upon the loom of existence. He would prefer to weave a pattern and to create a design. He is

Selected from *Best Jewish Sermons of 5717-5718*.

not satisfied to respond to God's roll-call of the living with a feeble and anguished "present." He would dare to ask the Almighty for more—"Inscribe us in the Book of Good Life."

The problem that confronts us, then, is what is a good life? When each of us addresses his appeal to God for an inscription in the book of good living, what kind of response does he expect? Simply put, it is the ancient question of Koheleth, "For who knoweth what is good for man in his life. ..."

Perhaps it would be well to approach this problem by stating at the outset what does *not* constitute a good life. For one thing, there is the life of indulgence. In every period of human history, in one formulation or another, it was proposed that the optimum program for living is expressed in the slogan—"Let us eat and drink; for tomorrow we shall die!" This is the hedonistic view of life, and is generally associated with early man in his primitive state. We pride ourselves that civilized man has long ago abandoned that view.

But has he? Are there not many, even in our own day, who in Rousseau's strange phrase, consider the ideal life as "a good bank account, a good cook and a good digestion." That, of course, is a very crude way of putting it. Let us, therefore, transpose it into a more recognizable idiom.

When we speak of a high standard of living, what do we mean? To some it is a chicken in every pot and a car in every garage. To others it is a fat envelope, with substantial take-home pay. To many it is a television in every room, well stocked deep-freezers, and homes with wall-to-wall carpeting. To all of us, it is high employment, a reasonable cost of living index, and a wide variety of consumer goods.

Let us reflect a moment. Those two words, *consumer*

goods, seem to be a subtle intimation of what the ideal of our day is. What is good? Whatever can be consumed. The quest and the attainment for pleasure, the maximum satisfaction of desires, the abundance of creature comforts, the achievement of social success and economic security—put them all together and they spell out the modern conception of the *good* life.

To be sure, this view of the good life has its consequences. These consequences are discernible when, for example, one studies the problem of delinquency. There was a time when delinquency was associated exclusively with slums and poverty and underprivilege. Today, alas, we have learned that moral corruption, the use of narcotics and the disintegration of personality may be associated with over-indulgence, even as with deprivation. We call them delinquents when they come from the underprivileged. We refer to them as "spoiled" when they hail from the overprivileged. In the one case, need and want are responsible; in the other, overabundance and boredom are responsible.

At the opposite pole of indulgence stands denial. A life of denial, or in its philosophic designation, a life of asceticism, is also hardly a good life. Once an entire religious philosophy was founded on the notion that the ideal life is one of denial, of repression and of abstention. Life is sin and lust and evil. To be good, therefore, one must flee from life, seclude himself in the wilderness, isolate himself in a monastery, hide in a nunnery.

Judaism not only dissented from such a view; it considered it sinful. The Nazarite who took the vow of abstinence and mortification was considered a sinner— "for he sinned against a soul." And the Talmud explains that the sin consisted in that he imposed affliction upon himself through abstention.

Judaism takes the reverse view. It not only sings with

the poet that "life is real, life is earnest, and the grave is not its goal," but it adds—life is beauty, life is joy, life is holy. The Jew is bidden to partake of food, of drink, of love, of pleasure. Even for those foods which are forbidden, our sages provided permissible substitutes. "Eat your bread in joy and drink your wine with good cheer." There is an obligation to enjoy life.

When others said that it was better to marry than to burn, the Jew countered with the exhortation to "enjoy life with a wife whom thou lovest." We repudiated the morbid and the melancholy and denied the crown of saintliness to those who escaped from life or sealed themselves off hermetically from society. Even God cannot reside in an atmosphere of gloom.

This leads us to the first criterion of the good life. Not escape from life nor absorption in it are the means by which ideal living may be achieved. Not indulgence nor denial are the keys to real fulfillment. The magic word is balance. Balance is to life what symmetry is to art, what rhythm is to the dance, what harmony is to music. Without balance one may reel through life like a drunkard, stumble through it like a weakling or flee from it like a coward. Without balance, life is lopsided and he who lives it is devoid of poise and grace.

One arrives at this conclusion out of a realization that life is not monolithic but variegated, not uniform but diverse, not consistent but paradoxical. Within the span of a single lifetime, how varied are the moods, how incongruous the experiences. Wealth and poverty come on the heels of each other. Failure and success appear cyclically. Birth and death arrive often simultaneously. Tragedy and triumph frequently intermingle. The stockmarket of life is never steady. It is nervous and fluctuating. It is sometimes "bearish" and sometimes "bullish" and often both at the same time.

From fibers of pain and hope
and trouble
And toil and happiness—one
by one—
Twisted together, or single
or double,
The varying thread of our
life is spun.

If this be life, then the good life consists of blending all these contrasting colors, shades and moods into a medley. He who balances the good against the evil, the hope against the despair, the laughter against the tears, the dreams against the disappointments, and makes the transition from mood to alternate mood—he who does this bravely and ungrudgingly lives the good life.

History abounds in glorious examples of such living. The once rich and happy but then stricken and suffering Job could rebuke his complaining wife and say, "Shall we take the good from the hand of God, but not take the evil." (Job 2:10). The triumph of Job consisted in his capacity to maintain a balanced life. He proved his ability to pass from wealth to poverty and back to wealth; to proceed from health to crippling illness and back to health; from joy to misery and back to joy. His was a good life.

"Give me neither poverty nor riches . . ." prayed the author of Proverbs, "lest I be full and say, who is the Lord, or lest I be poor and steal and profane the name of my God." Is it hard to recognize personalities all about us who might be guilty of similar sentiments? Prosperity softens and spoils them, adversity embitters and crushes them, and the transition from one to the other engenders either greed or gluttony or frustration.

The biblical portion for this Holy Day provides an interesting example of our thought. Hagar is the charac-

ter in mind. According to tradition, she was the daughter of a king or chieftain. Reduced circumstances compelled her to take a job as Sarah's handmaiden. How she
must have chafed under that ordeal. Then, in accordance with the practice of the day, she became Abraham's concubine. She bore him a son. From princess to
maidservant to expectant mother was the saga of her
brief life. How did she take this change of fortune?
"And when she saw that she had conceived," the Bible
recounts "her mistress was despised in her eyes."

Here was a lady who apparently could not make a
graceful transition from adversity to prosperity. Read
what follows. She fled from Abraham's home, she
returned, she gave birth to the child, she fled once again
and wandered aimlessly in the wilderness. And then,
"when the water was gone from her pitcher, she cast
away the child under one of the shrubs . . . and sat herself down . . . and wept." So, as long as there was water in
the pitcher, everything was fine and dandy. When there
was no more, then came bitterness, tears and despair.

How many of us can recognize counterparts of such
behavior. Business is good, profits are high, inventory is
low—in a word, there is water in the pitcher—so we go
merrily along on the highway of prosperity, confident
that this state of affairs will continue indefinitely. Then
something happens. Investments decline, profits dimin-
ish, prosperity vanishes—the water is gone from the
pitcher. Like Hagar, we no longer find joy in our home,
comfort in a trusting wife, delight in a child that needs
our love and interest in a society of which we are a part.
We retreat into ourselves, lost in the wilderness of our
own confusion, and weep. If our depression is not too
deep, we may be directed to the psychiatrist's couch in
the hope of finding relief and understanding for our
frustration and bewilderment. Actually, however, our

trouble originates in our incapacity to lead a balanced life, to maintain proper poise and perspective, and to make the transition from stage to stage, from experience to experience, with courage and with grace. Is not this thought confirmed by the most distinctive ritual of this day, the sounding of the *Shofar*? There are three dominant notes that issue forth from the ram's horn. There is the joyous blast of victory; the sharp wail of defeat; and the quivering groan of misery. These, my friends, are symbolic of the moods of life, the conditions of existence. To give a balanced tonal quality to each of these is to achieve a harmony—a harmony which is symbolized by the *Tekiah Gedola*—the ultimate triumph of the good life.

There is another quality that characterizes the good life. It cannot be lived alone. It must be shared. Fundamentally, that is why the indulgent life and the ascetic life can never qualify as being good. The indulgent man thinks of no other. The ascetic man runs away from all others. The one is greedy in the physical sense. The other is selfish in the moral sense.

Our sacred literature reports an imaginary conversation between Noah and Moses. Noah contends that he is greater than Moses because God saw fit to save him from the destruction of the flood, whereas Moses, on the other hand, was forbidden to enter the Promised Land. To which Moses replies: "You have saved yourself, while your generation perished. I died in the wilderness but my generation entered the Promised Land."

It is ever thus. "Only a life lived for others is a life worthwhile," says the immortal Albert Einstein. The good and righteous man conceives his goodness in terms of what he can do for others. So Moses prayed: "Let Moses die and a hundred like him, but let not the finger of a single Jew be hurt."

Is it not remarkable that when we appeal to God to be inscribed in the Book of Good Life, we say: "Inscribe *us* in the Book of Good Life." Not *me* but *us!* This is the glory of Judaism and its mark of supremacy over all other faiths. It never stressed personal salvation. It teaches and strives for social salvation. To recline in a paradise of infinite bliss all alone, while others are denied admission, is to transform such a paradise into hell.

Our tradition teaches us that on this day of judgment the Jew must pray for the well-being of all mankind. Examine our liturgy. "Lord our God, inspire veneration for Thee in all Thy creatures ... may they all become one fellowship to do Thy will with perfect heart." Look further. "Who is like unto Thee, merciful Father, who in Thy compassion rememberest Thy creatures for life,"—not Thy people alone, but *all* Thy creatures. Look still further. "As a shepherd musters his sheep and causes them to pass beneath his staff, so dost Thou pass and record, count and remember every living soul,"—not every *Israelite,* but *every living soul.* We exclude no one from salvation. "The righteous of all people have a share in the world to come"—is the verdict of our sages. We are bidden "to feed the non-Jew, even as we do the Jew." We are admonished that "whosoever saves a single life, it is as though he saved the entire world." The good life can never be self-centered. It must be social-centered.

As one contemplates this thought on this Judgment Day there flashes before his mind's eye the somber vision of what is transpiring this very moment in a sovereign state of the American democracy. What is transpiring there? Is it merely the defiance of the American Constitution? Is it the dignity of the Federal courts that is in jeopardy? Is it law and order that are threatened? Is it violence that is feared?

Something far more basic is involved. Recall the faces in the mob that blocked the way to school for the colored children of Little Rock. They were young faces that we saw in the public press. But they were snarling, sneering and scornful faces, distorted by hate and disfigured by venom. I remember those faces, for I saw them once before. They belonged to Hitler's youth and there was the same savagery written over them as they stood in their bestial brutality over helpless Jews.

In both instances the principle at stake is the same. The good life, which includes housing, employment, education, freedom and equality, cannot be selfishly cornered for one's self. It is good because it is the property and the prerogative of all. "All God's chill'n need wings!"

In all languages of the world, the word "life" is a singular noun. In all languages except Hebrew. In the sacred tongue of our Bible and prophets, life is *chai-im*. It is a plural form and there is no singular for it in the holy tongue. Why? Because a good life cannot possibly be lived in the singular. It must be in the plural.

It should now be apparent that the good life is not achieved by praying for it, but by laboring for it. It is not the gift of God, it is the creation of man. God does not give it—man chooses it.

One of the great principles of Judaism is that man may exercise free choice. At birth he is not stamped, as others would have it, with the stigma of Original Sin. As he emerges into life, he is neither good nor bad. Only the physical conditions of his being are imbedded within his genes, or, as the Talmud puts it, are predetermined for him. His mortal character becomes his own business: "To be or not to be," that is for God to decree; to be good or not to be good, is for man to determine.

"Behold, I have placed before you this day life and

good, death and evil. . . . Do thou choose life?" If this verse means anything at all, it means that God is the Author of life but that man must write the commentary on it. When, therefore, we pray to God to inscribe us in the Book of Life, we are acknowledging God's authorship. When we qualify the request by expecting Him to inscribe us in the Book of Good Life, we are evading a responsibility which is exclusively our own.

Similarly, we may appeal to God for the material conditions of existence: health, strength, abundance. These gifts are His to bestow. What we do with them depends entirely upon us. He may settle us in an Eden of abundance and place at our disposal, "every tree beautiful to behold and good to eat." It is we who fall prey to the wiles of the serpent and surrender to the blandishments of the tempter. He can give us a world of staggering dimension and of endless wealth with room for all in it. It is we who, in our envy and passion, become the Cains who slay their brother. "Behold, I have placed before you this day life and good, death and evil. . . . Do thou choose life?"

Modern man may well ponder this thought. The new psychology and psychiatry may have given him some erroneous notions. Too many of us fallaciously feel that we are now relieved of all responsibility for our action and conduct. Let us be done with blaming every abnormality and every neurotic behavior upon our grandmothers. To be sure there are pernicious influences in the environment that affect us. Of course there are festering cesspools within the soul of man that began in childhood and which, over the years, distorted and polluted his personality. Most of us, however, are mature and normal and all of us can, with effort, rise to our full stature as men and women. Most of us are capable of the right choice. If we do not choose the right and the good, it is primarily due to the fact that we do not choose to choose.

Perhaps then, our prayer on this day ought to be slightly revised: Inscribe us, O God, in the Book of Life. Enable us to provide balance and stability to that life. Permit us to share that life with others. Make us understand that such a life can be our choice.

34

Importance of Knowing Oneself

Rabbi Bernard Mandelbaum

AN ATTITUDE which permeates the atmosphere these days reflects the same mistake which is made again and again in the history of human affairs. People are really very much like the legendary "wise men of Chelm." It is told that the road approaching the city of Chelm had a dangerous precipice. On dark nights, people would misjudge their steps and fall off the cliff. Even during the day vehicles would slip off the steep side of the hill. It was a source of great concern to Chelmites, who sought a solution to the problem. They deliberated for seven days and seven nights until they came up with the idea that the thing to do was to build a hospital at the bottom of the hill.

It might have been more sensible to build a large fence barrier on the top of the hill; it might have made better sense, but it would not have been typical of the way of the Chelmites and, unfortunately, not the way that all men do things. For in all human affairs, we do not spare ourselves and are extremely resourceful in building hospitals, we have boundless energies when it

Selected from *Best Jewish Sermons of 5713*.

comes to rallying to help the underprivileged, we become strong and dependable in eliminating evil and tyranny. But we are weak, unenergetic and terribly unimaginative when it comes to preventing ills, when it comes to preventing conditions which give rise to the underprivileged. We do not seem to be able to create an order of society which will crush unhappiness, evil and tyranny before they have a chance to make their sinister appearance.

And there is a very good psychological reason to explain this weakness in people. For when there is a disease, an evil, or a common enemy that has to be eliminated—when, for example, there was a Hitler on the scene—we have the task of *fighting someone else*. But when we talk about preventing evil, of making it impossible for tyranny and injustice to ever root themselves in human affairs—then we are faced with the task of *fighting ourselves*, of correcting our own shortcomings and setting our own house in order.

Jewish tradition has always insisted that we can only hope to remake the world by first remaking ourselves. And in order to achieve this we must first acquire a new attitude in life. The new attitude that we must acquire for the New Year is expressed in a pithy phrase of the Rabbis of the Talmud: *K'shot atzmha ve-ahar kah k'shot aherim*—"First correct yourself before you get involved correcting others."

Our tradition teaches the importance of this lesson in many ways. We were given *Rosh Hashanah* and *Yom Kippur* for rethinking our past behavior and for rededicating our lives to God's truth. Each one of us rethinks his or her life of the past year. Each one of us rededicates himself to truth and justice, to ways of consideration and kindness. *K'shot atzmha*—correct yourself, look at yourself! Our primary task, our most difficult responsibility, is to correct ourselves.

Indeed a rabbi once asked his disciples why the Bible states that God created *a man* on earth; why didn't the Bible say that God created *man* on earth? And the Rabbi explained that each one of us must serve God and govern his life as if there were only one man in the world. Each one of us has enough of a task of remaking himself. The Bible, the Talmud, our prayers, all stress the power of each individual man to shape the destiny of mankind by living a good life in his own little world.

It is interesting to consider the extremes to which Jewish tradition goes in order to underscore the importance of *k'shot atzmha*, self-criticism and exposing oneself first to self-correction. Even God, as it were, puts Himself in circumstances where He shows men that He, God, is willing to correct Himself. God, too, is willing to check His own ways, to consider the justice and fairness of His decrees before chastising human beings.

We find this attitude reflected in God's relationship to Abraham. On *Rosh Hashanah* we read a portion of the Torah about the life of Abraham, the father of the Jewish People. Abraham discovered the One True God. He recognized His law, had faith in His commandments, even to the point of being ready to sacrifice his beloved son, Isaac, if God should demand it. And yet when this same pious, godfearing Abraham was approached by God's messenger and told that God wanted to destroy the two evil cities, Sodom and Gomorah, Abraham boldly challenged the Almighty with the words "Wilt thou then destroy the righteous with the wicked? What if there are fifty righteous people in the city. Will you destroy them, too? Will the Judge of the earth not exercise justice?" According to the narration in Genesis, God is not at all impatient of Abraham's challenge. Quite the contrary. The Almighty carries on an extended conversation with Abraham in which He proves the justice of His decision.

God permits Himself to be questioned and challenged by man. If it were conceivable that He was wrong, the Almighty was willing to listen to the arguments of Abraham.

Throughout Jewish history—in the days of Moses, the Judges, the Kings and prophets—God declares that He is answerable to man for all that He does.

"Oh My people, what have I done unto thee? And wherever have I weaned thee? Testify against Me." (Micah 6:3).

There even developed a unique familiarity between God and man, a questioning of God's ways, as expressed in many Yiddish folk sayings:

"Only one God and so many enemies."

"Thou hast chosen us from among the nations—why did You have to pick on the Jews?"

It is interesting that all this is part of the attitude which God cultivates in His relationship to man. It is not considered arrogant or presumptuous. For, through this unique relationship between a Jew and God, Judaism presents a dramatic lesson to mankind. If the Almighty is willing to submit His ways to the questioning of men; if God permits man to suggest that He—God—must correct His own ways before He metes out justice to mankind—how much more must we in our relationship with one another, in our approach to the circumstances in our own lives, follow the principle of *k'shot atzmha*. Correct yourself before blaming others, before finding fault with everything that surrounds you.

Much of the unhappiness and frustration in our lives is due to this inability to see ourselves as we are, the inability to correct our own ways, to change our own habits and dispositions. If we but scratch the surface of any area of human relations, the same symptom is to be found. Consider briefly the relationship between parents and children. Raising children raises many problems. But how frequently are major difficulties that parents have with children due to our failure to correct ourselves. Have we been too impatient as parents, have we given enough time, thought, attention and affection to our children? How often are tensions over choice of a mate or a profession due to the failure of parents to evaluate their own prejudices, a failure to follow the principle of *k'shot atzmha*. If this is true of a parent, it is at least equally true of the attitude of children to their homes and folks. How often do children consider parents "old-fashioned," "inconsiderate," or just simply "unintelligent," when it is they who are being *wildly unreasonable*, or selfish or simply immature.

In all these instances we must cultivate the new attitude of *k'shot atzmha*, evaluate your own shortcomings before you blame or try to change others.

In our times, the peace of mind and soul of people is disturbed by discontent with their life's work. Housewives may blame it on difficult children and an unpredictable husband. Workers may blame it on the boss or foreman. Businessmen may blame it on competitors. Professional men may condemn the injustice of a society which is blind to their unusual talents. But how many of us stop and take stock of our own impatience? How many of us are blind to the blessings we have and are simply envious of other pastures which always appear greener?

Correct yourself before you start blaming the whole world. See yourself and life's conditions as they really are, before you permit a greedy eye, an envious ear and an evil imagination to surround you with seemingly insurmountable obstacles and impenetrable darkness.

If this is true in the private lives of little people, it is no less true in the arena of world affairs. The world body consists of cells of individual human beings, with the same human faults that we have. This history of the two world wars of this century can be traced to selfish, self-righteous nations who ignored the principle *k'shot atzmha*, correct yourself. Individual nations played the god—seeking power, authority over others. But we must remember that they played the role of false gods. They wanted unbridled power, unquestioned authority. God, you remember, subjects Himself to criticism, is willing to be brought before the bar of morality and justice.

In our own day, two sets of ideologies—what we now call the East and the West—are vying against each other for the right to rule the world. The greatest blessing of the democratic forces of the West is to be found in the principle of *k'shot atzmha*. We know the meaning of self-criticism, self-correction. The challenge to us in the West is that we don't forget that principle. For here again, Judaism calls to us to learn a lesson from God. Why does God permit man's criticism and objections? Because God knows that His ways are the ways of truth. The Father of justice does justice all the time. Truth can always withstand the challenge of falsehood. As a matter of fact, our tradition tells us that falsehoods and evil were created for a purpose. We can learn from the challenge which they present to us. If the way of life of Western democracy plants the seeds which can blossom into a firmly rooted world order of peace and fellowship, then we can withstand the challenge of any false prophecies that may come from other parts of the world. We must be spiritually secure in our positions so as not to feel the need to suppress human liberties or to indulge in new imperialisms.

There is a charming, but endless children's song that

goes something like this: The bear went over the mountain, and what do you think he saw? He saw another mountain—which he climbed, and what do you think he saw? He saw another mountain. It mirrors a phase of the history of mankind. For we scale the mountain of war and conflict in one period of history only to find ourselves facing similar ominous heights of human tension. We can end the cycle by rising to the heights of the mountain which our father Abraham set as his goal, Mt. Moriah. Moriah, the rabbis suggest, comes from the word, *Horoah, teaching* the truths of God's law. Only when each of us, as individuals, and collectively as a nation, rises to spiritual heights of the new attitude of self-correction, of fashioning order and contentment in our own little world, can we hope to see a happy mankind walking the road of peace, hand in hand, with the light of God's law as their guide. On this Rosh Hashanah we pray for such divine guidance.

35

Our Self-Rediscovery

Rabbi Joseph R. Narot

IN 1913 FRANZ ROSENZWEIG was a young German
Jew in search of faith. The philosophy and the science
of his day did not give him the satisfaction he sought.
They did not answer his questions about man and God.
His Jewishness could not help him because he was far
removed from it. His most admired teacher was a Christian.

This teacher had found his faith and the answers to
the questions Rosenzweig was asking in Christianity.
One day Rosenzweig said to his professor, "What would
you do if all else in life failed you?" To which the in-
structor replied, "I would go to the nearest church, kneel
and try to pray."

Rosenzweig was so stirred by these words, coming as
they did from the lips of a scholar and thinker, that he,
too, decided then and there to become a Christian.
However, he wanted to enter the church, not by way of
the pagan world, but directly, from the religion of his
birth. For that reason he chose, as his last act as a Jew,
to attend synagogue services on the Day of Atonement.

Selected from *Best Jewish Sermons of 5715-5716.*

That Holy Day was to be the extraordinary turning point of his life. In the words of his biographer, "Rosenzweig left the services a changed person. What he thought he could find in the church only, that is, faith that gives one orientation in the world, he found on that day in the synagogue." According to Rosenzweig's personal testimony, "To become a Christian was now no longer necessary, and no longer possible."

Just what this rediscovery on Rosenzweig's part meant for him constitutes a heroic drama. A great part of his reclaimed faith was written in no less a place than the Macedonian trenches where he served in the German army of the First World War. From 1919 to 1922 he conducted an academy of Jewish learning in Frankfort. Then, in 1922, he was stricken with severe paralysis, through which he was to suffer agonizing pain for six long years. The use of his limbs slowly faded, all his nerves were gradually destroyed. Toward the end he could not speak, nor move his head. To communicate with his attendants, he would have them spell out the letters of the alphabet, and when they pronounced a letter which belonged to the words he was trying to convey to them, he would make some feeble gesture. In that pathetic fashion he continued to the last hour of his life at the age of forty-two to think, create and write.

The pertinence of his interesting personality to us at this time of the year is intriguing. Is it the echo of some of the searching we have done or ought to do? Does it remind us that tonight's and tomorrow's visits to the Temple are capable of being for us as well an opportunity for self-rediscovery? Surely the following elements must not escape our attention: the factor that drove Rosenzweig to look for faith acceptable to him in the first place; then the curious but significant step he took when he mistakenly felt the quest was over; finally, the real awakening that came to him on that Yom Kippur day in 1913.

As for the first, we find that the motivation for his struggle with himself is reflected in his writing. He called it "The Star of Redemption." One query concerned him—how was man to redeem himself? How was man to free himself from his fear of death, from his sense of aloneness, from his conflicts, from the evil in and about him? Where, as he asked his Christian teacher, shall man turn when all else fails him?

Of equal significance is the step Rosenzweig took, at the time apparently unrecognized for what it was, toward the finding of the answers to his questions. That step lay in his determination that if, as he thought he decided, he would become a Christian, he would do so directly from his origins as a Jew.

It was then that the atonement day liturgy, rich with ideas suited to his intellectual prowess, gave him final and full awareness that his redemption could be achieved within his origins in Judaism.

Thus, the relatedness of Rosenzweig to us. We, too, are in need of an all-sustaining outlook on life. We, too, would approach every possible solution from the vantage point of our own Jewish sources. For these sources would speak to us as they did to Rosenzweig of our final redemption, of the power that may uphold us when all else seems to abandon us.

Let us look at Rosenzweig again. The fear of death, loneliness and helplessness is a universal fear, but it is clear that some specifically personal problems inclined him to think about that fear to the extent that he did. We may certainly assume that he was seeking something to cling to because of his own feelings. It was therefore his own redemption he sought, not just "man's." We may say this without meaning to judge him critically, but only to point out that with him as with all men it is their personal needs that determine what they look for in life, the urgency with which they look for it, and the philosophy they weave around it. When we examine the possible relationship of this man's life to our own, it is then, not to find ways of imitating him, but to inquire how closely or remotely our personal needs coincide with his.

Well, then what are our needs? Are we in quest of spiritual security? Do these universal, natural and understandable fears of death and aloneness and of being left utterly without hope affect the character of our daily living? Let our first answer be one of admiration for the courage with which human nature is so often endowed. How frequently do we come into the presence of men and women who face agonizing crisis with confidence. They may never have embarked on a life-long search, they may never have developed a clearly defined philosophy. Nevertheless they meet peril with patient hope and calm acceptance.

At the same time, we must be honest with ourselves and fair with Rosenzweig and admit that there is room for added faith in our lives as there was in his and that it would help us as it strengthened him to search for such faith. Who is there among us that could not profit from greater confidence? Sometimes we prove this openly when we cry aloud that we have nothing left to live for. Sometimes our uncertainties drive us to panicky, striving for attainments questionable as well as worthy. And sometimes our problems are marked by our frantic need to run from ourselves and be like those around us.

One of the finest sociological studies of our times is hauntingly entitled, *The Lonely Crowd*. This book examines the changing American character in which individuality is being sacrificed in numerous directions for sameness. "The idea that men are created free and equal is both true and misleading," the text warns. "Men are created different; they lose their social freedom and individual autonomy in seeking to become like other people."

But for us this tendency assumes a special form and raises another problem. Our individual experiences with bigotry and our collective memories of prejudice remind us of the burden that is often borne by a minority group and renders us restless with our fate. Then, frequently, our discontent as Jews becomes confused with our perplexing personal problems as human beings. When that happens, the temptation arises to run from ourselves, to grieve that we are not like those around us, even to skirt at least the outer fringes of Christian religious experience. At that point, it is more difficult than we may think to know whether we are running from Judaism or from ourselves. At this point, too, our being here tonight may loom in our eyes as it did for Rosenzweig, that significant Yom Kippur day, as almost a last vestige of our Jewishness.

And yet it would be wrong for anyone to take for granted that this Holy Day really represents our last loyalty to Judaism, any more than Rosenzweig's entrance into his synagogue proved to be his last act as a Jew. We recall that he went to the services that Day of Atonement because he thought he had decided to become a Christian and because he believed he wanted to enter Christianity directly from Judaism. However, it is altogether possible that all this was more of a rationalization on his part than he sensed. It may well be that he was offering resistance to the idea of conversion and that he longed to end his quest for certainty in Judaism. In other words, he may well have been looking for a reason, other than his expressed or conscious reason, for going to his synagogue.

So it is that for many of us who have been wavering or groping, this Day of Atonement may denote more than we know the longing, not for the end of loyalty to Judaism, but for a deepening of our allegiance to it. We are here not only because we are in search of faith but also because we still feel, however vaguely, that it is here if anywhere, that we should find it. This is where we would like to realize our personal redemption, our strength for living. We are here, therefore, because we need to be here.

What then, and this is the last question of deep interest to us, did Rosenzweig find in the atonement liturgy that made him realize that he not only needed but now wanted to remain a Jew? Evidently, there leaped up at him from the pages of the prayer book the repeated, unbroken and insistent fact that Judaism is not a creed but a faith, that its message is not for one age alone but for all time, and that it speaks not only to the Jew as Jew, but to every man as human being who looks for hope, understanding and direction in life.

Please mark it well: there was no simple, magical formula he found for his life anymore than we may find it for ours. Rosenzweig brought searching thought and intense feeling with him to the synagogue and we must bring them with us too. Without such thought and feeling our prayers are mere words; with them they are indeed a great revelation.

Our prayers tell us, for example, and we need to think about this seriously, that despite the stress of the centuries in other directions, it is not doomed with guilt and sin that we stand before our Creator today, but forgiven and cleansed. Note how many times our prayers will reiterate this conviction tonight and on the morrow. Note how they anticipate spiritually what we have discovered in other ways today, that man cannot endure the weight of his sense of guilt, a sense of guilt that only drives him to further sinfulness.

Our prayers tell us, further, that if God is ready to forgive us for our sins, we must be prepared to forgive those who offend against us. Note, again, how we stress this tenet now and tomorrow. Note how it anticipates spiritually what is being learned in other ways today, that only forgiveness can lead to the restoration of the friend, to the rehabilitation of the wrongdoer. The unforgiving spirit, be it in the individual or society, is another burden which man cannot endure.

Our prayers have told us tonight that it is God who "sets us in life." This we must remember when the physician tells us that he has done all he can do and we still walk in the valley of the shadow. These too are burdens we cannot bear, Judaism teaches, the idea that man can heal without God and the notion that God can heal without man.

Our liturgy will tell us tomorrow, through the re-reading of the words of Isaiah, that fasting is nonsense unless it be another means of rededicating our lives to the clothing of the naked, to the feeding of the hungry, to the loosening of the fetters of wickedness and to letting the oppressed go free. Our liturgy will tell us tomorrow afternoon, through the life of the prophet Jonah that no man may look down on another and regard him as unworthy of God's blessing. Our liturgy will tell us all through the day that while we pray for the Jewish people, we pray not for our people alone but for all men and for the day when, washed of superstition and freed from idolatry, mankind will be as one.

Now we are perhaps better prepared to hear the two words which Rosenzweig used to describe his rediscovered faith: "Redeeming love." Nature and human nature, God and Man, the earth and its inhabitants, all

share in this redeeming love, this forgiveness, this healing, this charitableness, this justice, this universalism of
heart and mind. It was the grasp of these concepts on
his part that dispersed the clouds of his doubts and permitted the star of his redemption to shine through.
Here he found a faith which he felt, defied death and
linked him to eternity.

Tomorrow when the shadow of dusk will begin to
lengthen, when the full-throated note of the shofar will
echo against these walls, and when we depart for our
homes, will we espy the stars of our redemption in the
heavens above? We will if our hearts take hold of the
ideas in our prayers as firmly as our hands take hold of
the printed page. Then this will become more than just
another Day of Atonement in a monotonous, futile
cycle of years. It will be a day of self-rediscovery. It will
be a day in which we shall share in the redeeming love
of our faith. And we shall pray more meaningfully than
ever in the closing words of our concluding service:
"May the Lord bless our going out and our coming in
from this time forth and forever."

36

The Pillar of Salt

Rabbi Ahron Opher

IN THE PLAINS of the Negev, in Southern Israel, near the Dead Sea, there is a human-shaped rock which the desert Bedouins call "Lot's Wife."

The Bible tells us that when Sodom and Gomorrah were consigned to flame and only Lot and his family were permitted to escape, they were cautioned by the angels: "Look not behind thee; neither stop in all the plain." Then a curious incident is related in typical biblical brevity: "His wife looked backwards and became a pillar of salt."

What is the significance of this strange story? What was the nature of the woman's sin and the meaning of her punishment?

Shipwrecked sailors tell of their irresistible urge to keep their eyes fastened upon their sinking vessel as they sit in their life boats. Was this the sort of urge that compelled Lot's wife to look backward to catch a last glimpse of her native city as it was going up in flames? If so, what's wrong with that? Is it a sin to look back at one's past?

The question is what kind of past. What manner of

Selected from *Best Jewish Sermons of 5717-5718.*

town was this that she was looking back upon so long-ingly? What kind of a past was it that she was so at-tached to that she could not tear herself away? It was a city of filth and decay, a community of bestiality and horror—Sodom and Gomorrah. That is what she looked back at with such fascination. It is that which turned her into stone.

This is the lesson of the story and it is applicable to our own lives. The morbid wallowing in the ugly chap-ters of the past, the holding on to unhealthy bygone incidents, has a paralyzing effect upon life.

There are pages in history which may well be torn out of the records, in order to guard the face against their morbid fascination for the diseased minds and cor-rupt souls. A Hitler or a Stalin might never have taken hold of the hearts of multitudes if they and their co-horts were not bred on the demoniac lure of a Nero or a Ghengis Khan or an Ivan the Terrible.

A pious and sensitive medieval chronicler, who had witnessed the monstrous cruelties inflicted upon inno-cent men, women and children by the crusading mobs, stated that he refrained from detailing the atrocities in the record, lest their memory "desecrate the image of God imprinted upon the human soul." Indeed, some events in the past ought not to be looked back upon lest we turn into stone.

This is equally true of the individual as of society. There are dark corners in the lives of each of us which we would do well to tear ourselves away from and to grow out of.

They are, in the first place, the sins of the past, which sometimes have an unshakable hold upon us, so that we can never escape the shame of an incident in our child-hood or adolescence. A failure at school, a moral breach in our youth, an indecent act long ago, may keep one's soul forever captive, paralyzing it into permanent help-lessness and resignation. Many, thus, literally turn into stone. They cannot move out of the rut. They go through life reliving a sordid pattern woven in child-hood. "What chance is there for me with my back-ground," is the plaint of these chained souls. They let the memory of a past sin act like an inner blackmailer, demanding payment over and over.

But we must learn self-forgiveness which alone can turn the mistakes of the past into future wisdom, like mother earth who takes all the dross and decay and fail-ure of yesterday into her bosom and converts them into lifegiving fertilizer for tomorrow's plants.

"Look not behind thee, nor linger in all the plain." Life stretches before us. It is the foreground that holds out hope and promise.

Secondly, there are the pains and fears of the past which may lay their paralyzing hold upon us; the frightening experiences which mark the path of life; the sad and torturous memories of past humiliations and sufferings may have a petrifying effect upon the human soul, blinding us to all else.

If you saw the sad and lonely victims of battle fa-tigue, with their haunted faces, absorbed in the morass of past horrors, you will understand what psychiatrists mean when they refer to the perpetuation of a moment. There are sick and tortured souls, living and reliving frightful moments in their past. They, literally, have turned into stone. For them and many of us who to a lesser degree are crippled by sad or sordid memories the story of Lot is intended.

"Look not behind thee, nor linger in all the plain." We must learn to turn our back upon yesterday's clouds of fear if we are to benefit from tomorrow's sunshine of hope.

In the third place, there are also the hates and the angers of the past, which may pursue us through life, drying up our souls. Frequently, the original reason for our hate is forgotten, or lost its meaning, but the bitterness remains; and we preoccupy ourselves with fanciful rationalizations to justify the baseless prejudices and pet peeves which petrify our minds.

The Hatfields and the McCoys, which have become legend in the blood feuds of the Kentucky hills, are an example of the perpetuation of a hatred whose origin is lost in the distant past but whose potency has never lessened.

I know a woman who for many years suffered from an incurable malady—the hate for one man—and yet she always went out of her way to torture herself with the sight of him. Whatever the origin of her resentment, it absolutely had no present significance yet she persisted in looking backward into some vague and dismal past occurrence which turned her heart into stone.

So many of us are blinded to all that is beautiful in life by some ancient hate, fear or sin which haunts us throughout our life. Like Lot's wife, we cease to be human. We dry up like salt and become petrified, imbedded in the ugliness, fright or pain of the past. "Look not behind thee," for behind thee lies Sodom and Gomorrah; before thee the land of promise.

This, finally, applies also to the loves of the past, from which we must learn to free ourselves as we grow from stage to stage in life. Here is a man in love with a *memory* of a woman whom he knew when they were both adolescent and because of that he has refused life's happiness all these years.

Here is a woman who lost a son in the war and from that moment life ceased to have any meaning and, although she has a husband and other children and many friends, she has no interest in anybody or anything but lives continually with the memory of her dead son.

Who has not seen such bereaved persons walking through life in the valley of the shadow of death? Like a hero in the Arabian Nights who is condemned to carry the body of his dead wife on his back throughout his life.

Life must go on and as we pass from one stage to the next and from childhood to adolescence, from adolescence to manhood, from maturity to old age, we must learn to part from past loves and attachments. Otherwise, like Lot's wife, our hearts would dry up, our souls would close up, we would turn to stone.

"We who refuse to part with our past are idolaters of the old," says Emerson. "The voice of the Almighty sayeth 'Up and onward forever! We cannot stay amid ruins nor can we walk for long with reverted eyes like those monsters who look backward.'"

In the plains of the Negev in Southern Israel in the midst of the wilderness a new civilization is growing. Its planters and builders are Jews who lived through many Sodoms and Gomorrahs. They are a new breed of people—strong, confident and creative. What is most fascinating about them is their refusal to look back upon the past. That is why they are turning desolation into habitation and broken souls into men of valor.

"Look not behind thee, neither linger in all the plain."

37

The Heights of Faith

Rabbi Ely Pilchik

YOM KIPPUR LIFTS US to heights of personal faith.
"*A'Shabbat Shabaton hu lachem*—This shall be a Sabbath
of Sabbaths unto you—An eternal statute—for on this
day shall He grant you atonement to purify you—Before
the Lord shall you be pure," proclaims the Torah. The
Talmud refers to Yom Kippur as "*Yoma*—the day," the
day par excellence! "On Yom Kippur," claims a medieval
sage, "we mortals grab hold of the fringes of the super-
nal holiness above and pull it down to us here below."
Our own prayerbook in our Memorial Service tomorrow
afternoon calls this day, "The Sabbath of the Soul." Yom
Kippur is our most sacred day. Yom Kippur lifts us to
heights of personal faith.

When we ascend the heights of personal faith, what
do we see? We see ourselves. We behold ourselves bound
in a three-fold relationship. Bound to ourselves, bound
to others, bound to God. There is an I and I bond. There
is an I and you bond. And there is an I and Thou bond.

On Yom Kippur we examine this three-fold bond
closely. We read the small print of the life contract. We
try earnestly to understand the nature and the meaning

Selected from *Best Jewish Sermons of 5717-5718.*

of the contractual relationship. For just this purpose of personal title searching has Yom Kippur been commanded us.

The obligations in the first relationship, the I and I, may well be the hardest. Do I know myself? Do I care about myself? Am I at peace with myself? Are I and I in harmony?

When I open the windows of my inner self and allow some rays of insight to light up the corners of my heart, I am not so sure I like I. Here and there are evidence of my skirmishing with I. There be hours, even days, when I find myself at war with I. My reason and my emotions seem in constant conflict. Increase the light and behold much hateful, much lustful, much destructive in me. My outward manner frequently belies my inward feelings. And when it does, and I become aware, I develop a contempt for myself, I begin to hate myself; yes, there are times when I think I would destroy myself.

I read James Gould Cozzens' recent masterpiece of fiction, *By Love Possessed*, powerfully portraying the overwhelming urge of lust in the most respectable of us, and I say, "this is not fiction." It describes me, were I to be perfectly honest. When I think about my attitudes, my prejudices, my perspective on life, I ask myself, is this I? This mixture of selfishness and self-hate? This highly sociable creature so desperately lonesome at the festive social functions? This seeker for truth invariably finding uncertainty? This pursuer of happiness catching up only with dull misery? This self-appointed judge of all things yet no more than a lowly worm of the earth? Is this I? This compound of good and evil? So the Rabbis of the Talmud were right in telling me that within my breast rests the *"Yetzer Hatov*, the inclination for the finer," alongside the raging *"Yetzer ha'ra*, the inclination for the baser." They anticipated Sigmund Freud by 1,800 years in informing me that I am caught between the two poles of pain and pleasure, and that my personality is forged in this crucible of tension. I and I. I fear myself, I suspect myself, I impose guilt on myself, I bear grudges, vengeance, hostilities against myself. I don't seem capable of loving myself, I am afraid to love myself. I is separated from I, I is estranged from I.

Comes Yom Kippur. Yom Kippur literally means the "day of at-one-ment," the day for uniting I with I. On Yom Kippur, as I recall all my grievances against myself, I would insist that I am not so bad. I would forgive myself. I would accept myself. I would strive to like myself. I would give myself a chance to fall in love with myself. This re-linking of I and I we see on the heights of personal faith. Out of the charming mysticism of *Chassidic* lore comes the profoundly simple teaching of Rabbi Zusya: "When I ascend to the gates of the world-to-come they will not ask me: 'Why were you not Moses?' They will ask me, 'Why were you not Zusya?'"

When I have resolved to be myself, I will be prepared to examine the second bond of relationship—I and you—I and my fellow man. I stop to take the temperature of my feelings and the nature of my conduct toward those about me, and I hear the echo of an ancient prophetic thunder: "Why do we deal treacherously brother against brother." Focus the searching Yom Kippur light on the darker recesses of our hearts, and it will uncover the terrifying truth expressed by the great German philosopher Immanuel Kant: "There is something in the misfortune of our best friends which does not displease us."

We bristle with hurt. We hurt our parents. We hurt our children. We hurt our mates. We hurt our friends. We hurt in open and in secret. We hurt in stubbornness or in error. We hurt in the evil meditations of the heart.

We hurt by word of mouth. We hurt by abuse of power. We hurt by disrespect. We hurt by cheating. We hurt by exploiting. We hurt by outdoing. We hurt by doing in. I hurt you and you hurt me, and we hurt others and others hurt us, and our society hurts another, and one nation hurts another, and a whole world suffers and aches and hungers under a fantastic burden of all-destructive armaments because one suspects the other of plotting hurt. The I and you relationship is constantly strained. I am estranged from you; I am separated from you.

My good people, Yom Kippur literally means the "day of at-one-ment," the day for united I and you. Our prayers will not bring it about. Our fasting will not draw I and you together. The Talmud Yoma says very clearly: "Yom Kippur will atone for the sins between man and God; as for the sins between man and man, I and you, Yom Kippur cannot atone for them until a man becomes reconciled with his fellow man." Reconciliation, face to face, hand in hand, personal forgiveness, reconciliation, releasing the flood of love pent up in each one of us for the other. How desperately we want to be loved. How eagerly we want to do for others—scrape away the barnacles of our spirit, and all glisten with a goodness, a fairness, a loving kindness. When the I and I are mature and whole, and the I and you becomes joined and at one, then are all prepared to turn to the third, the ultimate relationship, the bond between I and Thou, man and God.

We have such difficulty in finding God, don't we? We have broken sound barriers and plumbed the depths of the earth and promenaded on the ocean floor; we have split atoms and regimented electrons and harnessed the elemental forces of the sun. We have searched above the earth and below the earth and inside the earth and have not found God. There is no Thou. It's all just one great big complex It. But it is a nothingness.

Neuter "It" neither seeds life, nor conceives life, nor nourishes life. It has no interest in life. Albert Einstein once told me in his backyard in Princeton that all the cosmic forces and laws are oblivious of little man on this insignificant planet. It is outside.

Thou is inside. Thou creates life. Thou sustains life. Thou is, we believe, the Father of life. Thou cares about life. Living man needs a living God, and a living God needs living man. I and Thou are inextricably bound together.

The whole I clasping the hand of the whole you, reflects on fleeting time and realizes that past is gone and future is yet to be. There is but present, and present is real and not illusory because present is infused with eternity, that which always is. I and you cleave to the Eternal *Now* and become part of the Eternal *Thou*. Seek not God—meet Him. He comes as the flash of a brilliant idea in the mind, as a streak of sun on the maple twig. He comes as a flood of light, as a cosmic demand for right. "He is the unity of all that is, the uniformity of all that moves, the rhythm of all things. ... He is the creative flame that transfigures lifeless substance. ... He is the faith by which we overcome the fear of loneliness, of helplessness, of failure, of death. He is the spirit which broods upon the chaos men have wrought, stirring into life the formless beginnings of the new and better world."

Ah, but all this is too poetic, too mystical, too philosophical. The Torah reading for Yom Kippur morning puts it much more simply. I and Thou? "It is not too hard for you nor is it afar off. It is not in heaven that you should say, who shall go up to heaven and bring it to us—neither is it beyond the sea, that you should say, who shall go over the sea and bring it to us—but the word, the word of God is very near unto you, in your mouth and in your heart."

Yes, and I remember from my childhood the little Jewish folksong which sums up the I and Thou relationship—

"*Rebono Shel olom*—Master of the Universe." I will sing Thee a *dudel*:

"I would sing Thee a Thou song—
Du-du-du-du-du—Thou, Thou, Thou, Thou, Thou,
Where can I find Thee and where can I not find Thee.
Wherever I go—Thou. And wherever I stand—Thou
Only Thou, Always Thou, Ever Thou.
If all goes well—Thou. If God forbid, ill—Thou
Thou art now, Thou wert then—
Thou art, Thou wast, Thou wilt be.
Thou didst rule, Thou rules, Thou wilt rule.
In the heavens—Thou. Here on earth—Thou.
Above, Thou. Below, Thou.
Wherever I turn, Wherever I reach out—Thou."

Simple faith, philosophical faith. Biblical faith—I and Thou—personal faith at the summit.

Yom Kippur literally means the "day of at-one-ment," the day of union of I and Thou. The hard shell of inertia around our hearts is cracked by the pliers of prayer and penance—an overwhelming love surges in, the estranged comes home, the separated is united, the lost soul finds its source. A new I emerges. I touching the Eternal Thou, embraces the you. The curtain rises on a mighty drama of togetherness, a symphony of at-one-ment. I and I are one, I and you are one, I and Thou are one, on this Sabbath of Sabbaths, this most sacred of days, this Yom Kippur which lifts us to the heights of personal faith.

38

Purification and Renewal

Rabbi Stanley Rabinowitz

ONE OF THE PROBLEMS of urban society is that of finding a way to rid our communities of accumulated waste. The more highly developed the community, the more challenging the problem, for these impurities pollute the air, corrode the skyline, and contaminate the water.

Some may think this an inappropriate subject for so sacred a day. But that is what Yom Kippur is all about: purification. The original function of Yom Kippur was to cleanse the sanctuary and to rid it, as well as those who worshipped in it, of accumulated defilement.

Though the ancient laws of purity are no longer to be taken literally, we retain the realization that man can still become defiled; the purity of his goals are contaminated and the stream of his life is polluted by the corrosive acids of hypocrisy, sham, self-seeking, the lust for power. To cleanse the sanctuary of man's soul, our fathers practiced a spiritual form of urban renewal. They designated a day for personal renovation when, through prayer and sacrifice, they washed away the impurities

Selected from *Best Jewish Sermons of 5717-5718.*

that desecrated the sacred domicile of man's image.

An ancient ritual of purification is outlined in the Bible. The instruction begins, "And ye shall take a red heifer. ..." The red heifer was to be slaughtered, burned, pulverized, mixed with the dust of the earth, and sprinkled over the impure person who, thereupon, was restored to the state of purity and rendered eligible to enter the sacred precincts of the sanctuary.

To compound the strangeness of the procedure, the Bible suggested that those who prepared the mixture of the dust of the red heifer would, themselves, become defiled in the process of its preparation. A strange and exotic ancient ritual which purified the impure and defiled the pure, and which required that some would sacrifice their fitness in order to produce the means whereby others could recapture their purity.

The formula is recalled annually in the synagogue calendar in the weeks preceding the Passover but is no less appropriate to the sacred season of the Holy days.

In the ritualized rehearsal of this procedure year after year, has it ever occurred that anyone should ponder the plight of those who were called upon to prepare the formula of purification, those who had to contaminate themselves in order that society could maintain the integrity of its purity? Surely they were someone's children, someone's husband, or someone's father. What happened to the people who had to suffer defilement in order to purify other people and who were thus forced to drop out of the mainstream of the camp?

The text is vague, the commentary cryptic, allowing us free reign of insight. Though we have abandoned the biblical rites of purity, there is something significant to be learned from this armchair procedure, for its purpose remains timeless.

Pollution, defilement, contamination are not out-

moded words. More than slums need renewal—we need
the renewal of the soul. More than streams can become
polluted—the social swim is also polluted with hypocrisy and sham. More than air is subject to contamination—the atmosphere of our civilization is contaminated with prejudice, intellectual dishonesty and the strait-
jacketed mind. These pollutants defile democracy, contaminate the land, and render us unfit to enter the sanctuary of our sacred aspirations.

There are those who seek to remove these defilements. Those who seek to prepare the potion of purification come in various shapes and in several colors.
Some have long hair, some have beards, some may be
unwashed. We call them by names which cover a multitude of deviations. Invariably, whatever their label, they
rebel, they reject, they demonstrate, they march, they
sit in, they talk in, they sleep in, they wade in, or they
just happen in. Some drop in, and some drop out. Some
are activists who seek to change society through political means; others, disinterested in politics, take refuge
in the lovely, passive and placid symbolism of the
flower. But whoever they are, they are united by revul-
sion and concern for the impurities of our society. The
two contaminants which they regard as the ugliest defilements of an indecent society are the war in Vietnam
and racial inequality. In varying reactions, they identify
other defilements: a draft law unfair to selective consci-
entious objectors, corruption in Congress, the differen-
tial between the treatment of a Senator Dodd and that
accorded Congressman Powell, the growing federal
octopus and the CIA involvement in student affairs.
The non-political seek to rid society of the contamination of hypocrisy inherent in its conventional attitudes
toward marriage, sex, drugs, and even God. The political activists see the source of contamination residing in

what they call "the establishment," or "the power structure." Those most reviled as responsible for the contagious defilement of duplicity are "the white liberals."

This attitude of the political activists toward the liberals is an indication that we now have a different breed of radical. The new breed, or the new left, differs from the old left of the pre-World War II popular front in several ways.

We Jews are strangers to neither the new left nor the old left, for we have always had an empathy for liberals, more than a casual identity with radicals, and even close association with revolutionaries—an affinity which is the result of both theology, sociology and the pain of experience.

Throughout the years of their dispersion, Jews have seldom had a stake in the status quo and little reason to identify with the establishment. In our history we have been more the victims of the power structure than its beneficiaries. We have never been comfortable when forced to cooperate with those who wield power over others. Our heroes have been those who turned their backs upon luxurious palaces in order to alleviate the pain of the enslaved. Therefore Jews were always an important segment of the liberal left, and are still to be found amongst the new left, far beyond our proportion in the population.

The differences between the new left and the old are important and instructive. The old left included not only Jews, but Jewish organizations. The new left includes Jews, but *no* Jewish organizations. The old leftists were proud of the liberals in their midst; the new regard the liberals as part of the contamination. The old left included Communists and Socialists; the new left is not as much non-Communist as it is anti-anti-Communist. In other words, Communism is irrelevant.

The old left tried to give dignity to labor; the new left is disillusioned with labor. It tries to give dignity to the poor. In fact, the poor is to the new left what labor was to the old left . . . its power base and its mass.

The old left included labor unions; labor and liberal were synonymous. The new left is disenchanted with labor and regards the unions as defiled beyond purification: "Unions have become petrified into lumps of reaction and special privilege, interested only in take-home pay, a bigger piece of pie, and easier working conditions. And in many instances, they are the most stubborn opponents of integration, equal opportunity and open housing. Labor has no interest in the arts and no cultural aspirations higher than the bowling alley, and none of their leaders except for Walter Reuther has entertained a fresh political idea in twenty years." (John Fisher, in *Harpers*, March, 1966.)

The old left rebelled against the corruption of poverty; the new left rebels against the corruption of affluence. The old left rebelled against the power of the upper class; the new left rebels against the vulgarity of the middle class.

We cannot ignore the promptings of the new breed of leftists, for their program is a prescription by which man can remove from himself and his society the defilements of social corruption and communal contamination. Segregation, poverty, exploitation, and war are contaminating evils from which society must be purified lest we remain corrupted beyond salvation. The goals which the new left proclaim are consistent with those of prophetic religion and consonant with the aspirations of all who seek to create a better society.

But recall the price of producing the dust of the red heifer. Those who formulate its prescription run the risk of defiling themselves in the process, and are thereby forced to dwell outside of the majority camp. The ancient insight is brilliant in its perception.

Those who attack the conventional institutions of marriage and sexual patterns in which hypocrisy is the mask for privilege, in the momentum of their derision, may reach a situation in which love is the mask for irresponsibility. Those who ride to the fray to joust with God, in the momentum of their challenge, may end up as cynics to whom everything is permitted.

The political left has stumbled into the pit. The momentum of their opposition to America's tragic involvement in Vietnam has carried them from a position which affirms that there is nothing good in America to a position which proclaims that there is no evil in Hanoi. So intensive is their opposition to the war in Vietnam that it has swept them into supporting all "national liberation movements," including struggles in the Middle East where, to our sorrow, they endorse the Arabs' war against Israel.

In attacking the American brainwash, they have plugged the channels leading to the open mind.

Israel is a test of the open mind. Never in the history of man has any war's beginning been more open and vividly revealed, in depth and width, in color and in black and white. Despite the fact that full publicity attended the massing of Arab armies, and their proclamation for all the world to hear that they intended to destroy Israel and to leave no survivors; despite the fact that the television screen unmasked the Arab threat in all its stark ruthlessness, the leftists, ignoring both fact and reality, were so intent to embrace within "the movement" all peoples of color, that they included even the Arabs. On the premise that the United States is always reactionary and Russia always progressive, they condemned Israel and supported Egypt.

There is tragedy in the new polarization of left and right. For the first time in our history, Jews are identified with the status quo, the establishment, the contented fat cats, rather than with the forces that would improve society. We have become the scapegoats of revolution.

What shall we say to our friends of the left? There is little that we can do to change the minds of those who are so self-brainwashed that they regard Israel as an imperialist power. We must, however, seek to deprive them of future converts; we must deny them an appeal to our sensitive young people. We must abort their attraction to idealistic Jewish youth whose honest idealism and sincere sympathy for the poor and the disinherited may attract them to the good words and the noble phrases mouthed by the new breed of leftist.

We must instruct our young people that Jews have always heard the cry of the oppressed; that it is no accident that Jews have always been identified with liberal movements, as activists and as supporters.

We must inform them that while it is true that too frequently religion has been the opiate of the masses, often a mask for privilege, and even an ally of the upper dominating classes, this has never been true of Judaism.

While it is true that religion has been insensitive at times to the need for social change and too often has opposed efforts to improve the living conditions of the working classes, we must not allow this to be true of Judaism.

In our schools, we must emphasize the moral teachings of our faith; we must make Judaism relevant to contemporary problems; the link between Judaism and social problems must be brought home. Judaism is more than ritual and prayer; it has something to say about charity, about the poor, about the treatment of the laborer, about the pain of old age, about civil rights and racial relations.

When there is legitimate grounds for protest, we must encourage our children to demonstrate. We must expose our young people's groups to the idealism and self-sacrificial commitment of Israel. We must teach them about the kibbutz movement where self-sacrifice is religion.

We must always identify with the persecuted and not with the persecutor. The day we forget to recite the phrase, "We were slaves in the land of Egypt," the day we forget to proclaim, "Thou shalt love thy neighbor as thyself," the day we forget to rephrase the classic question as declaration: "I *am* my brother's keeper," we forfeit the right to survival let alone the sympathy and loyalty of our young.

The time has come when we must isolate and identify Jews who are involved in the business of exploiting the poor, the ignorant and the rejected. Any slum lord is an abomination; if a Jew, he is a contaminating perversion.

Caveat emptor . . . let the buyer beware . . . has never been a tenet of Judaism; Judaism operates on the principle: Let the *seller* beware. The seller must protect the innocent buyer who may be blinded by the stumbling block of ignorance and need. And the day we forget that principle, we forfeit the respect of our young.

Our religion, beginning with Abraham, has been a religion that has smashed the idols of special privilege. Our heroes, beginning with Moses, have been those who have turned their back on the oppressors of any establishment, even when they were reared in it. We must not lose this momentum.

For all we know, the new left, whether they meet in convention or in flower-circle, may serve an important purpose. They are symptoms of our inconsistencies; they remind us of our hypocrisy and lack of integrity. Out of our confrontation with them, we may be forced to examine, if only to defend, our conventional attitudes. Perhaps we will begin to ask penetrating questions about marriage, love, sex, civil rights, and even about God. And by asking those questions or by answering their questions, we may discover some answers which, while they may not convince the rebel, may help us regain the purity of our integrity.

We need to examine our attitudes and our institutions occasionally to make certain that we are not defiled by expediency, that we are not contaminated by self-interest, or tainted by smug complacency. It is good to be so questioned and we owe a debt to those who challenge us.

What emerges from the biblical ritual of the red heifer remains a brilliant insight. The Bible insists that only those who are willing to be excluded and maligned as the price of creating the means of man's purification can help us rid ourselves and our society of the dross of impurities. Even though the new breed of leftists have betrayed us, we must not allow them to bring liberalism into disrepute or to push us over into the arms of the far right. They must not succeed in identifying the Jew with the far right or with those who oppose social improvement.

For the sake of the purity of our integrity, we must remain identified with those who seek to solve the world's problems and not with those who create the problems nor with those who resist their solution.

Someone must assume the responsibility for producing the ashes of the red heifer in order to cleanse man of his impurity. And if in the process those who formulate the means of doing so are forced to drop out of the camp, the Bible offers the invitation of reentry:

"And those who make the dust of the red heifer shall wash their clothes, bath their flesh in water and shall remain unclean until it grows dark. Thereupon they shall return."

39

Repentance from Love

Rabbi Emanuel Rackman

OFTEN HAS IT been said that Christianity stresses the role of fear. One has reason to wonder how the libel originated. Indeed, there are churches that survive by the dread of hell that they inspire in their adherents. However, Jews almost never frighten their children with grim portrayals of the universe's warmer spots. Nor does one ever hear a Rabbi urging religious loyalty on the basis of the promise of heaven, not to mention the fear of Hades.

Particularly with regard to *Teshuvah* (penitence) does our literature stress the return unto God because of a love impulse. The penitence we prize is the penitence *mai-Ahavah*—the penitence that is born of the love of God and His law. If one returns unto God because one fears punishment, one's return is hardly significant. Soldiers who suddenly become religious because they are afraid of death, or men and women who suddenly make vows because they sense danger—the danger of surgery or the danger of a stormy flight—may not be ridiculed. But their penitence hardly makes us regard them as saints.

Selected from *Best Jewish Sermons of 5713.*

And this will help us to understand one of the most difficult passages of the Bible which is often read on Shabbath Shuvah. We read that God spoke unto Moses, saying:

"Moses, you are about to die. Alas, however, that after your death the people of Israel will go a-whoring after the strange gods of the lands whither they will come, and they will forsake Me and My Covenant. I shall become very angry and cause great misfortunes to befall them. As a result, they will confess that they have come upon evil times because I, God, no longer reign among them. Yet on that day, their regret, their confession, will be to no avail for I shall hide My face from them. Their crime will not be forgiven."

Moses conveyed this message to the people of Israel but the people of Israel have never tired of asking whether the words of Moses do not contradict the assurance which the prophets gave us on many occasions that the road to penitence is ever open? Didn't our prophets and sages assure us that we could atone for our sins at any time? Even one moment before one's death one can atone for all of one's transgressions, and if one is but sincere, one can thus come to one's Maker in judgment as a saint. Why, then, did God indicate through Moses that even when Jews would recognize that their misfortunes were due to this disloyalty to God, their penitence would not avail them?

However, if you will examine the text I summarized you will see that the type of penitence which Moses regarded as unavailing is the penitence that comes not because the sinner is truly remorseful but rather because the sinner is frightened by the evil that God has wrought. That type of penitence is not penitence. To return to God because one is in distress over God's wrath is not a genuine return at all. And that is why Moses said that the penitence that comes from the dread of God's punishment is not the penitence of which the prophets spoke. It is rather like the penitence of the criminal before he goes to his execution. Real penitence does not arise from a fear of what will happen to our bodies externally but rather from an inner recognition of the great joy to be derived from returning to God. Real penitence is an inner recognition of the rightness of the way by which man shall live. It is born of exalted feelings of love and consecration. And it is when I read Jewish literature on this subject that I smile when I recall how *we*— *we* of all religious people—have been accused of emphasizing a religion of fear—we who shunned the method of inducing religious loyalty by the fear of hell!

Yet, friends, I call this to your attention on this Sabbath of Repentance because it is a point that is relevant to many phases of our communal and individual existence as Jews. Permit me to demonstrate how.

For many years now, Jewish organizations on the American scene have been trying to make themselves great by exploiting the fear that the average Jew has of anti-Semitism. The heads of these organizations have tried to gain members and solicit large contributions by appealing to the fears that Jews have because they are Jews. Their professional executives made anti-Semitism the great catch-all slogan. The fear of anti-Semitism is the slogan in all literature mailed out. It is the slogan for all fundraising speeches. It is slogan for all membership drives. I do not mean to indicate that these organizations do not do some good but it is remarkable that they have taken from the American Jewish community more money every year than all the Jewish institutions of higher learning put together. And because they took so much money—and money is power—these national organizations that thrive on the fear Jews have of anti-

Semitism have greater influence and control over American Jewish life than the forces in America that are working for a Jewish loyalty that is born of the love of Judaism, instead of the fear of anti-Semitism. Who can compare, for example, the influence of any federation of synagogues with the influence of the Anti-Defamation League or the American Jewish Congress or the American Jewish Committee? Who can compare the influence of any Rabbinic organization with the influence of the National Community Relations Advisory Council whose principal members are defense agencies? The truth is that we have been building an American Jewish community on the theory that to induce Jewish loyalty one must keep Jewish fears alive and that is why we spend so much more on fear projects than on higher Jewish education. That is also why even in our community you can get hundreds of Jews to work for the defense agencies while only a handful will work for a synagogue or school.

But friends, even these Jewish organizations, without as yet altogether changing their "lines"—they hardly can do that without discharging their deeply entrenched professional staffs—even these organizations have come to learn the folly of their ways. They have learned that you cannot inspire Jewish loyalty forever by fear. If a Jewish organization wants members and supporters it must ultimately base its appeal on the love of Judaism that Jews have. That is why many of these national organizations are flirting with the idea of doing something constructive for Judaism—for Judaism as a faith and a way of life. The two AJC's have already begun, and as usual the ADL will follow close behind. But the interesting thing is that they are learning that just as penitence because of fear is not significant, so the Jewish loyalty they sought artificially to induce by fear will not give their organizations lasting vitality of purpose.

The same idea has even begun to penetrate the Zionist leadership of the world. At the last World Zionist Congress in Jerusalem it was recognized that though Israel needs American Jews as much as ever, American Jews were leaving the ranks of Zionism. What could be done to make American Zionists stay in line? Some Zionists suggested the fear technique. Make American Jews understand that what happened to German Jews could happen to them. How tragic it is that those who proposed this idea did not realize that for altogether too long a time Zionist propaganda was based on the fears it induced—the fear of persecution, the fear of homelessness, the fear of second-class citizenship wherever Jews live. But alas, that is not the way to make a lifelong Zionist. You cannot inspire genuine Zionism by appealing to fear impulses. Rather must one sell a positive philosophy. Rather must one convince Jews that the dream of Zion is the dream of our Prophets to establish a state whence Torah, truth and righteousness, will come forth; to establish a state that will be a beacon of light to all the world; to establish a state wherein an aged civilization will enjoy a renaissance that will move us, inspire us and guide us. My Zionism was never the product of fear and it is, therefore, not subject to the ebb and flow of fear. It is rather part of my whole philosophy of Americanism and Judaism. And if Israeli and American Zionists want to retain American Jews in the Zionist ranks they would do better to make Jews better Jews, more Torah-minded Jews, more Judaism-conscious Jews, more Hebrew-speaking Jews, more Jewish-culture-minded Jews.

But what is true of the national Jewish organizations and the Zionist movement is also true of us as parents who want our children to remain Jews, to marry Jews, and to raise still more Jews. Let us face the truth. What do we consider the most important reason for giving our children a Jewish education? Let us admit it. Most Jews want their children to be able to face anti-Semitism a little more courageously. We want Jewish education as an antidote for the bites our children will get from the snakes in our environment who delight in Jewish hurt. What do we consider the most important reason for opposing intermarriage between Jew and non-Jew? Again it's fear—the fear that such marriages can't be successful. That is the principal reason we give our children. Furthermore, what do many Jews consider the most important reason for building synagogues and maintaining them in most small communities in America? Again it's the fear that if we don't build synagogues the Christians will think that we are atheists, communists, materialists. But friends—as good as all these reasons may be, Jewish loyalty cannot be induced either in Jewish adults or children by fear alone. The truly lasting, inspiring, and meaningful Jewish loyalty is one that must be conceived in love—because we love our faith, because we love our way of life, because we love our cultural heritage. I want my children to know Judaism, to love Judaism, to love Jews and to marry Jews, as well as to be close to synagogues and institutions of Jewish learning, because nothing gives me greater personal happiness and peace of mind than being Jewish. Nothing gives my life—character, my thought—significance, and my activity—*zest*, as much as my Jewish loyalty. As one great thinker put it, "I love being Jewish because it is the least difficult way I know of being human."

And that is the type of return to Judaism for which I plead on this Sabbath of Penitence. Not a return from fear but rather a return from love.

But alas, you may ask—how does one come back through love? How does one get to feel that way about one's faith, one's traditions, one's cultural heritage? The answer is simple. You learn to love music by listening to it. You learn to love art by exposing yourself to it. And everyone can learn to love Judaism by living it. No messenger from heaven will drop the love into your heart. No angel will induce it. But you can acquire the love by living Jewishly, by coming to the synagogue to read and hear the word of God regularly, by making the Sabbath the day of meaningful family togetherness that it is, by reading books and magazines that relate the eternal insights of our faith to all modern personal, social, economic and political problems, by learning Hebrew and sharing directly in the tremendous literary creativity of the greatest little republic on the face of the earth, by spending some part of every day of the year cultivating one's appreciation and one's life of everything Jewish. And it is for that that I plead this morning. I plead for a return to Judaism in love, and the way to learn to love Judaism is to expose oneself to it. I pray all of you to start that very process. Leisure time you have. May God but help you and inspire you to use that leisure time most significantly for your own personal happiness and spiritual edification as well as to insure the survival of Judaism.

40

If You Had Three Wishes

Rabbi Bernard S. Raskas

WE NEVER TIRE of fairly tales. They delight us, they charm us and they instruct us. Once we have heard a fairy tale, we never forget it. I remember such a story from my childhood. It is called "The Three Wishes," and it goes something like this:

A poor woodsman was granted three wishes by a fairy. The man was dazed by this great gift and he stumbled home. When he arrived he found that his wife had not yet finished preparing supper and so he said, without thinking, "I wish I had a piece of pudding before me." The slice of pudding appeared. His wife, seeing his folly in wasting a wish declared, "You are so foolish, I wish the pudding would stick to your nose," and up it flew to the poor man's nose. They tried to pull it off, but to no avail. They could not remove it. It looked so terribly funny that they had to spend the third opportunity wishing the pudding off his nose. In a twinkling they had good fortune and then they lost it. How sad.

Now I wonder if this fairy tale is not the life of every man. Take Rosh Hashanah. We come here to pray and

---

Selected from *Best Jewish Sermons of 5719-5720.*

seek wishes and blessings for the coming year. How desperately we want our heart's yearnings to come true. But, if we were granted three blessings for the coming year, with the assurance that they would come true, what would we ask for? Would we act in the manner of the woodsman and his wife and dissipate our good fortune into nothingness or would we be wiser to choose more intelligently? I have my doubts.

If we truly desire guidance on how to choose blessings for a New Year, we can find such direction in the Torah. As our ancestor Jacob approaches his end he gathers his twelve sons about him and proceeds to bless his children who are destined to father tribes in Israel. The threefold blessing of Joseph is especially worth remembering. *"Ben porat Yosef, ben porat alai ayin, b'not tzaadah alai shur.* Let Joseph be as a growing vine, whose branches run over the wall and whose roots are by a fountain of water." This combination of wishes is the finest blessing one could receive for the coming year.

The first one is *"ben porat,* a growing vine," which is the symbol of a growing mind. One of the greatest and noblest virtues a person could hope for in life is a growing mind. A developing and constantly maturing personality is a tremendous asset to the fund of a worthwhile life.

Bertrand Russell points out very well that half the sins of mankind are caused by the sins of boredom. We commonly speak of children and say: "Idle hands are in the devil's workshop," and we forget to add that idle minds can also be the source of untold human harm and mischief. An empty mind is a ready field for hate, distortion and unhappiness. We all know what it is to feel bored and how miserable boredom can be, and how depressed and angry it makes us feel. But, on the other hand, there is nothing more rewarding than the perpetual search and growth of the human mind. For with growth comes happiness.

I know a woman in her fifties who during the past year mastered the Hebrew language, and I tell you that millions could not duplicate the pleasure she now derives from worshipping with us. I know a man in his thirties who just learned to type and you can actually hear a joyous refrain as he rhythmically clicks his letters. I know a woman in her forties who learned to drive a car and you cannot even begin to imagine the immeasurable delight her new freedom gives her.

It is common nowadays to harp on the emptiness of our lives. Most critics of contemporary culture attribute this to the swift modern tempo which only permits us to skim the surface of living and never take the time to really learn to appreciate the finer and better things of life. We forget that some things cannot be hurried and must be tasted, savored and digested.

This can be well illustrated by an American couple who were touring France. As they came to the great Cathedral at Chartres the lady looked at her watch and, noticing it was late, she said "Well here we are. You take the outside and I'll take the inside."

Some things in life one must truly enjoy from the inside and the outside. Our life begins to take on meaning when we embark upon a venture or a study and we do not stop until it is thoroughly known and mastered. Moments of achievement are the most satisfying moments of our lives.

This is true whether it means wining an Oscar or a Nobel Prize, or just once, going the course in par, or serving a perfect dinner party, or giving a good book review, or to be so wise or gracious as to have your mother-in-law say you are wiser than your spouse.

These are but some of the products of mental and emotional growth and they ought to help inspire us to attain the ever growing goal of a *ben porat* . . . growing mind.

The second blessing of Jacob is to be found in the image of the "*b'not tzaadah alai ayim—*branches running over the wall," which is a beautiful symbol of the helping hand reaching forth to know, understand and help others. The symbol takes on added meaning when we consider the fact that too many people are walled in by their inability to grow branches of love and have never learned to extend the helping hands of friendship. In terms of theology it may be said that fellowship is Heaven and lack of fellowship is Hell. Or, as one of T. S. Eliot's character's in the *Cocktail Party* says: "Hell is alone, the other figures in it, merely projections. There is nothing to escape from and nothing to escape to. One is always alone." This is the undeniable truth. Hell is apartness; Heaven is togetherness. Hell is egocentricity and the inability to give of oneself to others. It is the failure to discover that the more we give of ourselves, the more we forget ourselves in loving concern for others, the better off we are—the stronger, the more truly contented.

I was deeply moved by the story of the little girl who was showing off her collection of dolls. She had many fine and expensive dolls, but when she was asked to show her favorite doll she picked out the oldest one. It was tattered, dilapidated, the hair was off, nose chipped, and cheeks scratched. When she was asked why she liked this one best, the little girl said: "I love her most because if I didn't love her no one else would."—If I didn't love her no one else would!

Do you wish to experience Heaven, then love where and when no one else would? Open your business to the handicapped and give him a chance. Be a sitter when your neighbor has to attend to an errand. Defend a person when all are against him. Take the initiative in keeping your family together. Invite the child down the block to join your child's club. Work in the kitchen, help with the picnic and decorate for the dance and you will find why the hands that help are sometimes holier than the lips that pray. God does not want us to do extraordinary things; he wants us to do ordinary things extraordinarily well.

In this classification of those who give, I see at the head of the list the teacher. Not only the teacher in College, or Public School or Hebrew School, but also the Scout and Cub Master, the Youth Leaders, the father who instructs his son in responsibility and the mother who enables her daughter to love in wholesomeness and kindness. Teaching is a true act of giving for it leaves a vestige of oneself in the development of another. If you have ever seen the light of understanding shine in another's eyes, where no light shone before, then you have gathered the treasures of teaching. If you have ever guided the unsteady and unpracticed hand and watched it suddenly grown firm and purposeful then you have had the gain of giving. If you have ever watched a young mind begin to soar to new heights and you have helped to launch a career then you have felt within you the sense of being a humble instrument in the furtherance of mankind.

One of my favorite musical scores is *The King and I* and in that wonderful work of art the finest selection expressed the creed of the teacher, which is also a fulfillment of the second blessing of having the capacity to give. Anna greets the charming Siamese children of all ages. She looks at her new pupils and she bursts into the following song:

It's a very ancient saying,
But a true and honest thought,
That "if you become a teacher
By your pupils you'll be taught . . ."

To be blessed with friendship is truly to experience the benediction of something beautiful and new every day.

The third blessing that Jacob extended to Joseph is to be found in the phrase, "*alai ayin* . . . roots deeply implanted by fountains of water." This symbolizes Faith. For just as waters nourish a growing plant, so does Faith provide the nourishment of a growing soul. From the fertile soil of the soul generously watered with Faith comes the courage for living. Courage is the fruit of Faith, even as belief and trust is the source of courage. The real test of the qualities of a person is not to be found in a readiness to die for a cause, but rather the determination to live on meaningfully despite personal unhappiness, pain, suffering and even great tragedy. Real Faith means a readiness to observe the words of the Torah: "*v'chai bohem*—and you shall live courageously." Real courage implies the willingness to stare facts and reality in the face and not to flinch.

There comes to all of us moments in our lifetime when we feel that our mental walls are caving in, our minds reel under the impact of events whose tragedy is tornado-like, and our ground shakes beneath our feet because of an emotional earthquake. We feel literally that we have no grounds of Faith on which to stand. It is precisely at this time that we should turn outwardly and inwardly and call upon our hidden springs of stored up Faith.

Outwardly we should turn to the synagogue, to the doctors, to the professional help of the social worker and the counselor. Inwardly, we should turn to God and the recognition that we all have within us the courage and the capacity to develop spiritually and emotionally, let our personality grow beyond our problems. We must recognize that to be human means to have problems; but to be godly means to rise above them.

Dr. William Menninger, addressing the National Association for Mental Health, said "we all suffer from mental pressures. There isn't a person who does not experience frequently a mental or emotional disturbance severe enough to disrupt his functioning as a well-adjusted, happy, efficiently performing individual." While this is certainly so, it is equally true that having the courage to be honest enough to admit the truth and possessing the determination to act on Faith and trust we can right our balance and restore ourselves to useful and happy living.

It is rather easy to separate the immature person from the mature individual. One may recognize the immature person by his lack of balance. He is overwhelmed by the first assault of misfortune and swept off his feet by the first piece of good luck. Then he believes, through his own slender store of experience, that what happened to him is utterly unique and nobody ever suffered his problems or met his good fortune. But, the mature person knows that to be human means to have spiritual ups and downs and to love means to experience both joy and sorrow for the sake of those whom we love. He knows that the Psalms, the Prayer Book, the love of a friend, the steadfast faith of a spouse, the skills of the professional, the balm of time and the healing hand of God, are the great power reservoirs of the human spirit. For behind the creation of every man stands the fact of a God—a God of mercy—who wanted us here and who put us here. And though we know not why we suffer, we have Faith that His wisdom is just and, in time, we shall know why our love brings us sadness as well as satisfaction. Until that time, we continue to live in courage and count our blessings. For in the blackest hour of distress, our despair must not block our determination to understand that there is no loss without gain, no hurt without healing, and no manner of death without leaving some measure of immortality.

A minister in Pennsylvania has expressed this thought in the following words:

> Today, upon a bus I saw a girl with golden hair
> She seemed so gay, I envied her, and wished that
>   I was half so fair.
> I watched her as she rose to leave, and saw her
>   hobble down the aisle.
> She had one leg and wore a crutch, but as she
>   passed—a smile.
> Oh, God, forgive me when I whine: I have two
>   legs and the world is mine.
> Two legs to take me where I go,
> Two eyes to see the sunset's glow,
> Two ears to hear all that I should know.
> Oh, God, forgive me when I whine;
> I'm blessed indeed, the world is mine.

Yes, when we have balance, perspective and the fortress of inner faith the world is truly ours.

During the remainder of the service and now through Yom Kippur, I would like you to reconsider your wishes and your desires. Do not lose what you already have by desiring that which you do not really need or truly want. The only worthwhile blessings that are really ours to have and to hold are a growing mind, a helping hand and a faith that endures. Those who have these three gifts will also be blessed with the concluding words of

Jacob: *"V'yafozu zroeh yadav mideh abir Yaakov, meshom roeh ehven Yisroel*—Joseph shall be as a growing vine, whose branches run over a wall and who is planted by a fountain of water."

The arms of his courage and achievements are made strong, by the hands of the Mighty One of Jacob, who is even the Shepherd and the foundation of the Faith of Israel.

41

No Rest for the Righteous

Rabbi Jack Riemer

THE RABBIS OF THE Midrash make a poignant comment on the first words of the *sedra* of Vayeshev. The *sedra* begins with the words: *"Vayeshev Yaakov b'eretz migurei aviv* . . . Jacob *settled down* in the land of his fathers."* The Rabbis say it wasn't so. *"Biskesh Yaakov leshev bishalva miyad kafats alav rugzo shel Yosef."* Jacob *wanted* to settle down in peace and he thought that at last he was going to be able to do so, but just then the tragedy of Joseph came upon him. The Rabbis go on to say that Jacob should have known better. He should have known that *ein shalva l'tzadikim b'olam haze*, there is no rest and there is no peace for the righteous in this world!

It is a grim statement that the Rabbis make, but is it not true? The entire life of Jacob, *from before his birth until after his death*, is one continual proof of its truth. It was one long struggle and one constant crisis from beginning to end. Before he was born, he wrestled with his brother in his mother's womb. As a child, he fought with his brother to obtain the birthright and the bless-

Selected from *Best Jewish Sermons of 5721-5722.*

ing. He ran away from Esau, and ran into Laban, who was in his own cunning way an even more wicked man to live with. He worked for Laban for twenty years, scorched by the sun by day, frozen by the cold at night. He married wives who bickered and quarreled over him. He fathered sons who disobeyed him and fought among themselves. On the way home, he wrestled with a stranger and was wounded. Then he had the heartache of seeing his only daughter, Dinah, molested by the people of Shechem. And then, when he is old and weary after so much sorrow and strife, when he comes home to his father's land, hoping to find peace at last, there begins the last and saddest chapter of his life, the tragedy of Joseph. He lives to see his favorite son sold as a slave by his own brothers. He is told that this child has been killed, and he mourns for him for twenty years. Then when he finds out that his son is still alive, he must leave his home because of a famine, and he must go down to live out his last days in Egypt. At the end of his life, this old man who sought peace and quiet all his days and never found them has to beg his children's promise that after his death they will carry his bones back and bury him in the land of his fathers. The life of Jacob, from beginning to end, is proof of the truth of the comment of the Rabbis: *ein shalva l'tzadikim b'olam haze*, there is no rest, and there is no peace for the righteous in this world.

The world is so made that each and every person in it, good or bad, is destined to have his full share of sorrow and strain, of tension and pain, of anguish and aggravation. The world is so made, and we might as well know it, that few if any of us, can ever expect to have permanent peace of mind and constant tranquillity. Suffering and sorrow, hardship and disappointment, toil and trouble come to us all.

What then is the difference between the good man and the bad? Only this: They both suffer, they both have pain, they both know tension and trouble, but there is a difference in what they suffer *for*, in what they have trouble *from*, in what takes away their peace of mind. The measure of a man is that which bothers him and that which disturbs his mind, that which annoys him and costs him pain.

He who would live a life without pain has come to the wrong world. There is no such choice here on this earth. But we can choose, at least to some extent, the kind of pain we want to have. We can choose between creative pain and pointless pain, between holy pain and petty pain, between pain for a purpose and pain that has no purpose.

A woman, for example, can choose between the pain of having children or the pain of not having children. The Hebrew word for childbirth is *chevlei leida*, which means the agony of childbirth, and this is exactly what it is. No man can understand how much it hurts for a woman to have a child. Even today, with all our anesthetics, all our obstetricians and all our medical care, it is still a painful process. And yet women choose this pain every day, and they choose it again, voluntarily, after they have gone through it once. They choose it because they prefer the pain of having a child to the greater pain of not having a child. The pain of having a child is temporary, and it is forgotten the moment a mother first sees her newborn child. The pain of not having children is a constant gnawing pain that never goes away.

There is one passage in the Bible that has always fascinated and baffled me. As a man I cannot understand it, but every woman can. We know that Rachel had a great deal of difficulty bearing a child. Yet when she finally gave birth, after all that pain and anguish, her first words were, "*Vatikra et sh'mo Yosef leymor: yosef Hashem li ben acher* . . . She called his name Joseph, [which means may God add] and she said: 'May God give to me another son.'" She had just gone through excruciating pain, and yet her first reaction was: May I be able to go through it again. She felt this way because this was creative pain, and when she saw her child, she felt that it was worthwhile.

A man can choose between the pain of having and raising children and the pain of loneliness if he doesn't. In Hebrew the term for raising children is a very realistic term, it is *tsa'ar gidul banim* which literally means: the *pain* of raising children. This is what it is. As our parents used to say, "Little children—little pains, big children—big pains." Raising children involves pain. What father can honestly say that he has peace of mind? There is noise and tumult in my house the moment I walk in the door. There is crisis and quarreling between my infants a dozen times a day. There is aggravation and excitement and tension every minute, and yet I would not trade with any bachelor for all the money in the world! It is pain, and responsibility, and fear, and annoyance, but it is creative pain, and it is worth it. It is a hundred times better than the emptiness and unfulfillment that would be mine if I had no children.

Every day in my life there are a good many hours of sweat and strain, the effort and frustration that is involved in studying. I spend many hours of each day, and many nights as well, sitting at my desk, preparing lectures, reading books, writing essays, working on sermons, and each one of them comes hard. It is work, and often painful work at that. It is what the sages of old called *yigia b'torah*, the work of learning.

But what choice do I have? I cannot choose to live

without work. I cannot choose to support my family without struggle. And I cannot choose to have knowledge without effort. I can only choose between the strain of working and the greater strain of not working, between the pain of learning and the pain of being ignorant, and I gladly choose the former over the latter.

There is a passage about study in the *Ethics of the Fathers* that is very interesting. It says:

> This is the way to learn Torah.
> You must be willing to get along on a salty crust
>   of bread.
> You must be willing to live on a measured amount
>   of water.
> You must be ready to sleep on the ground.
> You must be willing to live a life of pain.
> And you must work at the Torah.
> If you do,
> Then you will be happy,
> And it will be good for you.
> You will be happy—in this world,
> And it will be good for you—in the world to come.

We can understand that it will be good for you in the world to come if you live this kind of life. A person who subsists on such a diet and undergoes such difficulties in order to learn Torah deserves reward in the hereafter. But this is not all that the text says. It says that if you live a life of difficulty and hardship in order to learn, you will be happy *in this world*. How can this be? How can a person live on a crust of bread, a rationed amount of water, sleep on the earth, and be happy in this world? He can, if it is for a purpose, and if he accomplishes that purpose. There is such a thing as the joy that comes with suffering for the sake of something worthwhile, the joy that comes from a sense of accomplishment, even if, and perhaps especially if, this accomplishment comes at the cost of pain and effort. There is greater joy in an achievement that comes at the cost of pain and effort than there is in a gift given to us on a silver platter.

There is a choice that is open to us each and every day. We can choose between becoming emotionally involved in the lives of other human beings, with all of the fearful risks and pains that that entails, or we can choose to keep our hearts to ourselves, to live alone and to trust no one, with all of the certain hurt and pain that that entails. In Hebrew there is a precious, almost untranslatable term for sympathy. We say: *tsa'ar baalei chayim*, which means to feel the pain of every other living creature, to feel the hurt of all that lives. You run a great risk when you become emotionally involved with others. You may be disappointed, you may be cheated, you may have pain, but is this pain not better than the pain of those who keep their hearts to themselves, and live in selfish isolation? Is this pain not better than that suffered by those who lead petty lives, who are concerned only with their own welfare and with their own honor, who are annoyed and disturbed and upset when their own interests are involved, but who do not feel the heartbreak of their fellow men? A small man is one who feels pain each time his toes are stepped on or his honor is abused. A great man is one who suffers when any other human being suffers, who feels himself part of the entire human race, who grieves for those beyond himself.

There is ultimately only one choice that is open to us. Suffer we must. We cannot escape it. But we can choose between suffering by and for ourselves alone, or suffering with and on behalf of something that is bigger than ourselves.

The story is told about a certain Chasidic Rebbe from the East Side who became ill and had to be taken to a hospital in mid-Manhattan. In the morning of his first day in the hospital, the Rebbe got up, and as was his practice every day of his life, he put on his *tallit* and his *tefillin*, and began to pray. He said his prayers in a loud voice, and as he came to each new page he sighed and groaned and cried out in contrition and confession. The director of the hospital came in and asked him to stop making so much noise. While they were talking, a patient in the next room let out a shriek. The Rebbe asked:

"*For vos lost fyr ehm*? . . . Why do you let him cry out?"
"*Em tidt vey* . . . Because he is in pain," explained the director.
"*Mir tidi och vey* . . . I ache too," answered the Rebbe.

I ache too. The Rebbe was in pain, not for himself, but for the *galut Hashechina*, for the Holy Presence that is in exile, for the world that has gone astray, for all mankind that is separated from its Maker, for the Lord Himself who is ignored and forgotten in the world that He has made.

The measure of a man is what ails him, what hurts him. Does he hurt because of the ache of his body, the sores in his mind, or the scars on his soul? Does he cry for the world that is in agony, or for his own vanity that has been insulted? The measure of a man is not whether he has pain, for this all men must have in common. The measure of a man is what gives him pain.

Let us finish this study with one comment of the Rabbis of old. There is a verse in the Book of Psalms that says: "Blessed is the man whom God causes to suffer, and whom He teaches out of His Torah." The Rabbis

explain the verse in this way:
The Rabbis said:

There is no one in this world without pain.
There is one who has a toothache, and therefore
he cannot sleep.
There is one who has a sore in his eye, and therefore
he cannot sleep.
And there is one who is working in the Torah, and
therefore he cannot sleep.
Therefore it is written: "Blessed is the man whom
God causes to suffer, and whom He teaches out
of His Torah."

Blessed is the man who suffers for God's sake, who is bothered by a Divine discontent, who cannot rest because of worthwhile things. If suffer we must, then may all of our sufferings be of this kind. If there is no rest and no peace for the righteous as well as for all other men in this world, then at least let there be the pain of achievement and the joy of accomplishment, the struggle of building and the blessing of fulfillment, the pain of being part of something holy and the reward of seeing the fruit of our labors.

42

Our Alimony Jews

Rabbi Solomon Roodman

THE SAGE, Rabbi Aaron Karliner, when seeking to differentiate between Rosh Hashana and the other holidays of the Jewish calendar, made the following observation: where the Pilgrim Festivals of Passover, Pentecost and Tabernacles resemble the extremities of the human torso and the Day of Atonement is analogous to the heart, Rosh Hashana, he noted, may be compared to the head. This day, dedicated to the theme of soul searching and character testing, calls upon us to employ intelligent pursuit when endeavoring to evaluate our individual and national accomplishments.

Like everything else, Jewish life has been influenced by the strains and stresses of our tense times. We are witnessing a radical change in Jewish thinking which bodes evil for the future of Jewish survival. Basically it is a perversion of a fundamental attitude, the nature of which is expressed by a biblical incident. In the Book of Samuel, in one of the Jews' encounters with the Philistines, the enemy captured the Holy Ark which the Israelites had brought onto the field of battle. Thinking that they had

Selected from *Best Jewish Sermons of 5715-5716.*

finally captured the God of Israel, the Philistines transported their precious booty back to their homeland and placed it in the temple of their most revered deity. The following day they entered their temple and to their chagrin they found their deity prostrate on the floor before the Ark. This incident initiated a series of painful experiences for the victorious Philistines and after seven months they decided to return the Ark of the Covenant to its rightful owners.

Thereupon the Philistines sought the advice of their diviners and priests who recommended that a new wagon should be procured to which they were to hitch two milch cows, which had never borne a yoke. They were then instructed to place the Holy Ark on the wagon with a coffer filled with priceless trinkets. They were to send the milk cows on their way. No one was to direct the holy caravan, which was expected to reach its destination by itself. They simply said, "Send it away that it may go." Their responsibility ended there and then. They disregarded the biblical injunction which commanded that the sole method of transporting the Holy Ark was on men's shoulders and at no time was it to be placed on a vehicle.

This unique procedure amazes the average student of biblical lore. How could they expect the milch cows to find their own way? Yet, when we examine the present day attitude toward Jewish responsibility, we discover that we are guilty of similar folly. Is not the American Jew prone to place the Holy Ark on a vehicle together with coffers filled with priceless trinkets, conveniently forgetting that the Ark must be personally transported from place to place.

To the average Jew today, Judaism is not a system of observances which affect him personally, but one which deserves only his financial support. He may respect its ethical stance but he refuses to integrate it into his personal life. To revere Judaism as one does Greek culture or Roman art is relegating Judaism to the status of a fossilized museum piece. Just because one contributes generously to Jewish support does not mean that Judaism will survive. An impersonal Judaism, a Judaism by proxy, is an inadequate Judaism. Merely stressing the social and philanthropic aspects of Judaism while refusing to bear it personally is folly in the highest. Such an attitude recalls to mind the explanation offered by Rabbi Karliner when asked why the Almighty should punish Satan in the End of Days for his treacherous dealings when his prescribed duty is to tempt with sin. "Satan deserves punishment," answered the sage, "not because he tempts people with sin, but because he has them believing that they are not committing sins but rather performing *Mitzvos*." Such is the case with Judaism lived vicariously. It has its disciples believing that they have fulfilled their obligations to Judaism by virtue of their magnanimity.

This "alimony approach" to Jewish life, supporting but refusing to live with it, has had many injurious effects on the structure of the American Jewish community. Religious predilection no longer serves as the criterion for communal leadership. Thus, too many of our Jewish community leaders operate not as barons of organizational ingenuity but as slaves of religious indifference. Seldom do many of them maintain a semblance of religious affiliation. Though their numbers include those who have never crossed the threshold of a synagogue this does not prevent them from being acclaimed the master of Jewish destiny. It explains further why many soon become anonymous entities once their specific duties have been discharged.

The gross failure of vicarious Judaism becomes very obvious when we consider the attitude of the average worshipper who frequents the synagogue but three days of the year. Lacking religious enthusiasm, it is only normal for him to become bored and uneasy, regardless of the type of service being conducted. The spiritual leader who believes he can improve his situation by innovation and drastic change becomes an unwitting victim of delusions of grandeur. He is attacking the problem from the wrong direction. People may clamor for change and they may demand further doctoring of the synagogue service, but surrender to these and other demands by the spiritual leadership will not meet the challenges of indifference, decorum, and general migration from one house of worship to the other. Any obvious improvement will be of temporary duration.

It is not our services which are lacking, but it is the American Jew who is at fault. Ready proof are those places of worship which have capitulated to the whims and fancies of their parishioners. There, too, the same problem exists. Their leadership constantly complains of lack of attendance and total apathy. Place one individual in a situation and his whole being exalts with enthusiasm; place another individual in a similar situation and he wilts and falls by the wayside. This is because the average worshipper lacks a sense of personal devotion to the faith of our fathers. Too many believe they have discharged their obligations to Judaism by contributing to its support. It was Mark Twain who noted, "when some men discharge their obligations you can hear the report for miles around." Because the fire and zeal which motivated our ancestors is absent in Jewish life, Jewish life and progress are being squandered on the *moloch* of innovation and change.

In our synagogues today we need congregations, not audiences; participants, not spectators. The Ark of the Lord must be borne on one's shoulders. The aspirin remedies of the television screen and Hollywood may succeed for a while but one soon tires of a repeated performance. Some of us remember a member of an orchestra whom the conductor asked to play more softly. Despite his efforts to please, the conductor still was displeased. Finally in disgust the player put down his instrument and refused to play at all. It was then that the conductor commended him by saying, "Now your performance is really superb!" This is a poor method of solving the challenge of synagogue life. The self-appointed conductors will never be satisfied unless we reduce Jewish observance *ad absurdum*.

One learns to appreciate good music by learning its basic principles. One can appreciate the overpowering beauty of religious resolve by familiarizing himself with its motifs. It is time that the American Jew began living his Judaism. He must carry the Ark on his shoulders instead of endeavoring to salve his conscience by the philanthropic approach.

Vicarious Judaism brings us face to face with a similar challenge to present day Jewish life, namely, vicarious parenthood. Next to his Torah, to the Jew his child constitutes his most precious possession. It was through him that his Torah took on new life and inspiration. Thus, the Jewish parent of yesterday was wont to bear his child on his shoulders; he actually included his child in his every pursuit. He was constantly concerned with his child's thinking and sought every possible means to integrate his child's thinking with Jewish success. What is the attitude between children and parents today?

Compared to yesterday's children, the modern child enjoys many more physical and psychological advantages. He is better fed, better clothed, better housed, and offered greater opportunities for educational pursuit and recreational endeavors. Despite these advantages do our children show a greater sense of appreciation than we did when we were children? Do our children readily assume their fair share of family responsibility? The utilitarian approach has invaded our homes. If we meet the demands of our children, then we can hope to receive a semblance of gratitude in return but should we not be able to satisfy their demands, then we can be prepared for the inevitable.

The reason for this sad state of affairs hearkens back to ancient times. It's the old story of loading the Ark on a wagon accompanied with valuable gifts and then letting it make its own way. We give our children everything but ourselves. Parents and children no longer grow up together but tend to grow away from each other. We leave the discipline of our children to others, expecting the teacher to serve as an adequate replacement.

A fine educator noted significantly that every parent must pass through three stages in coping with his progeny. The first is dedication. Complete and unstinted care should be given the child. The second is education. The parent must provide every educational opportunity for his child. The third is abdication. The parent must learn to take hands off and give the child the liberty he must learn to use. The three stages must follow in sequence. Before abdication, there must come dedication and education. Unfortunately too many of us invert the process. We are prone to abdicate before the other two have run their course. The average Jewish child enjoys too many liberties. We allow teenagers to stay out until all hours of the morning. We encourage their social escapades, so that when they reach maturity, courtship is no longer a novelty. Our children grow old without years. They miss the fun of youth, the pleasure of growing up under the guidance of intelligent parenthood.

The increasing selfishness of American Jewish par-

ents, the pleasure seeking, the longing for social prestige, is widening the cleavage which separates parents
from their progeny. We have ceased being pals with our
children, we avoid doing things together with them. We
are alimony parents; we support but we do not live with
our responsibility.

On this day dedicated to a reappraisal of our lives we
would be wise to abandon the modern mode of vicarious living. Blessed would be our lives if we were to emulate the sagacity of the venerable sage Rabbi Chanina
ben Dosa, who being too poor to bring precious gifts to
the Temple in Jerusalem made his way to a nearby
desert and fetched there a huge rock which he smoothed
down and bore on his shoulders to the Holy City. When
reading this incident the average reader is somewhat
puzzled by the rabbi's actions. Could he not as easily
fetched a rock in Jerusalem proper? However, this odd
effort expresses the true meaning of faith. Genuine giving invokes the idea of giving of one's self. It carries with
it the task of self-involvement. Though poor and bedrag-
gled, Rabbi Chanina was blessed with character. True
faith requires personal involvement. It invites us to become an integral part of Jewish endeavor. It summons us
to attend services and bring our children with us. It
chides us to expose our children to the best that Jewish
education has to offer. It appeals to us to allow the spirit
and fervor of our faith to motivate our every thought
and action. Alas, Rabbi Chanina ben Dosa, if your spirit
were present in Jewish life today how much happier and
richer we would be!

Let us bear the Ark on our own shoulders, let us not
transfer our responsibilities or exchange privilege for
pottage. The Philistines who would allow the Ark of the
Lord to flounder and be waylaid are many. We alone
can lead it safely on the road of Jewish success.

43

Basic Needs in a Changing World

Rabbi Max Routtenberg

WE FACE A STRANGE paradox as we enter the synagogue on Rosh Hashanah to inaugurate a new year. We
leave, for a few days, the world of our daily lives, a complex world of rapid and bewildering change, and enter a
world that was fashioned several millennia ago and
which has remained basically the same all through the
centuries. We move out, as it were, from the age of
space, of nuclear fission and atomic energy, and seek
meaning for our lives and directive for wise and coura-
geous living from the age of nomads and sheep-herders,
of the ox-cart and the hand-plough. In a time when we
send Sputniks, Explorers and Vanguards into outer space,
we pick up the old-fashioned ram's horn, the Shofar, to
tell us how to live.

What does the ancient world of our fathers have to
teach us about this world of the 20th century which
fashions new marvels and creates miracles every day?
What does the age of tradition, with its fixed, unchanging rituals and ceremonies have to say to this revolu-

Selected from *Best Jewish Sermons of 5719-5720*.

tionary age of change with its tremendous problems and awesome challenges?

It is often helpful, when we face a conflict such as this in our minds, to turn back the pages of history and to see that we are not the first generation of men to be so perplexed. This conflict between tradition and change turns out to be an old tug-of-war that has been going on since ancient days. It was a problem that faced no less a person than our great teacher and law-giver Moses. He saw this people Israel whom he had led through the wilderness about to enter the promised land. What a change this was to be in their lives, to be transformed from a desert people, wandering about with no fixed abode (whose entire career was captured in the recurrent phrase *vayisu, vayachanu*)—into an agricultural community settled on its own land! He foresaw the whole complex of problems that they would have to face in adjusting themselves to this new society, the challenge of new neighbors, a new culture, new religious patterns. And so, in his farewell address, just before he died, Moses gave them this instruction:

"*Zechor yemot olam, binu sh'not dor vador.*

Remember the days of old, in order that you may understand how to live in each generation."

What did Moses mean by this terse command? He was saying simply this: each generation will be confronted with new demands and new challenges. Society changes and the world changes. New social patterns, new economic systems, new forms of government, new scientific discoveries—all those things happen (*sh'not dor vador*) generation after generation. But (*zechor yemot olam*) remember the days of old and you will see that there is something which never changes, something which always remains the same. That is man himself. His basic, fundamental needs, these go on, these remain with him through all the ages. And, if you would know how to meet them, then seek the guidance and the wisdom of the unchanging truths about man, turn to the tradition and it will tell you how man's unchanging needs can be fulfilled.

What are these basic needs of man of which the tradition speaks and to which our attention is drawn as we enter the world of the synagogue and participate in the pageantry of prayer, ritual and ceremony of the High Holy Days?

If we may couch it in modern terminology, our tradition addresses itself to the three basic needs of all human beings: the need to belong, the need to believe, and the need to become. These are the three dimensions of human experience which no one can ignore, except at the peril of personal fulfillment and happiness.

Our Torah reading properly centers around the career of Abraham, the first Jew to whom we look for guidance. We are reminded that this new fellowship which Abraham created is our fellowship to this very day. We are the *Zera Avraham*, the seed of Abraham, and it is as *"b'nai Avraham avinu,* children of Father Abraham," that we fulfill our need to belong.

We are reminded that it was Abraham who faced the new world with a great faith and a deep belief in the one God of the universe *"v'he-emin badonai vaye-chash'veihu litz'dakah*—he believed in God—and God knew that it would lead Abraham into a life of righteousness." And we are reminded that when Abraham was told to leave the old world and to explore the new he was assured, *"va-e-es-cha l'goy gado! . . . ve-he-yei vrachach*—I will make you a great nation and you will become a blessing." That is what sustained the Jew through the ages: he belonged, he believed and he grew to be a blessing, bringing the light of God, of truth and justice to all the world.

When we examine our own situation today, we may be inclined to feel that insofar as the need to belong and the need to believe are concerned, we are meeting them quite adequately. Certainly, here in America, belonging does not seem to be a problem. More than 125 years ago, Alexis De Tocqueville, after a visit to these shores, wrote in his report: "The one conspicuous trait of Americans is that they are a nation of joiners." If anything, we "belong" too much. We join anything and everything. Who can say that we are not meeting the need to belong?

The same may be said of our need to believe. We are living in a land that has stamped its belief on its coins—"In God We Trust," and we may well be called a "nation of believers." Do we not so proclaim ourselves daily in our pledge of allegiance, "One nation under God?" Surely we are meeting this second basic need, the need to believe, adequately.

It is largely in the third dimension of our lives, the need to become, that most of us will agree we fall short. It is here that we feel keenly our inadequacy and our failure. We all know that the law of life is growth, development and the negation of life is stagnation and decay. Every human being is a whole bundle of potentialities and all of life is a continuous process of seeking to actualize them. When these potentials for growth are not expressed, we become stunted and dwarfed. We have failed in the art of living.

Of course, we do continue to grow in our physical and mental powers, otherwise we would never achieve what we do in our lives. From infancy to early adulthood, we develop rapidly, our bodies grow and mature, our minds expand as they become filled with knowledge and understanding of the world about us. But then, somewhere on this ladder of change, at some given point, usually between our twenties and thirties, we stop; our growth is arrested, our development halted, and we become stagnant pools in which nothing new, fresh and challenging ever enters. Indeed, external changes take place, outward manifestations of growth—our incomes grow, our houses become bigger and more beautiful, our cars longer and our possessions greater. But there is no corresponding inner growth—our attitudes become fixed, our habits, our conduct is unchanged, and the great, fundamental need to grow, to become is never realized.

Long ago, President Butler of Columbia, observing this phenomenon made the observation: "The epitaph of the average American should be 'died at thirty, buried at sixty.'" And more recently, we read in the *New York Times Magazine*, the testament of Premier Nehru of India in which he declared: "The tragic paradox of our age is that in a world which is characterized by a tremendous pace of change, our civilization finds itself spiritually exhausted, and man, with his complacency and fixed ideas, is at a virtual standstill."

The fact is, of course, that standing still is intolerable. The chemistry of the human being simply won't permit it. You either go forward or you deteriorate. You just don't stand still. One cannot live in terms of the title of a recent best-seller—"Where are you going, out? What are you doing, nothing?" That is the essence of boredom, the greatest curse of human life.

So a great portion of our lives is devoted to escaping the deadening and intolerable burden of boredom. Two of our largest industries are devoted to helping us in this escape—the liquor and the entertainment industry. Having ceased to grow, we can no longer face ourselves as we are, and so we must run away from ourselves. We are forever "taking a drive," "making the rounds," "going places." We are desperate, hungry for change—and so we seize upon all the externals that our society provides us in such abundance. We are constantly buying new things, changing our styles, our friends, even the color of our hair. We call in the interior decorator to feed our hunger for change, rearrange our furniture, the decor of our homes. But it is of little avail. We have failed to do the main job of interior decoration, on ourselves, our minds, our spirits, our values, our purposes in life. We have betrayed our best selves, we have ceased to become.

And so, in this age of space, this age of modern marvels and miracles, we turn to the old world of external values and we pick up an ancient instrument, and we let the Shofar speak to us: *"U-ru yesheinim mish-natchem v'nirdamim hakitzu*—Awake ye slumberers from your sleep." The great sage Maimonides interprets this summons to man: *"Eilu hashoch'chim ha-emet behavlei haz'man.* Who are they who have fallen asleep?" This refers to those who ignore the true values of life and spend their days in things that are but vanity and illusion.

Do you seek to know, this Shofar says to us, why you have fallen asleep, why you have not grown into the fullness of your powers, why you have not become a blessing, to yourselves, to your fellow-man? Because you have not fulfilled the basic conditions of growth, because you have lightly and carelessly and amateurishly dealt with the need to belong and the need to believe. Your belonging is no belonging and your believing is no believing. It is as though, seeking to reach a certain destination, we have failed in the elementary task of first learning how to get there.

What does belonging mean? It means identification

with a group. How do most of us identify? We carry a membership card, we are a name on a list, we are a plate in the addressograph machine. We belong. But what rewards and what fulfillment can there be in this kind of superficial external belonging? Certainly it reaches nothing deep and central in our need for identification.

But there is another kind of belonging, the kind in which one feels part of the purpose, the ideals and destiny of the group. It means identifying with its hope and aspirations, its struggles, triumphs and defeats. It means involvement in its affairs, participation, fusion with its very essence, in body, mind and soul. (*Zechor yemot olam*) It is in that kind of belonging that the Jew of the ages became a blessing. He didn't carry a membership card in the Jewish people. He achieved identity because his whole life was a mirror of his belonging to the Jewish people. How did one identify a Jew? He was a *ben Torah*—he studied and knew the Torah, he lived a Jewish way of life centered in the synagogue and in the observance of the *mitzvot*; he shared in the memories and aspirations of his people—he was a link in a long historic chain; he belonged to Moses and Isaiah, to Akiva and Hillel, to Maimonides and Rashi; to the Jews of Vilna and the fighters in the Warsaw ghetto. He did not just belong to a club, an organization. He belonged to an eternal people with a mission and a covenant with God. It was this kind of belonging that gave him the vital seeds of growth, of development, as he rose in intellectual and spiritual stature through the ages and became a blessing to all mankind.

There is a kind of believing which is no believing at all, which touches only the surface of our lives and fulfills a basic need. It is the casual, halfhearted affirmation of so many of us when we say we believe in God, but it sounds so hollow and empty when we measure it against the quality and content of our lives.

Do you ever ask yourself, as I do, what practical difference does it make in my life when I say "I believe in God?" How does it affect my daily life, my conduct, my relationship to my family, friends, business associates? Is this belief my own, or is it something I just picked up, something I'm expected to believe in? Just look at us: We believe in God, in America, in the sanctity of marriage, in morality, in education. What difference does it make? Is it only non-believers who stay away from their churches and synagogues all the year round? Only non-believers who show no concern for the great issues of American democracy, only they who will stay away in overwhelming numbers from the polling booths in the coming elections?

We believe in the sanctity of marriage, but family life is disintegrating, divorce is on the increase, infidelity in marriage the major theme of our popular movies, TV dramas, and the most popular joke of comedians in our nightclubs. We believe in morality, when all about us is corruption in politics, in business, in labor unions, in government, everywhere there is a moral laxity and a breakdown in the moral fiber of the people. What kind of beliefs are these? What kind of convictions do we have when all the vital concerns of life are disintegrating before our very eyes.

Perhaps Max Lerner, in his *American Civilization* is quite right when he says these are not our beliefs at all; this is the lip service we pay to respectability. The central beliefs of the American people are the belief in success, in money, in power, prestige. It is in these that we seek to realize our need to believe, and it is here that we meet disaster. These are the *havlei hazeman*, the things of vanity and illusion. What is more tragic than the emptiness and frustration of a man who having achieved success, money, power, prestige, looks at himself and wonders what was it all for and what is there left to live for? He learns the bitter truth that success is not what a man *has*, but what a man *is*, and if his life has not been linked to the changeless and eternal truths of human existence, to love, friendship, mercy, justice, then all his other achievements turn to ashes and are naught but vanity.

"*V'heye bracha.*" Wouldst thou become a blessing? Then remember that true belief means commitment to the highest and best that we are capable of achieving. Belief in God means having the will and the power and determination to resist all the pressures and temptations of the environment, to remain stubbornly faithful to the ideals and values which our tradition at its best and noblest has bequeathed to us. True belief is the path to man's best self; and the discovery of his best self is man's only meaningful success.

Is all this too late for us? The years have passed us by, and while we nod understandingly, are we still asleep? Listen then to the Shofar with its call to *teshuvah*. That is the keyword of these days, return, return to the authentic tradition, the source of life's deepest meaning, and return to true belonging, to true believing, "*ve-heye vrachah*"—and you will become a blessing.

There is a famous painting in the Louvre which depicts the triumph of Mephistopheles over Faust. They are sitting over a chess game and Mephistopheles has made the move which checkmates Faust. A look of gloating on Mephisto's evil face, a look of despair and defeat on the face of Faust. And one day, we are told, a famous chess player stood before this painting and studied the board carefully. Suddenly, he looked about and exclaimed! He has one more move, Faust can still win!

We are not done with our lives. There is yet one

more move for all of us—the *am olam* summons—the
eternal people with its eternal values to which we
belong; the *el chai v'kayam*, the eternal King in whose
goodness and mercy we place our lives. Make your
move—*shuvah Yisrael*—that you may find life's deepest
fulfillment, that you may become a blessing to yourself,
and to all mankind.

44

Curses and Cures

Rabbi Edward T. Sandrow

THE TORAH READING on this Sabbath (*B'hukotai*) expresses lines, usually read sotto voce, that contain a list of some of the most unbearable maledictions that can befall a people. There was a time when some Jews preferred to forego the solemn honor of an *aliyah* when this chapter was recited. One had to be a hardy soul to brave the sound of the frightful imprecations which thundered out of these verses. Usually the sexton or some other functionary took the risk of reciting the blessings over this section of the *Sidrah*. Times have changed! Jews today accept such honors, aware or unaware of the meanings of the words; but the chapter in many synagogues is still intoned in a whisper and with rushed impatience. The Talmud, in referring to these sentences cautions us, *En mafsikin baklolot*, There is to be no pause while reciting these curses."

Twice a year do we go through the procedure since there are two *Tohahot*—two occasions in the early history of our people when Moses warned the children of Israel how they would be punished if they violate God's

---

Selected from *Best Jewish Sermons of 5713*.

law. The punishment and suffering he described is found in our text and does not have to be summarized. One should read them since no summary can do justice to their agonizingly fearful and overwhelming eloquence. What gloomy and foreboding literary passages! "If you will not hearken unto Me and will not do all these commandments. ... I also will do this unto you: I will appoint terror over you, even consumption and fever that shall make the eyes to fail and the soul to languish. ... I will set My face against you, and you shall be smitten before your enemies. ... Your strength shall be spent in vain. ... I will send the beast of the field among you, which shall rob you of your children, and destroy your cattle, and make you few in number; and your ways shall become desolate." Only the milder sentences are being quoted.

In the Book of Deuteronomy, twenty-eighth chapter, another series of maledictions are pronounced, some of them more frightening than those in our Torah portion. Listen to such shocking lines—". . . thou shalt be mad for the sight of thine eyes which thou shalt see. In the morning thou shalt say: 'Would it were evening!' and at evening thou shalt say: 'Would it were morning!'—for the fear of thy heart which thou shalt fear, and for the sight of thine eyes which thou shalt see." Such gripping terror, unbelievable in its sheer destructiveness!

Why were these warnings uttered not once, but twice? The Rabbis themselves could have accepted the dubious contentment of reading *one* version during the year. Why two? With characteristic genius they observed a difference in the two *Tohahot*. *Hala-lu b'lashon yahid ne-emrot, v'halalu b'lashon rabbim ne-emrot.* "In the one group, all the curses and threats are couched in the singular number, while in the other, they are uttered in the plural." In other words, one is spoken to the individual, men and women as single personalities. The other is directed to large numbers of people, to nations as a whole.

The Ramban tells us that the *Tohahah* is prophetic of the destruction of the First Commonwealth in the year 586 B.C.E. when the Babylonians conquered Judea, reduced Jerusalem to ashes, and sent our people into exile. The second, he indicates, foretells the devastation visited upon the Second Commonwealth by the Romans in the year 70 C.E. when the Temple was destroyed and Israel was dispersed to all the corners of the earth. While Nachmanides' suggestion is intriguing, it is questionable whether one can read such historic events out of the text. Yet, the two sets of maledictions can imply two types of national disintegration. One occurs when a people loses its national and political identity—its land, its statehood, its self-determination. The other, more tragic and more heartbreaking, when the individuals who comprise a people or a religious group lose pride in their heritage, forsake their faith and the values that make life worthwhile. The people, the nation, the group thus disintegrate because the individual men and women who are part of the group have lost all hope in and all meaning for morality, social striving, human growth.

The first *Tohahah* deals, then, with the type of national collapse which comes from loss of land or statehood. Our text utters warnings in the plural number because it refers to the collective determination of a people and the destruction of its soil—the cities of that people, its national shrines and institutions. The dynamic verses in the Book of Deuteronomy are directed principally to the breakdown of the morale of individual Jews, the crumbling faith—"Thou shalt have no faith in thine own existence," as the very text expresses it.

There were moments in our history when our people survived meaningfully and purposefully in spite of the loss of land and country. When the first Temple was destroyed, Babylon became a center for the revival of Judaism. Without nationhood, the Jew managed to contribute intellectually and morally not only to his own survival, but he produced ideas that became part of world culture. The individual Jew—even in exile, believed, and studied Torah and helped keep the group intact. After the downfall of the second Temple, we lost individual Jews. Jews became diluted in the political and social streams of foreign lands. Of course, there were Jews who accepted auto-da-fe and faced death *al kiddush ha-shem* rather than surrender their identity. But the insidious process through eighteen centuries expressing itself in forced conversion, expulsion, assimilation, self-hate, affected the morale of many individual Jews bringing about disintegration, loss of faith—a tragedy far worse than the loss of national independence.

There is much we can learn for our day from the thoughts of our sages and from the lessons of our history. We have been privileged to witness the rebirth of our people on the soil of its ancient homeland. Prime Minister of Israel, David Ben Gurion, uttered these words when Israel was admitted to the family of nations, "The Jewish people, returned to its own land, has been the greatest miracle of world history." He is correct. Israel has persevered against the overwhelming challenges of economic problems, political strife, military attack. We have seen *ge'ulat ha-aretz*—a miraculous and speedy rehabilitation of the soil, the reconstruction of cities, the reforestation of hills. All self-respecting American Jews are proud that Eretz Israel is a new and powerful bulwark of Judaism and of democracy, rich in promise in spite of its manifold difficulties, marvelous in its social vision, a resplendent center of the Hebrew language and literature, vital in its spirit and culture. It is bound to have a positive and heartening effect on Jews everywhere. The imperishable epic achieved by our people in Israel will be written into the saga of our great history for all time. A curse has come to an end. We have seen a recovery of a land and even statehood.

Not so close is *Ge'ulat ha-am*, the spiritual recovery of all the Jewish people, there in Israel, and especially here in America. We still do not experience the restoration of universal Jewish morale, the renewal of the faith of Jews in themselves, their heritage, their religious ideals, the determination to contribute spiritually and morally to the growth and the development of the society in which we live.

We are interested at this moment particularly in American Jewry. We may be thrilled and inspired by Israel, but Israel alone cannot give us a will to survive, and a faith in our uniqueness as a people here in America at the present juncture in history.

In America, we Jews, reflecting the materialism of our milieu, have reached a stage of plenty. We have contributed nobly to philanthropic causes and to charitable agencies. We have built hospitals and community centers and magnificent synagogue structures. But we are no different than the rest of the non-Jewish society in which we live and have our being. We are no more immune than they from the economic, social and psychological forces which beset people and beat relentlessly against them. If we are to judge from what has happened to our society—reverence, humility, compassion, moral strength have given way to aggression, competitiveness, combativeness, material possessions. There is an element of *"Tohehah"* in our time. Spiritual values are unsteady in America, and the pattern of behavior of individual Jews reflects the actions and attitudes of all other individual Americans. How do we know? We see what people strive after—raucous, cheap entertainment, mechanical gadgets, the power and the glory that money can buy. Read the best short stories and prize novels of the last few years written by men and women, non-Jews and Jews—and literature usually reflects psychological and sociological facts—the futility, the emptiness, the frustration, the mayhem, the bitterness, the sensuousness, the lack of faith and hope, the hysteria and inhumanity rise like deafening crescendos on page after page. Read the Kefauver report and briefs of governmental trials on organized crime, reflecting the social life of a generation—the racketeering, gambling, cheap politics, narcotics, fraud in high places and in low, as though these are the highest goals toward which all free Americans have been striving. We meet people who have superficial religions and who are groping; disillusioned intellectuals among them. No one in communal work can avoid the sight of so many emotionally unstable and socially immature people who wrestle with themselves and with their personality problems and who need psychiatric help desperately.

Lastly, the war in Korea and the cold war everywhere have shaken the foundations of our morality. There is not a single newspaper that fails to illuminate our growing military power, and the progress of atomic weapons and hydrogen bombs calculated to produce casualties unheard of by civilized man. In addition, the overt attacks on all forms of international cooperation, the Covenant of Human Rights, the UNESCO; the insistence on loyalty oaths and the rise of witch hunts in colleges and universities; the establishment of new restrictive immigration laws; the campaigns by publicists, commentators, senators of distortion and xenophobia have shaken the spirit of many people of all creeds and races. A resolution passed by the Presbyterian Church in the U.S.A. in May 1950 realistically appraised the fear and insecurity of our day: "The corruption that eats away the foundations of democracy, and will bring about the crumbling of its structure, is not the work of enemies without our walls but the work of those among us. Under the stimulus of fear we adopt many forms of oppression and terrorism—the very things we despise in Communism. Some forms of loyalty oaths are required which stifle freedom of thought and inquiry. People, even in America, are afraid to speak their convictions for fear of reprisal. Thus is laid the groundwork for a society which would destroy the very freedom we seek to save."

Yes, we are witnessing the recovery of land and statehood, but the recovery of the faith of the Jew in his ability to share in raising the standards of our society, in the potential of his own spiritual heritage for the good of all—this has not come as yet. If we could only reevaluate our goals and believe with a deep and abiding conviction that we Jews as individuals have something universal to contribute. If we could only understand how the Jewish religion with its vast reservoirs of spiritual truth—this *Kesher shel kayama*, this enduring tie which binds our people with God and meaningful survival—can still give this land and this world a spiritual rebirth, we would embrace it and use it and preach it and live it. If we did, we would stop this travesty of spending meager amounts for Jewish scholarship and Jewish religious education compared to what is spent on the tangible, material values of our time.

The picture is by no means a completely dark one. There are hopeful signs. There are young people who seem to be regaining some of the idealism their parents lost in the rush for material success. There are congregations of young Jews growing up here and there in America. There are college students and G.I.'s who refuse to succumb to the disillusionment of temporary pleasures and frustrations. They yearn for inner health saying, "Heal me, O Lord, and I shall be healed." They reach out for a will to live which comes from religion—the religion of Torah, the synagogue, the prophet, the saint—"the Judaism which speaks of God, and the worship of God," our ethical commandments and the quest after God. There are no substitutes for these if we are to survive. America itself will benefit as we rededicate ourselves to these values.

Let us join them in working for *Ge'ulat ha-am,* the religious reawakening and spiritual revitalization of the Jewish people, of individual Jews, just as we labored and continue to devote ourselves to the redemption of the land of Israel. Let us rid ourselves of that moral vacuum which we and other Americans try to fill with all sorts of "negativisms and fanaticisms." We need to develop as free and mentally healthy human beings a faith in God which transcends the false gods and gilded idols of our generation.

Let us remove the second *Tohehah,* the second series of curses which have emptied the souls of so many individual Jews and non-Jews—*veheye beraha*—and let us become a blessing once again.

45

How to Face a New Age

Rabbi Wilfred Shuchat

SEVERAL WEEKS AGO an article appeared in a prominent newspaper entitled "Symbols of the New Age."
It made reference to two phrases which more than any
other appear to symbolize the new world in which we
live. The first is "The Broken Atom"; the second, "The
Displaced Person." The Broken Atom calls to mind that
chain of convulsive forces set off in the natural world,
in science and in international relations with the drop-
ping of the Atom Bomb. The Displaced Person calls to
mind those destructive forces that have been unleashed
on human beings in our generation, the entire process
of dehumanization and dislocation that has engulfed
modern man. This is the new age we are living in—the
age of the Broken Atom and the Displaced Person.

How are we to face a new year in such an age? What
program can we set up for ourselves which can retain
our spiritual balance in a world of such uncertainty and
such imbalance? Surely such a question, such a problem, such a theme is not unworthy of our attention on
Rosh Hashonah.

Selected from *Best Jewish Sermons of 5715-5716.*

In this connection I should like to call to your attention a very helpful biblical parallel which corresponds almost exactly to the human situation today. I have in mind that gripping scene in the Bible where a Broken Atom was first unleashed, not on Hiroshima or Nagasaki but on Sodom and Gemorah, ancient dens of corruption and wickedness. The same narrative tells us about one of the early displaced persons in history—Lot and his family, the only survivors of this ancient and terrible holocaust. The only difference between the biblical crisis and that of our own day appears to have been that Lot had the advantage of special angels, special messengers from on High, to advise him in his difficulties. In a most gripping scene Scripture describes the fire and brimstone falling upon Sodom and Gemorah while the lonely figures of Lot's household went their way out of the fiery catastrophe. At this moment the three messengers address words of guidance and comfort to the confused Lot.

Himalet al Nafshecho—"Save your soul." It is imperative that you escape and work out a future for yourself.

There then follows a three-fold program in which Lot is offered specific directions for his deliverance.

"Do not look behind thee; neither stay thou in all the plain; flee to the mountain-top lest you be utterly consumed."

It is a fascinating verse, richly endowed with double meaning. It speaks not only of Lot's generation; its teaching reaches across the ages speaking directly to the lives, the hearts and for the age in which we live today.

We, the generation of the post-war, have experienced a destruction not unlike in quality the generation of Lot. We too are looking for a way to carry on our lives with some degree of maturity. While we do not expect Utopia in our lifetime, we would at least be grateful for a measure of wisdom that would enable us to order our personal lives with some degree of balance and perspective. "How to save our souls" thus becomes a question of great urgency, and Scripture offers us a series of recommendations designed to regain for all of us our spiritual composure.

In the first place *Al Tabit Acharecho*—"don't live in the past." This tendency to regress to the past is noted particularly during times of stress and struggle. Very often when tragedy strikes a home, the bereaved are obsessed by the thought that had they acted differently at a particular moment in the past, the tragedy might have been averted. This constant preoccupation with what might have been—is one of the greatest obstacles to mental health. We cannot forever keep open the rear guard of our lives. We simply have to learn that once ultimate decisions have been forced upon us, we must live our lives from the point of that decision onward and not try constantly to reopen that which has been closed. "Don't live in the past"—is good guidance for today. We cannot help remembering the past. We cannot help being grateful for the past; but to live in the past is to regress into infantile behavior. Do you remember the picture called *Sunset Boulevard* which depicted a movie actress who could never forget that twenty years before she had been a great star? Not being able to understand that she no longer had the talent or the popularity of an earlier era, her life was completely bereft of any sense of maturity or balance. "Don't look back," the Bible says, "don't live in the past."

We would be helped in understanding this point of view if we realized, first, that not everything in the past was good, and, second, that even those things in the past which were of great value, cannot necessarily be reproduced in our day.

One of the really fine books that appeared recently is the volume called *Life Is With People*—the sociological study of the *Shtetl*, the Jewish small town of Eastern Europe. It is a book that is all sweetness and light, reproducing with great love the wonderful constellation of Jewish values and loyalties that permeated the life of the *Shtetl*—their great learning, the warmth of family affection, the high standards of ethics, their sense of humor, their generosity, their customs and ceremonies, Sabbaths and festivals. To read the volume is to be filled with pride and warmth in the knowledge that these were our ancestors, verily a noble past. How far away are we from the *Shtetl*? A mere twenty-five years, fifty years. In no case more than a hundred years.

Does anyone imagine for a moment that this way of life, beautiful as it is—worthy as it is—could be reproduced today in contemporary America? It could not. For in order to have that kind of community, in order to have a *shtetl*, you must also have a ghetto. You must also have a measure of isolation from the world at large, making it possible to turn completely inward, into Jewish life. What Jew of today would be willing to sacrifice his emancipation even for a way of life as worthy as that of the *Shtetl*? Very few. In the words of Thomas Wolfe, "You can't go home again." Even that in the past which is good cannot always be reproduced because we live in different times. Therefore "don't look back." You can't live in the past.

It so happens that Lot's wife did not heed this advice. She did look back and, in language that is wonderfully symbolic, the Bible tells us that she was turned into a pillar of salt. That is what happens when we try to turn the clock back. We become arrested in time. We congeal. We atrophy. "Don't live in the past."

That is the first lesson. Now Scripture offers a second

recommendation. *Al taamod b'chol hakikor*—"don't come to a halt on any part of the plain where you now stand." Unsatisfactory as it is to live in the past, it is equally futile to freeze yourself in the present.

Living in the present sometimes expresses itself in living for the moment only, without regard to consequences. Omar Khayyam, in his famous poem sang a panegyric to this philosophy:

> Some for the glories of this world; and some
> Sigh for the prophets paradise to come;
> Ah, take the cash and let the credit go,
> Nor heed the rumble of a distant drum.

This kind of devil-may-care attitude often crops up during periods of great uncertainty and distrust. It is, of course, demonstrably irresponsible.

There is, however, a much more subtle way in which living for the present can become such a dangerous thing. I refer to that almost inexplicable craving for modernity that seems to obsess so many people.

We have reached the point in our society where if you want to insult your neighbor, you have merely to say that he is old-fashioned. Truth has become equated with modernity. People no longer read the best books; they read the latest book—or, what is even worse, the best seller. They no longer see the finest movie but the most recent. A designer in Paris sketches a style and millions of people change their outer mode of life in order to conform.

What is behind this compulsion to modernity which the late Dr. Solomon Goldman calls "The Great Idolatry of Our Time"? It is the disappearance of the individual as a clearly distinct person. It is the disappearance of every mark of individuality and discrimination in the face of a mass pull of conformity, of being like everybody else.

To what end this obsession to live entirely by the standards of the present? Will it produce a better human being, one who is more generous, more tolerant, more truth-loving, more talented?

The story is told that a Jewish pilot was among the first to participate in a trans-Atlantic crossing during the early days of aviation. When the newspaper reporters seeking a human interest story, interviewed the boy's father and asked for his opinion on his son's remarkable aviation achievement, the father instinctively replied: *Tsu vos hot er es gedarft?*

What did he need it for? That is the question that can be directed to many of our contemporaries who worship the idols of modernity. To what end? For what purpose? To such questions there is no satisfactory answer. Bad as it is to live in the past, it is equally unconstructive to freeze your life in the present. "Do not halt where you now stand."

If we are not to live in the past, and not to live for the present alone, what program are we to follow? Are we to live for tomorrow? Is the future to be the scene of our greatest aspirations and hopes? Why should that be? What is there about the future that should make us risk feeling that it will be any different or better than the past? Time by itself does not possess the key to the good life. It itself must be sanctified and filled with significance. It is here that our text rises to a beautiful climax. First, "Do not look back at the past." Second, "Do not halt where you now stand." And finally, "Flee to the mountain-tops."

To the mountain-tops! That is the message of the hour. The onward march of human history is not forward but upward. The hope of mankind is not necessarily tomorrow. It can be tomorrow if it is lived on certain levels of value, on the mountain-tops of hope, in which case it can also be today as well as yesterday. *Ha-hara himalet.* "Flee to the mountain-tops lest you be utterly consumed."

It is interesting to note how often the mountain is used as a biblical symbol. "Unto the hills I lift mine eyes" or "who shall ascend the mountain of the Lord?" The symbol of the mountain brings with it two thoughts—a sense of direction and a sense of perspective. The mountain represents what a modern preacher has called "the upward look." It seems to suggest that in spiritual life it is not the tense that counts but the direction—not forward but upward. When a man possesses the upward look, it is then possible for him to live in every tense, past, present or future.

In the magnificent Rosh Hashanah liturgy we have a section known as Zichronot, "remembrances" where we remember the past. But what is it that we remember of the past? Abraham, Isaac, Jacob, the prophets, great personalities whose lives were suffused with purpose, whose days were lived on the mountain-tops of great ideals and values. The rest of the past is ignored but these men are remembered because they rendered their time significantly alive.

The same prayerbook speaks of Malchuyot "the kingship of God" teaching us that when life is lived in the present under the shadow of God as King, when our conduct is subject to His judgment, then life even in the present can be lifted up to the mountain-tops of aspiration and high purpose.

Our liturgy also speaks of Shofrot "trumpeting of the future," heralding the possibilities of a universal peace for mankind if the nations live up to the Divine conditions for a just world. Thus the future can also become a source of human confidence and enriching possibilities. That is what happens when life is lived from the mountain-tops of aspiration. Past, present and future converge in a world of meaning.

This is the manner in which we ought to face the new year. The age of the Broken Atom and the Displaced Person can only be confronted from the mountain-tops of life, from the perspective which gives life a goal and a direction, and from that upward look, that Divine discontent, urging us constantly to scale the mountain-tops raising the sights of our life. The vital problem in the last analysis is not what we were or what we have become, but what we ought to be. This upward look is the key to a better future.

Standing at the threshold of a new year and a new age, this is the spirit in which we ought to confront the future.

"Do not live in the past."

"Do not reduce your life to the level of the present."

"To the mountain-tops of life"—thence may God bless you.

46

Three Questions We Must Answer

Rabbi Hillel E. Silverman

HAVE YOU EVER paused for a heart-to-heart talk with yourself? Have you ever indulged in self-analysis for the purpose of taking stock of yourself? Have you ever asked yourself, "What am I doing, where am I going?" Have you ever wondered whether you are a success or a failure as a human being?

Would that we might prepare a testing instrument that could conclusively determine, on the basis of a level attained, our merits as human beings! I can think of a number of provocative questions for such a soul-searching examination. Are you a happy person? Do you feel that you get the most out of life? Do you enjoy your work? What is the most important value in all the world to you? What do you do with your leisure time? What is your real goal and purpose in life? What do you hope to achieve by the time you are sixty or sixty-five years old? How many close friends do you have? Who are your closest friends? How many people will really miss you when you pass away? These are intriguing though per-

Selected from *Best Jewish Sermons of 5721-5722.*

plexing questions. Your answers would be a good indication of your success or failure as a human being.

However, I can think of three even more significant and crucial questions which must be answered if we are to take an honest and realistic inventory of ourselves.

In the Book of Kings, an episode is related about Elisha, the successor of Elijah, one of the earliest of the prophets. Elisha is befriended by a woman called the "Shunamite." He lives in her household for a number of years. The Shunamite is childless and the prophet, Elisha, promises her that she will soon give birth to a child. The following year she is blessed with a son. Elisha moves away to another village. A few years later the little boy hurts his head severely while playing in the field. The Shunamite, beside herself with fear and anxiety, rushes to the next village to seek out her friend and confidante, the prophet. Elisha, after these many years of absence from her household, forestalls her in her hour of need, to ask three simple but penetrating questions: *"Hashalom lach* ... Is it well with you? *Hashalom l'ishech* ... Is it well with your husband? *Hashalom layeled* ... Is it well with your son?"

Those would appear to be simple questions, they are in fact not simple at all. If we knew the answers to these three questions, we could, through them, measure our own success or failure as human beings.

Let us together consider these questions. First, *"Hashalom lach* ... Does it go well with you?" The word *shalom* is one of the most versatile in all of the Hebrew language. Literally, *shalom* means "peace." Today in Israel there is no word for "hello" nor is there a word for "good-bye." For the word *shalom* is used in its stead. You greet a friend, *"Shalom* ... Peace." A person takes leave of you, *"Shalom* ... Peace." Many are the nuances of this word: *shalom aleichem,* a cordial greeting; *shaol shalom,* to ask how a person is; *natan shalom*, to give greetings; *sukkat shalom*, canopy of peace; *alav hashalom*, may he rest in peace; *Yerushalaim*, Jerusalem, city of peace. *Shalom* is derived etymologically from the word *shalem* which means complete or whole. And this is the meaning of real peace; it is a state of being in which there is completeness and wholeness, nothing amiss, nothing lacking. In English we resort to the idiom, "How are you?" This expression is an innocuous one. You meet someone at a dance and say, "How are you?" You have never seen him before. Are you really interested in the state of his health—or he in yours? In Hebrew we do not say "How are you?" when we meet on the street, at a theatre or in a synagogue. We ask, rather, "*Ma schlomcha*?" Is everything complete in your life? Is anything lacking, anything missing? Surely, this is far more significant than the blunt and casual "How are you?"

This, precisely, is what the prophet Elisha conveys to the Shunamite. He does not say "How are you?" but, "*Hashalom lach*? . . . What is the state of your peace?" How is your conscience? Can you live with yourself? By far, this is the most penetrating question that we can ever ask of ourselves. Can we live with our consciences? Can we live with ourselves, our real selves, not the selves that we pretend to be, not the self that we display to our friends in public, not our made-up self, but beneath all of that artifice and masquerade, the real self, the honest self, the private self, the self that is known only by you and Almighty God. Can you live with that self? Can you live with your conscience? When you rise up in the morning are you able to look into the mirror with pride and confidence that you will like what you see there? I do not mean your physical image but your moral and spiritual reflection! Can you gaze into the mirror in the morning, and say in all honesty, there is nothing wrong with this reflection, nothing tarnished, nothing ugly. My conscience is clean, my heart is pure, I am not hiding anything, I do not suggest subterfuge, there is nothing devious about that reflection. I am honest, above-board, pure. I say what I mean and I mean what I say, my yea is yea and my nay is nay. *Hashalom lach?* Can you live with your real self? This is what Elisha asks the Shunamite. And the Shunamite replies: *"Shalom li* . . . I can live with my conscience." Again, can we, in all truth, say the same? Can we say: There is nothing in my business that I hide from my customers, my associates, my employers, my employees, my competitors. I have nothing to hide from my family, nothing to hide in my home, nothing to hide from my neighbors living on the street, nothing to hide from my community, my synagogue, my rabbi. Can we say as the Shunamite said: I have not hurt a fellow man, I have not deprived anyone of something rightfully his, insulted anyone, embarrassed anyone, destroyed another's reputation, gossiped, slandered. I can live with myself. I can live with my conscience happily and freely.

Oftentimes, we delude ourselves into a clean conscience, but in reality it is only the gift of a poor memory. There are so many people in our midst who cannot answer this first question affirmatively. There are in this community practiced and cultivated hypocrites and phonies; there are those who are unethical, who lie, who steal, who cheat, who deceive, who gossip, who slander. It is time we asked our real selves: *Hashalom lach?* Can we live with ourselves? Can we live in truth and peace with our conscience?

The second question that the prophet Elisha directs to the Shunamite is: *"Hashalom l'ishech?"* How is your husband? How is your wife? How is your family? How is your home? This is the substance of his question: How is your home life? Consider this question, honestly and squarely: How is your home life?

Judaism teaches that the home is the great reservoir and fortress of our faith. The home is even more important than the synagogue, for Judaism could conceivably survive without the synagogue if the Jewish home was to remain intact. For the most part, whatever is done in the synagogue can be done equally well in the home. The Sabbath is observed in the home, the festivals, the rituals. When we pray in the home with a *minyan* and a *Sefer Torah* the home is virtually converted into a synagogue. Judaism instructs that the home is the *Mikdash M'aht*, the Sanctuary-in-miniature. Ideally, the Jewish home is holy and sanctified. There is religion in the home, there is learning in the home, values are taught, character is molded. In the home there is security, protection, beauty, warmth, serenity and inspiration. The home generates a feeling of being wanted, of being needed, of being loved.

Hashalom l'ishech? How is your home life? The question should be treated in all candor. How is our home life—not the life that the community sees, but our inner home life. Do we look forward to being in our homes? Do we anticipate leisure hours in our home? Do we enjoy our home? Or do we attempt, consciously or unconsciously, it does not matter, to run away from our homes? *Hashalom l'ishech?* How is your home life? Where do you celebrate the highlights of your life? In your home, or in a nightclub? In your home, or at a show? In your home, or at a dance? In your home, or on a vacation? It has been aptly said that "homes have never been so comfortable and people so seldom in them." Are you in your home merely physically, or do you exchange intelligent and warm conversation with the members of your family? Do you read together with your family, listen to good music together? *Hashalom l'ishech?* Do you live in a home, or do you live in a house? There is a great difference between a home and a house. In a house we merely eat and sleep and sprawl and tend our biological needs. Coleridge is reported to have remarked that "the largest part of mankind is nowhere a greater stranger than in the home." How true! In so many homes parents are strangers to children, children to parents, husbands to wives, wives to husbands.

Hashalom l'ishech? How is your home life? Is there religion in your home? Or is your home an empty shell stripped of all these lofty treasures? One of the most wonderful phrases of Judaism is *shalom bayit* . . . a peaceful home. This is the key to happy and successful living—the great ideal of a peaceful, beautiful, wholesome home life predicated upon harmony, mutual consideration, compatibility and love. Are these to be found in your home? Or when you enter your home do you find conflict, noise, argument, irritation, sarcasm? Ben Johnson said "The ultimate result of all ambition is to be happy in the home." Isn't it sad that so few people have really attained *shalom bayit?*

Elisha asked a third and final question of the Shunamite: *"Hashalom layeled?"* How is your child? Is it well with your children? What kind of children are you raising? This is certainly another leading question.

Are you a successful parent? Are you proud of your children? I do not mean this in a worldly and material way. I am not asking whether you are proud that they have acquired a college degree, or earn a good living, or live in a fine home, or associate with the right people. But, I am asking, have you raised children with an eye to developing character? *Hashalom layeled?* Does it go well with your children? Are they innately refined and just and well-mannered? Do they have integrity? Are they kind? Do they have compassion for others? Or, are they selfish, self-centered, pleasure-seeking, irresponsible? *Hashalom layeled*? What kind of children do you have? Are they respectful, do they respect you, have they acquired wholesome ideals and values from you? Do your children know the meaning and practice of sacrifice, loyalty, courage, patience, humility, temperance, honesty, hospitality, love? *Hashalom layeled*? How are your children? Do they feel that they alone exist in the world? Do they consider their luxuries and their pleasures and conveniences primary: How are your children? Are they thoughtful or are they spiteful? Are they smug, conceited, spoiled, cynical? Do your children love worship, the synagogue, the Jewish people, their fellow man? Are you close to your children? Can you have a heart-to-heart talk with your children? Do your children confide in you? Do you confide in your children? Do you see eye-to-eye with them? Is there between you a unity of purpose that binds you together in an inseparable bond?

We have reviewed three essential questions, penetrating, revealing, and deeply provocative. The answers will betray what you are, whether you have mastered life, if your days are worthwhile, if you are successful. You must answer these questions to yourself, silently, in your heart, and above all with complete honesty. *Hashalom lach*? Can you live with yourself, with your conscience? *Hashalom l'ishech*? Is it well with your home life? *Hashalom layeled*? Is it well with your children?

If after long and thoughtful deliberation you can say, as the Shunamite said, *shalom li*, all is well. Then it matters not who you are, and what you are, how much you own, and how much power and prestige you have mustered. You have won the greatest gift of all, for you are a success as a human being.

47

The Eternal Light

Rabbi Baruch Silverstein

IN EVERY SYNAGOGUE, just above the Ark, there is a small lamp with a dim mellow glow, called the *ner tamid*, the Eternal Light. This light, unlike others, burns continually and uninterruptedly, day and night, year after year, decade after decade. All the other lamps are switched on and off in accordance with the customary rules of economy in the house of residence as well as in the house of worship. This particular light, however, transcends such mundane considerations. The *ner tamid* may not be extinguished even for one minute. It must spread its luster upon the synagogue without interruption.

An aura of mystery surrounds the *ner tamid*. The fixture holding this unique light is artistically executed and ornately decorated. The wire that supplies the electric current is cleverly concealed. Carefully camouflaged beyond any recognition is the small, painted bulb. Very few members of the congregation have ever seen the hidden switch controlling this light.

The origin of the *ner tamid* may be traced back to the

Selected from *Best Jewish Sermons of 5721-5722*.

early beginnings of Jewish religious history, namely, to the ancient forerunner of the modern house of worship, the Tabernacle in the wilderness. Among the specific directions given by God to Moses with regard to the construction of the mobile sanctuary, we find the following commandment: "And thou shalt command the children of Israel, that they bring unto thee pure olive oil beaten for the light, to cause a lamp to burn continually. In the tent of meeting . . . Aaron and his son shall set it in order to burn from evening to morning before the Lord. It shall be a statute forever throughout their generations. . . ." In conformity with this statute, the *ner tamid* became a permanent fixture of the portable tabernacle which accompanied the Israelites throughout their journey in the wilderness. As the biblical text clearly implies, this commandment was to be binding upon all future generations and future sanctuaries. When the permanent *Beth Hamikdash* in Jerusalem replaced the portable sanctuary of the wilderness, the *ner tamid* was a significant part of its elaborate decorations. With the destruction of the Temple, the Eternal Light continued to be a required adornment of the local synagogues which replaced the national shrine. About two thousand years after the commandment of the Eternal Light was first given to Moses, the rabbis of the Talmud declared, "It is customary to light a *ner tamid* in each synagogue which is called 'the miniature sanctuary.'" The Talmud cautiously refers to this practice as "customary." Universal observance made it mandatory.

Since the commandment states specifically that the light must burn continually, precautions have to be taken lest it be extinguished accidentally. Some synagogues are so concerned over such an eventuality that they are reluctant to use electricity for the *ner tamid*, fearing that the electric current might be subject to sudden failure. Besides, bulbs must be replaced frequently, necessitating brief periods of darkness in violation of the law. Because of these objections, naphtha or oil is often used instead of electricity. Constant replenishment of the supply assures uninterrupted illumination.

The reasons for the burning of the *ner tamid* are not entirely clear, but are surrounded by mystery. Its uncertainty provoked, on many occasions, lively debates among the Rabbis of the Talmud and teachers of later generations. Some of our sages contended that the early origin of the *ner tamid* was primarily functional, and that it fulfilled an urgent practical need in the ancient house of worship. They stated, "*Mimenu madlikim et hanerot.*" The Eternal Light apparently served as a "pilot light" or "fire bank" from which all other candles and lamps were kindled. This torch which burned continually, constituted a readily available source of fire which was not easily obtainable.

Many rabbis, however, disagreed with this pragmatic interpretation of the nature of the *ner tamid*. With language revealing deep indignation they questioned the validity of this explanation. "*Hakadosh-baruch-hu shekulo or, tzarich l'or shelachem?* . . . Does the Lord of the Universe, who is the source of all light, need your light?" The Eternal Light, they insist, is not an illumination *for* God but a flame *from* God; not a lamp for the House of God, but a lustrous gleam from God's heavenly abode; not a tool of practical convenience, but a celestial spark of sacred dimensions. "It is not that I am in need of light, says the Lord, but you who are in need of it." The Eternal Light, these sages insist, is of symbolic significance. It serves as a visible reminder of the eternal God and of the eternal values that form the basis of religious faith. The emphasis upon its "perpetual burning," these teachers declare, serves to admonish us to include in our lives pursuits of permanent durability and of imperishable value. The *ner tamid*, shedding its uninterrupted illumination upon the worshippers, is a dramatic reminder that we should not waste our lives in fleeting and ephemeral interests, but must concentrate on important values.

Now, if this is the nature of the Eternal Light, it certainly contains a message of great significance to our own generation. "Modern man," a contemporary philosopher said, "is trying to win small prizes, and is gambling his life away." Most of our lives are occupied with petty wants and desires. Our precious time and our talents are spent on passions and aspirations that are temporary and evanescent. We concentrate all our efforts upon the acquisition of material possessions, and we neglect the spiritual treasures which time and tide cannot corrode. Our lives are occupied with means and not with ends; our obsessive interests consist in preparing for some future day when we shall be able to lead a life free from worries, but that day constantly eludes us. Like the reader who never goes beyond the book's introduction, so do we occupy ourselves with the periphery of life; we stop with the introduction to life; we never reach its essence, its real contents.

An enlightened American industrialist recently said: "It is a good thing to have money and the things that money can buy. It is, however, equally important to check whether we have not lost the things that money cannot buy."

The Eternal Light reminds us to hold tight to those aspects of life which are of eternal value. It warns us that if we would transcend the fleeting nature of human existence, we must attach ourselves to values that are of enduring significance. It admonishes us to acquire treasures that do not corrode and cannot be stolen.

Oddly enough, our grandfathers possessed these treasures in relative abundance. In spite of economic poverty, social ostracism and countless other deprivations, they did not consider their existence meaningless. Their lives contained spiritual riches of transcendent significance. Our ancestors of past generations did not suffer from the mental anguish plaguing our age. Their religious piety made them largely immune to the gnawing feelings that life is purposeless. Their daily acts were in response to the will of Almighty God, and therefore embraced imperishable values. Through the performance of *mitzvot* they became "partners with God" in His universal plan. The enmeshing web of ritual linked them with affectionate bonds to the Divine Master of the Universe, the Jewish people and Jewish history. It invested their lives with permanence. It gave them a sense of direction and purpose. It supplied them with anchorage.

Our generation is painfully aware of the lack of these values. Agonizing doubts of purposelessness and impermanence disturb our peace of mind and soul. Notwithstanding our advanced education and high standard of living we feel impoverished and insecure. A young British existentialist referred to our age as a "generation of outsiders." We are suffering because we lack a "magnificent obsession," an indispensable element in every meaningful life. The most obsessive occupation of our generation, namely, material acquisition, is the most illusive and unsatisfactory of all aspirations. Material abundance does not necessarily result in personal happiness. Strangely enough, those who are financially secure are often among the most insecure individuals of our society. Obviously, economic blessing alone is not the cure-all solution to life's manifold demands.

A story is told of a Chasidic rabbi who met one of his followers unexpectedly in the marketplace. The disciple, who was a moderately successful businessman, was rather embarrassed by this chance encounter. His rapid steps had shortened his breath and covered his face with prominent beads of perspiration. He seemed to be deeply upset by disturbing business matters, and was hardly in a mood for leisurely conversation. When the rabbi asked him where and why he was running so breathlessly, he haltingly replied, "To make a living, of course." The rabbi philosophically retorted, "How do you know, my dear man, that your living lies in the direction toward which you are running? Perhaps it is in the opposite direction, and you are actually running away from it."

The values set up as significant, the goals of life as expressed in its philosophy, define the essence of a religious way of life. Many centuries ago the Jewish sages of the Talmud drew up a list of eternal values in Judaism, and prefaced it with a most beautiful introduction: "These are the things, the fruits of which a man enjoys in this world, while the capital is laid up for him in the world to come." This table of eternal values was not allowed to remain hidden in the austere volumes of the Talmud, but was added to the daily prayer book in order to make it more readily available to the masses. The following practices were enumerated by the rabbis: "Honoring father and mother, deeds of lovingkindness, attendance at the synagogue morning and evening, hospitality to the wayfarer, visiting the sick, dowering the bride, attending the dead to the grave, devotion in prayer, making peace between man and his friend; but the study of Torah surpasses them all."

The validity of this table of eternal values remains basically unimpaired. Evolved by the authors of the Mishna close to two thousand years ago, it is equally applicable to our own day. Although the terminology may be old-fashioned, the true meaning and enduring value of these activities hardly need elaboration. By "honoring father and mother," the rabbis not only implied respect for parents, but emphasized the holiness of all family relationship. By "making peace between man and his friend" the rabbis underscored the enduring values of true friendship. By "synagogue attendance morning and evening," our revered teachers not only alluded to prayer, but affirmed the importance of personal involvement in the common endeavors of society and in community life.

The conspicuous omission of *tzedaka* or charity from the list of basic values is not accidental, for its inclusion might cause hardship to many well-intentioned individuals who have no financial means for giving. However, the rabbis substituted for *tzedaka* several other charitable deeds of equal, if not superior value. "Acts of lovingkindness" are not limited to financial gifts or even temporary loans. "Hospitality to the wayfarer" does not require affluence or a split-level home with a patio. "Visiting the sick" can easily be practiced by everyone, and as an enduring charitable act it is certainly not inferior to monetary gifts to the hospital fund. Similarly, "attending the dead to the grave" and comforting the bereaved are deeds of inestimable lovingkindness. Genuine expressions of sympathy—shedding a soft tear, extending words of encouragement—exert healing effects upon the tragedy-stricken, and restore their shaken faith in the worthwhileness of life. "Dowering the bride" may be expressed by extending the hospitality of our modest home for the wedding ceremony, baking a few cakes for the wedding reception, surrendering a few items of clothing to replenish a skimpy wardrobe or assisting the groom to find some suitable occupation.

The remaining two selections in this remarkable

table of eternal values belong to a somewhat different category. The "study of Torah" and "devotion in prayer" are distinguished by the uniqueness of their spiritual and intellectual demands. Yet if success in these endeavors is not easily attainable, it is not because they require rare talents, or unusual gifts. What study and prayer do require is concentration and reflection, sensitivity, inquisitive curiosity and a sense of reverence. These qualities are in various degrees of intensity, the latent possessions of each human being. Meaningful prayer is not the exclusive domain of rabbis and saints. Striving to attain a sense of nearness to God, the essence of all inspired prayer, is the privilege of all human beings. Similarly, all of us are invited to participate in the study of Torah and to draw from it as large a measure of wisdom as our capacities will allow. All of us are invited to rub shoulders with the great minds of all times, and to gain new insights in our understanding of man and the universe. Such acquisitions, undoubtedly, are of imperishable benefit and eternal value. No wonder, therefore, that in drawing up a list of life-enriching acts, the rabbis attached overriding importance to the element of learning. "*V'talmud torah k'neged kulam* . . . and the study of Torah surpasses them all."

While general practice dictates placing the Eternal Light in front of the congregation, there is sufficient evidence to indicate that in certain synagogues of post-exile times this lamp was installed over the exit-door, opposite the Holy Ark. Since the Ark invariably faced eastward, the Eternal Light located in the west, in the rear of the synagogue, became known as the *ner maaravi* or "western light." It is not difficult to speculate on the purpose behind the selection of this particular place. The message of the Eternal Light must be in front of our eyes not only while we find ourselves in the holy precincts of the synagogue, but, above all, while we are away from its embracing influence. By placing the Eternal Light over the exit door, it faced the worshipper while he was taking leave of the House of God, thereby serving as a dramatic parting reminder. The Eternal Light admonished him to carry its message with him into the street, the marketplace, and into his home.

By now, the custom of placing the Eternal Light in the east is too well established to allow for easy change. Wherever placed, however, the Eternal Light is a most significant symbol. No wonder so much precaution has always been taken to assure its uninterrupted radiance. No wonder so much awe and reverence surrounds its mellow illumination. For when the *ner tamid* sheds its mystical rays over the synagogue, the Jew senses the presence of God in his sanctuary, and exclaims, "How goodly are thy tents, O Jacob; thy Tabernacles, O Israel!"

48

Six Million for Six Million

Rabbi Ralph Simon

IT IS AN INTERESTING FACT that the Bible commands us to observe Rosh Hashanah as a Holy Day, but nowhere is it designated as Rosh Hashanah, the New Year. Even in our prayers we do not find this title. It is only by popular usage that it came to be so designated. The Bible and the prayer book give it an entirely different name. It is called Yom Hazikaron, the Day of Remembrance. Our tradition dedicates the first day of the year to the act of remembering. Why is remembering so important that we have made Rosh Hashanah the most important observance of the year? Our answer would be that remembering is the one act which makes us truly human. Man is, after all, a part of the animal world. The quality which distinguishes him from the brutes is remembering. Memory is practically non-existent among animals. They live by instincts and conditional reflexes, but they carry over very little from yesterday, and they have no conscious concern for tomorrow. The animal lives only in the present tense. Man however, has a faculty of memory which determines his entire life. He lives

Selected from *Best Jewish Sermons of 5733-5734.*

in three dimensions of time—the past, the present and the future. Because he remembers yesterday, his today is meaningful, and he is able to plan for tomorrow.

We often read accounts of people who are afflicted with a disease which psychiatrists recognize as amnesia. Because of some trauma or illness, it produces a total loss of memory. We must distinguish here between some symptoms that are associated with senility. A young woman recently told me that she was having trouble with her mother who is losing her memory. She forgets anything that happened yesterday, but remembers very clearly what happened fifty years ago. This is a form of selective memory, while amnesia is a total inability to remember. People who are so afflicted discover that life actually loses its meaning. They do not know who they are, nor anything about themselves; they remain bewildered until their memory is restored. Rosh Hashanah is therefore, a holiday that deals with a most important faculty. Because it is Yom Hazikaron, the day of remembering, it bids us to stay human and to maintain that quality which has raised us to the highest level of existence.

What are the most important memories of this generation? There are two events which exceed in scope anything that ever happened in the world history of the Jewish people. The first is the Holocaust, known in Hebrew as the *Shoah* (destruction). That catastrophe happened to our people between the years 1940 and 1945 when six million Jews were exterminated. The second great memory of this generation is the rebirth of our people after 2,000 years, the creation of the State of Israel. This day of remembering should bring to our awareness these two epochal events of our time. What do they mean? The tragedy of the Holocaust is so unique that we had to invent a special word which would indicate that an entire people were doomed to be murdered. It is the word "genocide," the extermination of a people. I would utter a word of caution about this word. It is being used carelessly by people today in a manner which belittles the Jewish tragedy. They refer to the war in Vietnam as genocide. Casualties in various riot situations are frequently called genocide. These are indeed tragic events, but they do not fit into the category of the Shoah. The most vicious attempt to belittle our catastrophe is now taking place in the Soviet Union. In the city of Kiev there is one of the saddest places on earth. It is an area known as Babi Yar where, during World War I, the Nazi forces had assembled some 10,000 Jews and machine-gunned them to death. That ravine ran with blood for days and became a vast mass grave. Tourists who visit there are shocked to discover that the local authorities have not permitted any monument to be erected there which mentions the martyrdom of our murdered brethren. One official cynically explained: "Jews were not the only victims. Other people died also." He overlooked one crucial fact that relates to the use of the word "genocide." War has many victims. Innocent people are killed when shells and bombs strike. Many people were put to slave labor by the Germans. But only for the Jew was there a special fate which makes comparison with other people impossible. Only for us was there a sentence of death on every man, woman and child who bore the name Jew. The Nazis invented a new crime. It had nothing to do with what one did. It did not matter whether one was an enemy national or not. For the Jew, the crime was to be alive. Anyone who had a Jewish parent or grandparent was systematically searched out and brought to ultimate destruction. The weak were killed immediately; the stronger were enslaved and reduced to living skeletons before they were exterminated. Under the Nazis, no Jew could escape. We should remember that if they had, God forbid, achieved a military victory the "ultimate solution to the Jewish problem" as they euphemistically called it would have occurred. This meant the death of every Jew in the world. American Jews should not forget that we were sheltered and reprieved by the Allied victory.

We have been numbed by the enormity of the atrocity that was committed against our people and have never come to grips with the meaning of the Holocaust. Rosh Hashanah bids us to remember in a meaningful way what happened to us over a generation ago. There is an uncanny similarity in numbers between the six million who died, and the six million Jews who live in this free blessed country of ours. The question that we must ask is, how do the prosperous six million American Jews relate to the other six million who were shot, gassed, cremated and buried alive: What is our response to that tragedy? An enormous literature has been growing up around this subject. Some of it is dangerous because it embodies certain evasions. One is an almost heartless judgment which has been uttered by Nazi apologists and even by some self-hating Jews. They say in effect, "It is true that Jews were murdered, but it was their own fault." We can dismiss this kind of explanation with contempt. It is the language of the vicious anti-Semite or the psychotic Jew. Some observers and writers are retreating into cynicism. If the Holocaust could occur, there is no God and no justice in the world. It is the cry that was uttered centuries ago by Jews who witnessed tragedy and proclaimed: *"Let din v'let dayan*—there is no justice and there is no Judge." If we think this today, the world is doomed. We might as well prepare ourselves for the ultimate destruction of mankind. The third evasion is most often heard and therefore, most dangerous. People do not want to hear and be reminded of the past. From the point of view of human drama, the Holocaust is certainly the most gripping and tragic event of history. A few good films on this subject, the "Diary of Anne Frank" and "Judgment at Nuremberg" were produced; yet people did not want to see them. They would rather forget and be entertained. They do not want to be confronted with tragedy. We recall that the Olympic games which ended so tragically, were opened with an attempt to hold a memorial service at Dachau, near Munich. The planners felt that it would provide an appropriate expression of contrition and sorrow. The Olympic games were attended by more than 10,000 people, yet when the memorial was held at Dachau, a handful of people attended—mostly members of the Jewish group.

The newspapers published an article written by a young journalist by the name of Bob Greene. In it he said: "It is not supposed to be very strong in us for we cannot remember. We are the young Jews born after Hitler, and we have never considered the fact that we are Jewish to be a large part of our identity . . . It is not supposed to be very strong in us, and yet, here I am sitting at a typewriter in a hotel room hundreds of miles from home trying to write a story, and I cannot do it. For the television has just finished telling the story, the story how once again people who hate the Jews have knocked on the door in the middle of the night and done their killing, and I can think of nothing else . . . It is not supposed to be strong in us, because all the barriers are down now; and a hotel will not turn us away or a restaurant will not deny us a table if our name does not sound right. And yet, when the killings began, they thought to take a young man named Mark Spitz out of Germany, because he may be the best swimmer in the world, but first of all he is a Jew, and no one wanted to think what might happen to him. Many of the people who thrilled as he won the gold medals were very surprised to find out now that Spitz is a Jew. Later, of course, they will say it doesn't matter what his religion is. But Spitz knew that it mattered. We all knew that it mattered, and that it would be smarter for him to go home . . . There are young men who are dead this week who should be alive, and it would be a horrible thing, no matter who they were. But of course, they were Jews, the reason that they are dead is because they were Jews, and that is why on this night there are so many of us starting to realize for the first time what that means."

What does it mean that we are designated as Jews today? It took an entire generation to begin to formulate some reaction to the tragedy that overtook us. We now have a young writer by the name of Elie Wiesel, who has produced a series of novels, in which he tries to describe what the Holocaust meant to him. A philosophic interpretation is offered by a teacher named Emil Fackenheim. He is a Professor of Philosophy at the University of Toronto, and was himself a victim of the Nazis in 1938 when he was a Rabbi in Germany. He was taken to the infamous Dachau concentration camp. Fortunately, he was released and came to freedom in America. Dr. Fackenheim has wrestled with this problem for thirty years and has sought the answer for himself. *Time* magazine published an article about the Jews which contained a brief quotation from this Professor of Philosophy. He said that the Torah contains 613 commandments ("taryag mitzvot") which were given to the Jewish people. Since Hitler, the Jews have added a 614th commandment: To stay alive! The greatest mitzvah that a Jew can perform today is to stay alive. Then he denies victory to Hitler. Every Jew who lives today proclaims that the Nazis failed. Every Jew is a living witness to the fact that the program of genocide was defeated. To fail to live is to betray the Jewish people and all of mankind. The warning that Rosh Hashanah gives is that the war with Hitlerism is not yet won. Any Jew who does not stand up as a Jew, gives a posthumous victory to Adolph Hitler!

This explains why the second event is so meaningful. The rebirth of Israel has resurrected a state which the entire world had declared to be dead. In the year 70, the Romans destroyed the Temple, and the City of Jerusalem, and commemorated the event when Titus, the conqueror, came to Rome. They erected the arch of Titus which is still standing, and inscribed in Latin the words "Judea capta-Judea is captured" and ended. The Jewish response to Titus, to Hitler, and to all who sought to destroy us is "Am Yisrael hai—the Jewish people lives." This is to us a double challenge. We, the six million, are the representatives of the other six million. We ask each Jew today, who represents another Jew who was murdered, how do you bear witness to that fact and how do you vindicate your survival? Have we conquered genocide and defeated Hitler by the meaningfulness of our lives? We have a program to fulfill. Each of us has to live for two people—for ourselves and for that alter ego, the Jew who died because he bore our same name. This means that we must study and discover our past. We must read our great treasures—the Bible and the Talmud, our poetry and our history. We must rediscover ourselves and proclaim that we are alive. The Jew today must discover his people, his soul, and his history. It is a challenge that we cannot evade.

Our second response is that we who are free and affluent shall keep alive the State of Israel. We witnessed the campaign of terror and murder which attempts to deter our forward march. We have to declare, as the prophet did in ancient times: "Every weapon that will be created against you will not succeed." No Jew must betray the mandate to preserve humanity and to keep sanity in a crazy world. This is Yom Hazikaron, the day of memory. Let us never forget that we are surrogates for Jews who died. Yesterday the Jewish world said Kaddish for its dead. We do not end with Kaddish, we begin with it. There is another word that is based on the same root, Kiddush, which means sanctification and joy. We shall convert the Kaddish to Kiddush and we shall declare to the world that we will not be deterred. On this day of remembering the six million that are gone, we the six million who are alive will proudly uphold our heritage. We go forth into the new year with bravery and energy to build a world of peace. We reaffirm the words of the Psalmist: "I shall not die but live and declare the works of the Lord."

49

Our Ends Are in Our Beginnings

Rabbi Jacob J. Weinstein

LESS THAN A MONTH AGO we celebrated the birthday of the world. In loving empathy, in a symbolic way, we placed 5722 candles on the birthday cake commemorating the moment the Lord said, "Let there be light." And six days later, according to the biblical author, God created man. In the ecstasy of the inspiration Michelangelo drew from this account, he pictured God on the ceiling of the Sistine Chapel as reaching out his finger to convey the spark of life to the outreaching finger of Adam, thus beginning an Adamic-link chain-reaction which has continued to this day.

Last Tuesday, we celebrated Simchat Torah and no sooner had we finished the last verse of Deuteronomy than we began the first verse of Genesis, like chain smokers, as though to say in matters of the spirit there is no beginning and no end; or rather more profoundly, as befits the people of Einstein, in the end is our beginning as in the beginning is our end. What a peculiar people we must indeed be to rejoice in a law that com-

---

Selected from *Best Jewish Sermons of 5721-5722*.

mands us to rein in our instincts and our appetites and live by the light of that order which is best for the larger community in time and space. Imagine our Supreme Court Justices dancing the Hora around the Constitution and its Amendments!

Today, on *Shabbat Beraishit* we read in full the account which we began on Simchat Torah. The first chapter of Genesis belongs to the top level of the mind. It is rational, scientific, studied. It is an account which might be appreciated by an architect, an engineer or a musician. God works by fiat, He creates by decree, but it is not an arbitrary decree. It is ordered, guided by a sense of reality, a sense of first things first. The light must be separated from the darkness, the earth divided from the water. The provender of grass and herbs must first be provided for the animals; and when all is in readiness, the stage is set for man—both male and female—who will reproduce according to their kind, as the grass and trees will yield seed according to their kind. There is a fine sense of balance and proportion, a division of function between earth and sea, moon and sun, man and beast. The Creator calls this planned universe "very good," and the seventh day—the *Shabbat*—a day of rest and fulfillment, the joyous celebration of the balance and harmony achieved by the work of the six preceding days.

This Sabbath has kept Israel more than Israel has kept the Sabbath. It is not merely the day of rest, the day of cessation of work. It is token and harbinger of the ideal world to come, the time of the Messiah, when the lion will lie down with the lamb and tears shall be wiped from all faces. The Sabbath is at the core of all reforms to extend the sway of justice in the world. The seventh year was the year of release: release for the soil, a sabbatical year for Mother Earth; the release of the slave from his bondage, the debtor from his debt. And when seven times seven years were counted, on the Sabbath of Sabbaths, the Jubilee Year was proclaimed on the Day of Atonement. In this year all land would revert to the original owners and the slate would be cleansed for a new fresh start. The Levitical legislation for the Jubilee provided 49 years for the natural differences between men to operate, but in order that these differences might not become frozen and thereby create impassable barriers between men—for men who live differently, think differently—it arranged for a radical new deal in the fiftieth year.

No wonder Moses Hess, a compatriot and co-worker of Karl Marx, envisioned in his *Rome and Jerusalem* a Sabbath of the world, when men's abilities and ambitions would be in balance, when the forces of production and the forces of consumption would be harmonized, when men and nations would cooperatively till the earth and justly share its ever increasing yield. Karl Marx, unhappily, was not seduced by the Sabbath spirit. He saw struggle and uncompromising hostility where Hess saw conciliation and adjustment. If one can still hold to the comforting illusion that institutions are the projections of men, one might say that the *kolhoz* and the Soviet State are the projections of Karl Marx; the *kibbutz* and the Social Welfare State of Israel are the projections of Moses Hess. And it becomes ever more clear that the political order which will best harmonize freedom and security, the one and the many, the person and his government will have more to learn from little Israel than from either the United States or the USSR.

I have told you only of the first account of creation when the Lord considered each day's work as good, and the culmination of his work in the creation of man and the Sabbath as very good. But this condition is not long-lasting. Eden and perfection are only sometime things. Even God's harmony cannot be static, frozen, like the youth on Keats' Grecian urn.

The fourth verse of the second chapter of Genesis begins another story of creation. This has always been more appealing to people. It is a much more primitive account. A mist comes up from nowhere and brings vegetation in its wake. God makes man of the dust of the earth and breathes into him the breath of life so that man becomes a living soul. Even Eden proves lonely for man, so God makes a helpmate for him out of one of his ribs. Now Adam and Eve are given the freedom of the garden and the care of its flora and fauna except for one tree in the middle: the Tree of Knowledge. Of that they are forbidden to eat. But the serpent slithers up to Eve and soft-talks her into eating of that tree and into persuading Adam to eat of it, too. Paradise is too much for men. They are driven from the Garden and sojourn East of Eden—and it seems are still going ever farther East, like that shining youth in Wordsworth's ode who daily *from* the East must travel.

That first careless rapture, that divine ecstasy of the first account of creation seems so far away from us. The Lord, it seems, prepared a second Eden for us in this good earth of America; but we do not obey the laws of harmony and justice by which we might enjoy it. The Sabbath which was the crown and purpose of creation has become a word of apprehension, of fear, of terror. It connotes not the end of harmonious equilibrium of working forces but a dreaded layoff, severance, and unemployment. Our great industries—steel, autos, packing—are caught in the constant throes of crisis, because we refuse to face new conditions with new remedies. We hold on to the old shibboleths of the sacredness of property rights, constantly increasing dividends, constant reduction of costs, constantly speeded-up automation, without considering the effect of these practices on the human beings involved.

Although automation makes it possible to provide economic security for all, it will forever destroy our hopes of a good society unless we reach, no matter how painfully, the conviction that the much multiplied power of the machine, even as it is the product of the collective intelligence, is a resource of the entire community and not merely of management; and that the combined wisdom and resources of government, management, labor and the consumer must be mobilized to work out greater equity than now prevails in the distribution of the benefits of this incredible power. It is encouraging to note the awakening of organized religion to this obligation; to see the many religious denominations which have established offices and provided personnel to study these complicated issues of social justice, so as to enable the church and the synagogue to set up effective guidelines for man's responsibilities in a highly industrial democracy.

It will require the best offices of religion to help our people overcome the traditional attitudes toward thrift, in a situation which requires ordered and built-in obsolescence, and to help them understand that the sanctions for severance pay, transfer expenses, stock options and retirement pensions are equally valid, though necessarily in different degree, for workers as well as management. There can be no true Sabbath for those whose rest is the rest of layoff, whose freedom from work is also the freedom to starve. Liberty without groceries is a mockery. No God worth the worship of man can hold a society guiltless which makes Nature's abundance and man's ingenuity the preconditions of want and insecurity.

If our domestic serenity is hounded by strikes, dislocations and distressed areas, how much more is the world scene harassed by the dogs of war! The *shalom* dove has no place to rest its weary wings. The olive branch goes begging and the rainbow is seen only at the periphery of the fallout dust. Nations think in the obsolete terms of the past, suffering national pride to blind them to the proximity into which science has squeezed the circumambient earth. Instead of getting down to the business of channeling the earth's abundance to the exploding populations and finding ways of subverting Malthus' dour prediction, the power blocs try to subvert each other and are more concerned that each nation carry a specific banner than that it provide for the people whose trustee it is.

What an immeasurable distance stretches from our day to that first Sabbath of Beginnings when God looked upon the work which He had done and called it very good. Eden appears as a far and distant dream. Few are the voices that speak with a sense of loyalty to the universe. Dire and compelling as the need appears to take sides in the ideological dialogue of our time, it is even more necessary that the church and the synagogue remain committed to God and the purpose and order of His Universe, remembering that national pride is no less vain pride because it is draped in a flag; remembering also that loyalty to the life-force and the continuity of the life-force is as noble a commitment as is national patriotism.

It is extremely difficult, I know, to hold to this larger loyalty. The Cold War is beginning to develop the partisan spirit of the hot war. Those who are not for us, right or wrong, are considered against us. The depredations of the Bear, the Kremlin's brash bullying are considered reason enough to suspend all objectivity, to close ranks and accept the discipline of the team. This may appear to many as the elementary wisdom of survival. It cannot be so for the servant of God. For him, the stern admonition of Father Mapple to himself in *Moby Dick* applies:

> Woe to that pilot of the living God who sights the duty to preach the truth to the face of Falsehood! . . . Woe to him whom this world charms from Gospel duty. Woe to him who seeks to pour oil upon the waters when God has brewed them into a gale! Woe to him who seeks to please rather than to appall! Woe to him whose good name is more to him than goodness! Woe to him who in this world courts not dishonor! Woe to him who would not be true, even though to be false were salvation! . . . for what is man that he should live out the lifetime of his God!

We who serve the Torah are the Swiss Guard of the Lord. We are committed by an old oath, sworn at the foot of Sinai, to help God keep the promise he made to Noah:

> I will not again curse the ground any more for man's sake . . . neither will I again smite any more every living thing as I have done. While the earth remaineth, seedtime and harvest, and cold and heat, and summer and winter, and day and night shall not cease.

50

Three Tests of Character

Rabbi Aaron M. Wise

WHAT FIRST IMPRESSED me in earliest childhood about Yom Kippur was the fasting. Before we ripen to a spiritual appreciation of atonement day, we become aware of it as a period of self-denial, when food and drink do not pass our lips for 24 hours. For many adults Yom Kippur still remains little more than an exercise of will-power, testing whether they can get to bed without the customary midnight snack, wake up with breakfast, and go through the day without partaking of food. Yom Kippur becomes nothing more than an endurance-contest.

What spiritual purpose is there to our fasting? According to Yehudah Ha-Levi, on Yom Kippur day the Jew becomes like an angel of heaven, free of earthly needs, not eating, not drinking, dedicating his complete time and thought to God and Prayer. This brief time we escape from the animal within us and become that creature of whom the Psalmist sang: *Va'techasreha m'at me' Elohim,* "Thou hast made him but little lower than God."

Truth is, we spend most of our lives not differently from our household pets, the cattle in the field, or the

Selected from *Best Jewish Sermons of 5723-5724.*

wild beasts of the jungle. We sleep and wake, we eat and void, we are born and we die, altogether like our animal-cousins.

The rabbis had this animal-like resemblance in mind when they told the story of Adam's creation. Before God began to mold the first human out of the dust, He called the animal world together and said: "Let us make one more creature in partnership. Each of you will have a share in him, and I will give him a portion of Myself." The animals agreed, and God proceeded to create the first Man.

When a human being comes into the world, he is in fact no more than a helpless little animal. A newborn baby has no awareness of humanity, of family, of parental love. What he knows is that he is hungry and wants to be fed; he is wet and dirty, and wants to be changed.

It takes time for the child to develop human qualities. That occurs when he begins to know that his parents love him, when he begins slowly to reflect some of that love toward them.

But the little animal is still there, and it comes out when he's tired or hungry, when he's jealous or cross. That's when he doesn't care how much they love him. He wants his own way. He can be impolite, unkind, cruel, even vicious: incarnating one of the beasts with whom God made His partnership.

The older the child grows, the more control he develops over the little animal. But it's always there. No matter how advanced in years, something can touch off his bad temper, his jealousy or his greed.

Rabbi Mosheh of Coucy, a French rabbi of the 13th century, once wrote: "The fight in man between the angel and the beast goes on throughout life. Not until the hour of death can man be certain which of the two won."

Judaism is bent on arming the angel against the beast. Hence the Ten Commandments which say, in effect, "Let there be an end to the life of the jungle in which man must kill or be killed. Let there be divine law governing men." Hence Yom Kippur, which makes us aware of the beast within us, and the divine power we possess to control it.

The ancient rabbis were shrewd judges of human character, and they gave us spears to track down the animal in man. They said there are three ways by which you can tell what a human being is really like: *B'koso, b'kiso, u-v'kaaso*, "by his wine-cup, his purse, and his anger."

Our people have since time immemorial abhorred the *shikkur*. When a man becomes drunk he loses control of himself; he becomes more animal than human. He diminishes the image of God he represents. Judaism restrains the Jew from overindulging in the wine cup. As it were, when drink tempts us, our grandfather whispers: *"Feh, es passt nisht!"* Jews have an enviable record of sobriety in America today, with the largest percentage of drinkers, and the smallest percentage of drunkards.

But we overindulge in other things. Food, for example. Harry Golden, in his delightful book, *Only in America*, has a section entitled: *"Ess, Ess, Mein Kind!"* in which he pictures how, from the cradle, the Jew acquires an obsession for food.

We eat too much! We eat every day the way our grandparents ate only on Shabbos. Even Jews who have drifted far from the tradition still keep their hankering for Jewish food. They practice "gastronomical" Judaism, as it is called. As we become less devoted to Jewish worship and study, we become correspondingly more devoted to Jewish delicatessen.

Come to a party and see the tables laden with a rich,

diet-defying, morale-corrupting buffet. Observing how people heap their plates with food, it seems as if they have taken to heart the talmudic warning: "Man will be held to account for every good thing in life he passed by and failed to enjoy."

Not that we need this food. Doctors warn us that we are eating our way more quickly to the grave. As Mark Twain once said: "Adam didn't really want an apple. He ate it only because it was forbidden!" The very first man was a nasher, and we have imitated him in our passion for the forbidden.

Could we but listen to what the body we seek to nourish tells us, we would hear: "Hold your appetite in check! Don't run amok! *Zei nisht kain chazir!*"

On Yom Kippur we call a halt for the day. We abstain from food and drink. We are reminded of the sins we commit against ourselves, against our own health and well-being, in our self-indulgence and lack of self-control.

The second index to human character is *b'kiso*, money. You can tell what a person is like by his attitude towards money, how he earns it, how he saves it, how he spends it, how he wastes it, how he values it.

The Talmud questions: "Why did the High Priest in the ancient Temple wear only white on Yom Kippur, and not his customary garments of gold?" And the sages explain: "On Yom Kippur God did not want to be reminded of Israel's sin with the Golden Calf. Hence the High Priest was to wear his white vestments and not the gold."

We, too, do not want to be reminded of money on Yom Kippur. That is why we have eliminated the Kol Nidre appeal from our service. But we cannot escape mentioning money, because for many of us it is the most important thing in life. To speak of our shortcomings and not refer to money, would be like describing Switzerland without mentioning the Alps.

The first problem I encountered as a rabbi concerned two men who had been friends for twenty-five years, and then business partners for six months. Not only was their friendship disrupted, but it turned into a bitter enmity that raged for years. Ah, what money can do to bring out the beast, and not the best in man.

How many times have we heard of family problems arising out of a *yerushah*? Sometimes I wish that the inheritance tax would be confiscatory. The inheritance so often elicits the worst in a family: greed, hate, vengefulness. We should let every new generation start on its own feet.

We Jews do not believe that money is the root of all evil. We know what good it can accomplish when used wisely. But all too often people use money to cajole, to bribe, to subdue, to demoralize. How many times do parents and grandparents shower little children with gifts, in order to buy their love? Unable to express their feelings in a healthy, normal way, they try to purchase affection with trinkets and toys. But affection and love are not marketable items, and if children don't really feel it, they learn how to pretend—all for a price.

We live in the Age of the Commercial. At times you feel that there is nothing which we will not sell. I have read of a Christian congregation where the offering is taken before the sermon and the minister announces: "The bigger the offering, the shorter the sermon!"

How easy-running a synagogue would be if we never had to talk about money. Nobody would ever call the rabbi to pour out his bitterness and rancor about the injustice of the Temple bill. The Temple is no ivory tower. The problem of getting and spending money affects it no less than it does you. What we must guard against is permitting money values to dominate our thinking, as unfortunately they have in many areas of American life.

Dr. Louis Finkelstein, President of our Seminary, writing in *Fortune Magazine*, describes the moral decay of the American business world, its dog-eat-dog competition, its bribery and dishonesty. Read it and you will see how jungle law has displaced the rule of kindness and justice in our society.

I discussed Dr. Finkelstein's article with a business leader in our community who had only this comment: "Competition is so ruthless today that you can't be honest and stay in business." With a shrug, he admitted the indictment and said: "What can you do?"

We have permitted the beast in *homo Americanus* to get out of control. The hunger for possession and the thirst for power have turned much of our business world into a den of lions. Can we call upon the lion tamers of conscience and reason to save us before we destroy ourselves?

When I say "destroy ourselves," I am not only speaking figuratively. The tensions of our money-dominated culture are destructive and devastating. Speaking with a friend in the advertising business, I learned about the alarming percentage of men in his field who die before the age of 40. By our way of living, by the guilt feelings we heap up, by the inward corrosion of soul, we hasten to an early death. We drop out of the rat race and leave behind us insurance policies and rich widows. With all the respect to the widows and the orphans: *men arbet far'n teivel!*

Yom Kippur is a day to stand apart, to contemplate this whirling merry-go-round on which our lives are caught. It is a time to remember the wise words of Albert Einstein: "Try not to become a man of success—

rather, become a man of value. A successful man gets out of life more than he puts in. A man of value will give more than he receives."

Third and last of these signs of character is *b'kaaso*. You can tell what a man is like by his anger.

Many times in life we hear only what we want to hear, because our anger blocks off our senses. Dr. Cyrus Adler was president of his congregation, Mikveh Israel in Philadelphia, when it dedicated its new building. One of the influential members was infuriated about the seat she had been given—it was behind a pillar. Dr. Adler was called out. He heard the woman's complaint, then he said in his courtly manner: "Madam, if it was for the good of the synagogue, I would not mind sitting in the gutter." Even more enraged, she rushed to the rabbi and said: "Dr. Adler told me to go sit in the gutter!"

Oftentimes after the holidays I hear of an argument which occurred between an usher and a Temple member, nearly always about a trivial matter, but one that led to sarcastic exchanges and bristling hostilities. Our anger seems always to be on tap. It takes no more than a word or gesture, and we arch our backs, our fur blows up, we hiss and prepare to scratch.

How often do we see a woman arguing with a sales-clerk in a department store, letting her have the sharp side of her tongue. A slight error on a sales slip, but it was enough to waken the fury. So many people go through life continually asking to see the manager.

Where does our anger come from? Much of it is kindled at home. We carry with us the frustrations and the disappointments of our family life, and then lash out at anyone who thwarts our will or stands in our way, wherever and whoever it may be.

Tonight is the Night of Forgiveness in the Jewish calendar. For the angers that seethe within us we must bring the medicine of understanding and love.

On this night when we are on trial for our souls, we summon the witnesses in our behalf, like that Hassidic Rebbe who was about to die. His disciples gathered around him. "How do you want to be buried?" they asked. He looked around the room. His eyes fell upon the table in the center of the room. "Take this table and cut from it the boards for my coffin. Bury me in these boards that were once my table! My family and I sat around this table. Here we ate, here we talked. Around this table we lived our lives. I want the table to be a witness either for me or against me."

In a profound sense, is that not true of every one of us? The pieces of furniture in our homes are the silent witnesses of that poignant drama which we enact with the members of our family. No matter what face we show to the world—there, within the privacy of our homes, we reveal our true selves. So often that is an angry, hurtful, vengeful, biting self, which we would be ashamed to expose to the whole world. That is the animal within us, which convention and morality have taught us to hide and cover up. But on Yom Kippur Eve, let us be honest enough to admit that the animal is there, to confess how little we have done to subdue it with intelligence and love.

I began my sermon with the legend about God's partnership with the animal world in creating the first man. Let me tell you how I would want the legend to end. After Adam sinned, God again called all the creatures together. He told them how Adam had disobeyed Him, how he had greedily eaten of the forbidden fruit. He had acted like an animal, and God was going to drive him out of the Garden of Eden. God said that He would punish man further by taking from him the divine spirit He had given him and let him become but another animal. But the birds and the beasts protested. They had been partners in the creation of man. They wanted God to give him another chance.

Thereupon God relented and gave man three gifts: the gift of wisdom, the gift of generosity, and the gift of forgiveness. These were to remain forever the tokens of the divine in man.

These are the gifts that Yom Kippur pleads with us to apply to our lives: the wisdom of self-control against the appetites which would destroy our bodies; the gift of generosity as antidote to our greed and our envy; and the gift of forgiveness to dissolve the anger and the hatred which poison our lives. Take these three gifts this Kol Nidre Eve and let Yom Kippur work their magic into your lives.

51

Growing Old

Rabbi Herbert Yoskowitz

"GROW OLD ALONG with me/the worst is yet to be." Such are the sad words of Charles Whitman in his recent review of Simone de Beauvoir's book, *The Coming of Age*. The book describes attitudes toward human aging. Is it shocking that old age, rather than death, is contrasted with life. The conventional and sensational issue of death is replaced here with the more repulsive issue of decay.

Parshat Noach has featured within it the sensational story of Noah's building of the Ark. It's a great story, one that film-makers would readily use as script material. Just think of the featured scenes: a great-sized ark being built, pairs of animals being herded inside, the rains that fell and didn't let up, the gradual abatement of the rains, the flights of the raven and of the dove to see if the water's height had lessened, the departure of all the ark's inhabitants to the newly-dried land, the sacrifices offered to the Lord by Noah and the Lord's promise never to allow the land to be so cursed again. Then the Lord pronounces what has become known as

Selected from *Best Jewish Sermons of 5733-5734*.

the seven laws of Noah. Finally, there is the sensational
scene which would probably be the end of a theatrical
production: the Lord causes a magnificent rainbow to
appear in the sky as a sign by the Lord that such a cata-
strophic flood will never happen again.

Such is the main emphasis of Parshat Noach and
only small attention is usually paid to what follows. Let
me share the story with you, citing a few medieval
Jewish commentaries to help understand the main message of the story:

> And the sons of Noah, that went forth from
> the ark, were Shem, and Ham, and Japheth;
> and Ham is the father of Canaan. These three
> were the sons of Noah, and of these was the
> whole earth overspread. And Noah the hus-
> bandman began, and planted a vineyard. And
> *he drank of the wine*, and *was drunken*; and he
> was uncovered within his tent. And Ham, the
> father of Canaan, saw the nakedness of his
> father, and told his two brethren without. And
> Shem and Japheth took a garment, and laid it
> upon their shoulders, and went backward, and
> covered the nakedness of their father; and their
> faces were backward, and they saw not their
> father's nakedness. And Noah awoke from his
> wine, and knew what his youngest son had
> done unto him.
>
> And Noah lived after the flood *three hundred
> and fifty years*. And all the days of Noah were
> nine hundred and fifty years; and he died.

Obviously by whatever standards were used to count
years, Noah was growing old. And the words, "Grow old
along with me/the worst is yet to be" obviously were
being felt by Noah. The commentator Nahmanides

wrote that in Noah's zeal to consume great amounts of wine, he planted rows upon rows of vines. With no other fruit trees did he make such a special effort. It's a very saddening picture: Noah running to and fro consumed by the passion to make more and more wine available to him. The picture of an old man consumed by such an unhealthy passion is sad to witness and sad to relate. Ibn Ezra explains that Noah was sick from the extraordinary effort he had put into constructing the ark.

When pressures are great, some of us, young or old, fall. Others of us rise from these pressures and grow as people. We become better able to help others and to live life with a zest we never knew existed.

In a few weeks, we are going to study the great pressure that was placed upon another elderly gentleman, The Patriarch Abraham. When he was in his solitary aloneness on Mt. Moriah, he was ready to make one of the most difficult sacrifices that one may be faced with in life—readying his son to be sacrificed for a cause thought to be greater than the life of any one man. Did he "crack" at this occasion or even afterwards? No, we do not see even a glimmer of evidence that Abraham succumbed to the pressures he faced as he was growing older. In facing his crisis in life in personal aloneness, Abraham could very well have made a wonderful self-discovery of his inner strength. We read of no faltering in old age by our first Patriarch. Indeed, too, that is one of the reasons why nearly all the Rabbis throughout the centuries have held Abraham in such higher esteem than they did Noah. Abraham devoted his latter years to a way of life which did not bring shame nor disgrace upon his name. Noah's name became tainted because he apparently did not have the inner strength in his advancing years to refrain from acts causing loss of respect.

In rereading Noah's response to the calamity about

to fall upon his generation, I receive the strong impression that Noah gave up on his society. Somewhat akin to Utnapishtim in the Mesopotamian myth, Noah did not pray to the Lord to save his generation. Perhaps he felt that it was a good idea to destroy the society in which he was living. Then a new better society could be built and justice and human understanding would prevail. No more violence! No more corruption! What beautiful idealistic aims. Unfortunately many people who do not see the old society destroyed in all due haste become so unhappy with the existing society that they find difficulty in living in it. Some people with such an attitude today seek to escape reality by turning to drugs. Perhaps Noah sought to escape the realities of his society by turning to the vineyards and to the wine that it could yield.

Abraham, in contrast to Noah, always sought to preserve life and to maintain existing societies. Abraham pleaded for such corrupt communities as Sodom and Gemorrah. Hopefully, even with just ten good people the society could be constructed anew without destruction of the old. Even evil societies could be corrected for good without first destroying them. And a person could live a full purposeful life in society even while the reforms were taking place.

You and I have a choice. And I'm addressing myself here to those under age thirty-one years, too. We can prepare for our advancing years by continuing to have goals. Martin Buber is quoted as saying, "To be old is a glorious thing when one has not unlearned what it means to begin." According to the Rabbis, Abraham had a goal. His goal was to continue his career as Jewish preacher, conveying the Judaism that was so much a part of his life. What was Noah's goal? The Rabbis tell us that even while engaged in the occupation of building the Ark, he did not actively seek a life-long goal, e.g., the one adopted by Abraham. In Noah's case, his aimlessness and his lack of preparation for his advancing years could very well have led to his episode of drunkenness.

This past summer I visited the Sistine Chapel in Rome where I viewed some of Michelangelo's great contributions to the world of art in his latter years. Or, how can I forget the appearance of our own Golda where she appeared in most elegant, but simple fashion, at the opening of the Israel Festival which I attended three months ago? I can't help but contrast such a way of living one's *later* years with the blank empty looks I see in some of the faces of older people. We can prepare ourselves *now* for our later years by cultivating worthy goals which will outlive us and give us a sense of pride. Just going to our work jobs, e.g., going to build the arks in our lives, isn't enough to sustain us in our later years. Then retirement can mean the end of a man's productive life, much as the marriage of a woman's youngest child may write "finis" in her own mind to her usefulness.

The question of how to deal with the elderly is not a question of what to do for our parents and our grandparents. The question is: what should we do with and for ourselves? At about the time we learn to make the most of life, most of it is gone. Prepare for advancing years now by making new beginnings, by developing worthwhile interests and by serving others in the community. Then we will be able to feel that like Abraham, even as we are *growing old* our lives are worthy.

About the Author

Saul I. Teplitz received his Bachelor of Arts degree from the University of Pittsburgh and was ordained by the Jewish Theological Seminary of America, from which he also he received his M.H.L. and D.H.L. degrees. Following ordination, he served as rabbi of New York's Laurelton Jewish Center (1944-1960) and Jewish Community Center of Harrison (1960-1963). From 1963 until his retirement in 1991, Rabbi Teplitz was spiritual leader of Congregation Sons of Israel in Woodmere, New York.

Throughout his career, Rabbi Teplitz has been very active in community affairs. He has served as president of the Synagogue Council of America, the Rabbinical Assembly, and the Commission on Synagogue Relations of the Federation of Jewish Philanthropies as well as vice-president of the New York Board of Rabbis. He has been chairman of both the New York Rabbinic Cabinet of Israel Bonds and the Rabbinical Advisory Committee of UJA-Federation.

In addition to editing all twelve volumes in the *Best Jewish Sermons* series, Saul I. Teplitz authored his own collection of sermons, entitled *Life Is for Living*. He has written countless articles for major Anglo-Jewish periodicals and has appeared widely on television and radio.

Since his retirement, Rabbi Teplitz has been a visiting associate professor of homiletics at the Jewish Theological Seminary.